KU-826-728

LIBRARY

Learning
Principles, Processes
and Practices

)07

Rosemary J. Stevenson and Joy A. Palmer

Children, Teachers and Learning Series

Series Editor: Cedric Cullingford

)07

NEWMAN COLLEGE
BARTLEY GREEN
BIRMINGHAM, 32

CLASS 370.1523
BARCODE N 0079075 3
AUTHOR STE

WITHDRAWN

CASSELL

N 0079075 3

Cassell Educational Limited

Villiers House	387 Park Avenue South
41/47 Strand	New York
London WC2N 5JE	NY 10016-8810

© Rosemary Stevenson and Joy Palmer 1994

All rights reserved. No part of this publication may be reproduced or transmitted in any form or by any means, electronic or mechanical including photocopying, recording or any information storage or retrieval system, without prior permission in writing from the publishers.

First published 1994

British Library Cataloguing-in-Publication Data
A catalogue record for this book is available from the British Library

Library of Congress Cataloging-in-Publication Data
Stevenson, Rosemary J.
  Learning: Principles, Processes and Practices. – (Children, Teachers & Learning Series)
  I. Title   II. Palmer, Joy   III. Series
  370.15

ISBN 0-304-32561-9 (hardback)
      0-304-32563-5 (paperback)

Typeset by Colset Private Limited, Singapore

Printed and bound in Great Britain by
Biddles Ltd, Guildford and King's Lynn

Contents

Foreword

The books in this series stem from the conviction that all those who are concerned with education should have a deep interest in the nature of children's learning. Teaching and policy decisions ultimately depend on an understanding of individual personalities accumulated through experience, observation and research. Too often in recent years decisions on the management of education have had little to do with the realities of children's lives, and too often the interest shown in the performance of teachers, or in the content of the curriculum, has not been balanced by an interest in how children respond to either. The books in this series are based on the conviction that children are not fundamentally different from adults, and that we understand ourselves better by our insight into the nature of children.

The books are designed to appeal to *all* those who are interested in education and who take it as axiomatic that anyone concerned with human nature, culture or the future of civilization is interested in education – in the individual process of learning, as well as what can be done to help it. While each book draws on recent findings in research and is aware of the latest developments in policy, each is written in a style that is clear, readable and free from the jargon that has undermined much scholarly writing, especially in such a relatively new field of study.

Although the audience to be addressed includes all those concerned with education, the most important section of the audience is made up of professional teachers, the teachers who continue to learn and grow and who need both support and stimulation. Teachers are very busy people, whose energies are taken up in coping with difficult circumstances. They deserve material that is stimulating, useful and free of jargon and that is in tune with the practical realities of classrooms.

Each book is based on the principle that the study of education is a discipline in its own right. There was a time when the study of the

iv

principles of learning and the individual's response to his or her environment was a collection of parts of other disciplines – history, philosophy, linguistics, sociology and psychology. That time is assumed to be over and the books address those who are interested in the study of children and how they respond to their environment.

Each book is written both to enlighten the readers and to offer practical help to develop their understanding. They therefore not only contain accounts of what we understand about children, but also illuminate these accounts by a series of examples, based on observation of practice. These examples are designed not as a series of rigid steps to be followed, but to show the realities on which the insights are based.

Most people, even educational researchers, agree that research on children's learning has been most disappointing, even when it has not been completely missing. Apart from the general lack of a 'scholarly' educational tradition, the inadequacies of such study come about because of the fear of approaching such a complex area as children's inner lives. Instead of answering curiosity with observation, much educational research has attempted to reduce the problem to simplistic solutions, by isolating a particular hypothesis and trying to improve it, or by trying to focus on what is easy and 'empirical'. These books try to clarify the real complexities of the problem, and are willing to be speculative.

The real disappointment with educational research, however, is that it is rarely read or used. The people most at home with children are often unaware that helpful insights can be offered to them. The study of children and the understanding that comes from self-knowledge are too important to be left to obscurity. In the broad sense real 'research' is carried out by all those engaged in the task of teaching or bringing up children.

All the books share a conviction that the inner worlds of children repay close attention, and that much subsequent behaviour and attitudes depend upon the early years. They also share the conviction that children's natures are not markedly different from those of adults, even if they are more honest about themselves. The process of learning is reviewed as the individual's close and idiosyncratic involvement in events, rather than the passive reception of, and processing of, information.

Cedric Cullingford

Preface

A major difficulty confronting teachers when they must decide which learning activities to give to their pupils is that of seeing how the activities fit together to achieve the overall learning goals. Different activities seem to have different purposes, such as practice or revision or the acquisition of new information, and so they do not form a coherent category in which they all contribute to a single purpose. In such circumstances, the choice of activities seems very haphazard, since there is no principle or rationale to guide the choice. One of our main purposes in writing this book is to provide such a rationale. We present a basic guide to what is currently understood about principles of learning so that these can be used to make informed choices about teaching and learning in the classroom. When these choices are based on a sound understanding of learning, they will no longer be haphazard and they will also allow a proper course to be steered between the extremes of 'traditionalism' on the one hand and 'progressivism' on the other, thus avoiding the pendulum swings that seem to characterize so much of educational policy. We hope that the book will enable teachers, teacher trainees and policy makers to develop principled guidelines for classroom practice, guidelines that are based on well-understood educational and psychological principles.

In the book, we discuss educational practice in the light of psychological principles of learning. We emphasize that learning should focus on an overall goal of conceptual understanding, even when the current activity is concerned with practising and revising known skills and concepts. We also identify three important principles of learning. One is the need to activate prior knowledge at the start of each learning activity. Without this, understanding will not occur, misconceptions will not be corrected, and the learning will be seen as arbitrary and abstract. A second is the need to foster the motivation needed to ensure that effort is invested in learning. This requires the engagement of prior beliefs about the nature of learning and about one's own abilities. It also requires instruction in the use of learning strategies so that effort will be followed by success. Finally, a third principle emphasizes the importance of good learning strategies to ensure that learning and understanding are successful. These strategies require metacognitive abilities: a capacity for self-reflection, a knowledge of good strategies, and the motivation to put the knowledge into practice. These and other themes are discussed in relation to teaching in the core subjects of the National Curriculum.

The book begins with two chapters that set the scene for those that follow. The first spells out some of the basic categories of learning while the second spells out the recent history of policy and practice in Britain and identifies current practice as it has been observed in recent large-scale research studies. Then come the chapters on the core subjects: science (Chapter 3), reading (Chapter 4) and mathematics and writing (Chapter 5). Chapter 6 looks more closely at the important roles of prior knowledge and motivation in learning, and is followed by two chapters more specifically concerned with practical classroom issues. Chapter 7 discusses the teacher's task and considers how teachers can match learning tasks to desired learning activities. Categories of learning tasks are also described. Chapter 8 draws together the themes of the book and discusses how the three learning principles of activating prior knowledge, good motivation and good metacognitive skills can be realized in the classroom. Two methods of teaching metacognitive skills are also outlined to show how practice might go beyond a preoccupation with traditionalism and progressivism towards a new synthesis that focuses on both process and product at the same time. By these means we hope to have shown how policy and practice are best guided by an understanding of the principles of learning.

In writing this book, we make one major assumption that needs to be defended. We assume that the basic processes of learning are similar whatever the age of the learner. We therefore draw on studies and examples from learners of all ages, from the early years through to adulthood. We hold this assumption because the major difference between young and older learners seems to be the extent of the prior knowledge brought to bear on new learning, not the learning processes themselves. A number of studies are discussed in the book that support this conclusion. We hope, though, that our adoption of this assumption does not mask our other belief that each person's approach to learning is unique and has its own special significance. That special significance, of course, may itself depend on a person's own unique set of prior beliefs and expectations.

There are a number of people who have helped us make the book better than it might have been. Early drafts of the chapters have been read and commented on by Charles Crook, Hazel Emslie, Michael Eysenck, David Kleinman, David McNamara, Deirdre Pettitt and John Richardson. We gratefully acknowledge their help and wish to point out that any remaining errors are our own. Rosemary Stevenson thanks the ESRC for supporting her research throughout the period in which the book was written. We also thank Naomi Roth of Cassell for her patience while the book was being written, Lynn Carrington for typing Chapters 2, 3 and 7, and Malcolm Rolling and Judith Warner for preparing the figures. Finally our sincere thanks go to the two Davids: to David Kleinman for continued intellectual and emotional support, and to David Cooper for sharing anxieties as well as enthusiasms, and providing unfailing encouragement and support.

CHAPTER 1

The Nature of Learning

Overview

Human learning is responsible for all the great advances in the world, philosophical, scientific, technical. It is also responsible for our ability to find our way around the world from one day to another, our ability to interpret and make sense of the world around us, and our ability to achieve wisdom and maturity with the passing years. Furthermore, human learning is so complex and so far-reaching that, no matter how hard they try, scientists cannot get even the fastest computers to learn a fraction of the things that humans learn with ease. What is it that makes human learning so powerful?

Human beings engage in two different kinds of learning: implicit and explicit. *Implicit learning* occurs without our being aware of it, whereas *explicit learning* requires conscious and deliberate effort. Our capacity for implicit learning may well account for the ease with which we learn to make sense of the world and find our way around it. However, our capacity for explicit learning reveals a vast potential for learning that few people ever fully achieve. We will briefly outline some features of implicit learning, but the bulk of this chapter is concerned with explicit learning. This is because explicit – deliberate – learning seems to be unique to humans and it is the kind of learning that is probably responsible for humanity's greatest achievements.

Implicit learning

Implicit learning involves noticing regularities in the world and responding to them in consistent ways, and it is an ability found in all animals. Such learning is usually referred to as *conditioning* when animal learning is discussed. Humans are affected by conditioning too, but the learning involved is very complex, more so than is usually the case in other animal species. Such highly complex learning is probably aided by biological constraints that are peculiar to our species. For example, young children are biologically constrained to learn their native language in the absence of explicit tuition and without there being deliberate attempts to learn. Adults too learn highly complex sets of relationships in the environment. This is illustrated in a series of experiments by Broadbent and his colleagues (e.g. Berry and Broadbent, 1984; Broadbent *et al.*, 1986).

In one experiment, Berry and Broadbent (1988) trained subjects in two dynamic control tasks. For example, one of their tasks required subjects to interact with a 'computer person' called Clegg and try to get him to become and stay very friendly. Clegg initiated the interaction by displaying one of twelve descriptions (e.g. polite, very friendly, loving) on the computer screen, after which the subject had to respond by typing in another description. There were twelve descriptions to choose from: very rude, rude, very cool, cool, indifferent, polite, very polite, friendly, very friendly, affectionate, very affectionate, and loving. The descriptions reflected an intimacy scale from very low to high and each description had a score from 1 (very low) to 12 (high) on this scale. Over a series of learning trials, the subjects had to get Clegg to display the description 'very friendly' and to keep giving that description on successive trials. Clegg responded to the subject's choice of description in a retaliatory fashion. If Clegg had typed 'polite', and the subject responded with the description 'friendly', then Clegg would retaliate with the description 'cool'. Clegg's responses were determined by the formula:

$$C = 2(S - C1)$$

where S = the intimacy score of the subject's last response
C = the intimacy score of Clegg's current response
C1 = the intimacy score of Clegg's previous response.

The subjects successfully learned to carry out this task. However, when questioned about the experiment afterwards, they were unable to describe the relationship between their own and Clegg's responses, even though they could not have performed the task successfully without knowledge of the relationship. Berry and Broadbent argue that the knowledge was learned implicitly and was unavailable to conscious awareness. The subjects in Berry

2

and Broadbent's experiment act 'as if' they know the mathematical principle that underlies their performance, but they cannot describe it. The inability to describe the knowledge gained through implicit learning is apparent in our use of language too. We can successfully use our knowledge of language to talk intelligibly and to understand what others say, but we are not able to describe this knowledge unless we have been explicitly taught about grammar in school. In general, implicit learning seems to be a form of learning that we cannot avoid. We cannot help learning the regularities and relationships in the world around us and acting on what we have learned. In other words, implicit learning is automatic and occurs without our conscious control.

Implicit learning results in implicit knowledge, knowledge that we use in our daily activities but that we cannot describe. Implicit knowledge can also be learned explicitly. This happens when explicitly learned knowledge has become automatic, and hence implicit, through repeated practice. We will encounter implicit knowledge of this latter kind later in the chapter, when we discuss learning through problem solving and practice. We will refer to such newly implicit knowledge as knowledge of skills that have become automatic. We will also encounter implicit knowledge in later chapters of the book, where we will reveal the pervasive influence of such knowledge on new learning. For example, a learner's implicit beliefs and preconceptions about a subject have a profound influence on learning science (Chapter 3), learning mathematics (Chapter 5), and even on the motivation to learn at all (Chapter 7). Implicit knowledge influences almost everything we do, and it is what we usually mean when we refer to the prior knowledge that a learner brings to bear on new learning. Implicit knowledge is easy to use but hard to describe, because we are rarely consciously aware of it.

Explicit learning

In contrast to implicit knowledge, explicit knowledge is hard to learn, although once learned it can be readily described. Explicit learning requires conscious and deliberate thought. It seems to be unique to humans, probably due to our use of language, and it may well be responsible for the sophistication and power of human learning. Explicit learning is the kind that is fostered in schools and other educational establishments, and because of the importance that we place on education, we concentrate here on spelling out what it involves. We can identify three different kinds of explicit learning: understanding, problem solving and memorizing. Most people are familiar with the last two, but the first one, understanding, is less frequently encountered.

Ideas about *problem solving* and *memorization* seem to form the basis of many people's beliefs about learning, whether the people are children or adults. Bereiter and Scardamalia (1989) investigated beliefs about learning, and their results suggest that children and adults view both problem solving and memorization as important activities of learning. The only difference between children and adults was that the adults mentioned learning goals whereas the children did not. For example, adults generally stated a goal for which the learning was intended, such as studying yoga in order 'to learn how to relax' (Bereiter and Scardamalia, 1989, p. 370). By contrast, children aged about 9 years (third graders) generally said that they wanted to learn a particular topic, such as spelling, without indicating a higher-level goal. Even so, the goals of the adults were problem-solving goals rather than ones of understanding. However, in all cases subjects' reports showed that they thought learning was a mixture of problem solving and memorization. When the learning concerned factual material, both children and adults listed memorizing activities such as reading, taking notes, rehearsing and so on. When the learning concerned skills, the subjects emphasized practice.

However, alongside these longstanding beliefs that learning is based on problem solving and memorization, another belief has been voiced on many occasions. This is the belief that learning concerns *understanding*. The view of learning as understanding seems to be a relatively late development, one that probably first appears during the college years (Chall, 1979). Säljö (1979) interviewed adults and asked them what they understood by learning. By analysing their responses, he identified five qualitatively different conceptions of learning:

1.　*as an increase in knowledge*: This approach views learning as a passive process, the gradual absorption of relevant information that becomes assimilated with prior knowledge. It is something that is done by teachers rather than learners and can be likened to the filling of a jug. The teacher possesses knowledge that is given to the students. People who hold this view of learning seem to be thinking of implicit rather than explicit learning.

2. *as memorizing*: With this kind of learning, the learner has a more active role. However, the information that is memorized is not transformed in any way. Instead it is subject to rote repetition. The learner is intent on 'getting it into his or her head'. This view sees learning as memorization, as the accumulation of unrelated facts, unrelated because the learner sees no need to relate them to pre-existing knowledge.

3. *as acquiring facts or procedures to be used*: This kind of learning leads to the acquisition of skills, such as reading, writing or mathematical skills, that can be used to do things now and later. However, there is still no transformation of what is learnt by the learner. The emphasis in this approach is on practice so that the skills become automatic.

4. *as making sense*: The learner who adopts this approach makes active attempts to abstract meaning while learning and to use the new material to update and modify existing beliefs. With this approach, learning is about trying to understand. It leads to the ability to explain things, not just remember them.

5. *as understanding reality*: This kind of learning is similar to the approach in 4, but there is an additional suggestion that learning enables you to see the world differently, and think about things in different ways.

Views 4 and 5 are qualitatively different from views 1 to 3. View 1 hardly counts as explicit learning at all, and views 2 and 3 see learning as either memorizing or problem solving. By contrast, views 4 and 5 see learning as understanding. Van Rossum and Schenk (1984) have found that university students who hold one of the first three views take what is called a *surface approach* to their own learning. The learning task is seen as one of reproducing the subject matter at a later date, in an exam for example. Students who hold views 4 or 5 take a *deep* approach to learning. They think about what they are learning, seeking to understand the material and use it to develop and change their pre-existing ideas. Of course, as Gibbs (1990) has pointed out, an approach is not the same thing as a skill, since it is primarily about the learner's intention. This means that it can be difficult to identify a student's approach just by looking at his or her lecture notes, for example. You might need to ask the students what they were trying to do when they were taking the notes, and what they were thinking about. Alternatively, the work of Van Rossum and Schenk suggests that a person's conception of learning – which of the above five views they hold – is also a good guide to the approach they take when learning.

It is important to point out that problem solving and memorizing are not unreasonable views of learning. They both have their place in enabling people to make their way in the world without having to think too much about what they are doing. Repeated practice in these two activities makes such automatic actions and skills possible. Nevertheless, to go beyond automatic and unthinking action, understanding is needed. To see why this is so, we will briefly describe and discuss each of the three kinds of explicit learning. Before we do that, though, we need to understand the role that memory plays in learning.

THE ROLE OF MEMORY IN LEARNING

Human memory can be thought of as having two functions. One is to store all the knowledge we have gained about the world as concepts, facts and episodes. The other is to provide a place where conscious thinking can occur. The first, storage, function is fulfilled by long-term memory, a memory store that holds everything we know and believe about the world. Some of this knowledge will have been learned implicitly and so we will not have conscious access to it, but we will be able to use it when we act on the world. Other stored knowledge will have been learned explicitly and can be consciously retrieved and reported.

The second function of memory is fulfilled by a *working memory* (Baddeley and Hitch, 1974; Baddeley, 1986). As the term implies, working memory is predominantly a mental workspace where conscious thinking occurs. Of course, it has a storage function too because we need to hold in working memory the ideas that we are thinking about. One of the main features of conscious thought is that it is only possible to follow one train of thought at a time (see e.g. Neisser, 1963). This is because working memory, where such thinking takes place, has a very limited capacity; it can only hold a small number of ideas at a time (seven plus or minus two, according to Miller, 1956), and it only allows one thought to be pursued at a time. This limited capacity of working memory, therefore, places severe constraints on explicit learning because the capacity can be easily overloaded. Hence, explicit learning is difficult because its demands may exceed the capacity of working memory. Indeed, one of the main functions of practice is to make what has been learned automatic (that is, implicit) so that it no longer occupies space in working memory.

The above are the key features of explicit learning: the initial involvement of working memory and the subsequent freeing up of working memory by making the learned material automatic through extensive practice. These features are apparent in the discussion that follows of the three different types of explicit learning: understanding, problem solving and memorization.

Learning as understanding

Understanding is the most difficult form of explicit learning. First, like all explicit learning, it requires working memory and, indeed, often exceeds the limits of memory. Second, as we shall see, it requires an ability not required by other forms of explicit learning. This is the ability to reflect on and control deliberately one's own knowledge and thought processes. Such self-reflection is a very high-level cognitive activity that usually takes many years to achieve. Third, it is hard to pin down exactly what is meant by the term 'understanding' and to explain how such understanding is achieved. Small wonder, therefore, as we shall see in subsequent chapters, that people find such learning difficult and that many people do not attempt it at all.

In order to achieve an approximate characterization of what is meant by understanding, we will use an account of learning that has been presented by Scardamalia and Bereiter (1991). They point out that there are two elements involved in learning: one's pre-existing knowledge and the new information being presented, as shown in Figure 1.1. As the arrows in the figure also show, understanding is seen as a two-way interchange between the two. Pre-existing knowledge is used to interpret the new material and, in turn, the new material yields information that may be used to modify our pre-existing ideas and beliefs, sometimes in major ways. This two-way process is the hallmark of understanding. The aspect that is most likely to be neglected, according to Scardamalia and Bereiter, is the journey from right to left in the figure. That is, people frequently fail to evaluate their pre-existing knowledge in the light of the new material. Such a failure leads to people holding conflicting beliefs because they learn new information that is inconsistent with their pre-existing knowledge, having failed to revise the latter in the light of the former.

It is important to distinguish explicit interpretation processes from implicit and automatic ones that occur each time we understand what we read or hear or see. These automatic processes enable us to read a book or participate in a conversation without having to interpret each word that we encounter consciously and deliberately. Such processes undoubtedly contribute to implicit learning about the world. But they are not what we have in mind when we talk about learning as understanding. Learning through understanding involves deliberate attempts to make sense of new material by using prior knowledge, and deliberate attempts to rethink one's ideas in the light of the new material. Explicit understanding, then, goes beyond the simple addition of new material

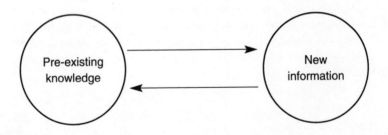

Figure 1.1 The two-way process of expert learning (adapted from Scardamalia and Bereiter, 1991)

to long-term memory. It even goes beyond simple integration, through which new material is incorporated with pre-existing knowledge already stored in long-term memory. Instead, it involves the deliberate use of pre-existing knowledge to interpret new material, and the deliberate use of the new material to modify and update pre-existing beliefs and ideas. Such deliberations are very hard to sustain, partly because they make heavy demands on working memory, but partly also because they require the use of high-level reflective processes that control and regulate learning. We shall say more about these self-reflective activities (known as metacognitive processes) in Chapter 2. For the moment, we will concentrate on showing how such explicit understanding processes are used.

Bereiter and Scardamalia (1989) have examined explicit processes of understanding in schoolchildren. They asked young high-school students (aged about 12 years) to read texts that conveyed new information. While they were reading, the students were also asked to report aloud everything that they were thinking. The researchers then used these *verbal reports* to examine how the students were reading the texts. Some of the texts contained new information that conflicted with the students' prior beliefs. For instance, one text segment read as follows:

> Harmful germs are not trying to be bad when they settle down in your body. They just want to live quietly, eat, and make more germs.

This passage contradicts the popularly held view that harmful germs are aggressors. Some students accurately paraphrased the text, showing good comprehension of the text at the implicit level; the words and sentences were understood and the information in the text was grasped. But they showed no signs that they realized the implications of the new material for their understanding of germs. An example paraphrase produced by one of these students is as follows:

> That means they don't want to really hurt you, but they just want to live quietly and eat the food you digest and all the things that could go on in your stomach and they just want to get more bacteria.

The above is an accurate paraphrase, but there is no attempt to relate the new information back to pre-existing ideas and beliefs about germs. It is as if the material has nothing to do with these preconceived ideas and so it cannot be used to modify and update them. On the other hand, some students recognized that there was a conflict between the new information and their pre-existing views. But although they recognized this, they did not go on to resolve it. An example paraphrase from one of these students is:

> That's hard to believe. Let's see. Then I always thought [of] germs moving around or fighting us. I didn't think that they would just settle down and raise a family. That's not exactly my idea of a germ.

Finally, a very small number of students not only recognized the conflict but set about trying to resolve it with their available knowledge:

> Well, they don't really know that they're bad, but they're just living their normal way but everybody else thinks they're bad.

In this last example, the student has used the textual material to gain a new perspective on germs and pre-existing ideas have been modified. Such 'expert' learning is rare in school-age children. Indeed, even adults find such learning difficult. For instance, there is a wealth of research showing that people frequently fail to make explicit use of prior knowledge spontaneously when trying to understand a text or solve a problem. An example of the difficulties schoolchildren encounter in this respect is illustrated by the following study.

Hasselhorn and Korkel (1986) presented 12-year-old children, who were either soccer experts or novices, with a short story about soccer that contained six inconsistencies. After reading the story, the soccer experts noted 30 per cent of the inconsistencies, compared to 15 per cent noted by the novices. Following this phase of the experiment, half of the novices and half of the experts were taught a reading strategy that depended on prior knowledge for its execution. These students were told to think about what they knew about soccer and to use this knowledge to aid comprehension of the text. The remaining subjects (controls) were taught some general monitoring strategies (e.g. check comprehension often) and some encoding strategies (e.g. underlining, self-questioning) that did not depend on prior knowledge.

Following this training, the children read the soccer passage again. The most important result was that experts who were taught the knowledge-activation strategies increased their detection of inconsistencies on rereading the passage (63 per cent compared to 40 per cent by expert controls). These results show that simply having the relevant knowledge is not sufficient to guarantee that it will be used spontaneously in new situations, since the experts did not explicitly use their available knowledge the first time they read the passage. However, when instructed that previous knowledge would be useful, the experts clearly did make explicit use of it and improved their detection rates accordingly. Gick and Holyoak (1980) have shown that undergraduate students similarly fail to use prior knowledge deliberately when solving a problem, although, like the schoolchildren, they will use prior knowledge if the experimenter tells them that it will be useful.

The knowledge that we are concerned with here, and that is enriched and revised through understanding, is conceptual knowledge; that is, knowledge that describes the world around us and that groups such knowledge into deep conceptual categories. Such conceptual knowledge is often referred to as *declarative knowledge*, and one of the major functions of learning through understanding is to revise and update our conceptual understanding of the world.

In summary, learning through understanding, then, consists of evaluation as well as the integration of new information with old. The new learning is evaluated in relation to pre-existing knowledge, while the pre-existing knowledge itself is evaluated in the light of the new learning. Such evaluations are very difficult, primarily because they require conscious attention (the use of working memory) and the deliberate use of one's pre-existing knowledge. These difficulties may account for the ease with which learners of all ages engage in problem solving or memorization instead. Let us turn therefore to these other two kinds of learning to see how they differ from understanding.

Learning as problem solving

Problem solving is a common human activity. Since it does not require the deliberate use and explicit awareness of prior knowledge like understanding does, people engage in it readily, sometimes at the expense of understanding. The following are all common problems, although the last three are normally confined to educational contexts:

- how am I going to pay this bill?

- where did I leave my gloves?

- what shall we eat for dinner tonight?

- what will I have left in my bank account if I buy this book?

- what groceries do I need to buy this week?

- what is 16 times 25?

- shall I take my opponent's rook on my next move (in chess)?

- how can I explain what problem solving is?

- what am I going to write for this essay?

- how am I going to pass this examination?

These problems have two things in common. They all have a goal, such as buying groceries or knowing the answer to a mathematical equation; they all lack immediate ways of attaining the goal. A problem, therefore, is a situation in which the goal is blocked, either because of lack of resources or because of lack of information. Whenever you carry out some action to achieve the goal, the problem is solved. In reaching the solution, something new is learned – about how to pass exams, how to multiply 16 by 25, or how to plan a dinner menu and so on. Then, when the problem occurs again, the same solution will be remembered and used once more. With repeated practice of the same problem, the solution will come to be retrieved from long-term memory rapidly and automatically whenever the problem is encountered. Compare, for example, a child's early attempts to add up two numbers with the later ability to retrieve the answer to a specific addition, such as $4 + 6$, directly from memory. Thus, not only is something new learned on finding the solution in the first place, but, after repeated practice, the learned information may subsequently become automatically available whenever the problem arises again.

What is involved in finding a solution? Newell and Simon

(1972) have given the best answer to this question. They say that finding a solution means finding the quickest route to the goal. This is not as straightforward as it sounds because there are usually a vast number of ways to solve a problem. Take the example of choosing a move in a game of chess. Chase and Simon (1973) have worked out that a typical game of chess involves about 60 moves, with an average of 30 alternative legal moves that could be chosen each time. This makes a total of 30^{60}, a number so astronomical that no computer, not even the fastest, can play chess by exploring every possible move sequence. So how do people decide which solution to try? They certainly do not contemplate every possible solution and then decide on the best one. Instead, according to Newell and Simon, people reach a solution in a series of steps, each one bringing the problem solver closer to the goal. Another way to put this is to say that each step in the solution reduces the difference between the current state and the goal. Thus, the solution that is chosen is the one that, as far as possible, is the quickest way of achieving the goal.

To give a concrete example, imagine that you are driving in a strange city that you have not visited before. You arrive from the south and you need to get to an office building in the north-western corner of the city. You have no city map to help you, so you have to do it by dead reckoning. You use the time and the sun to help you locate the points of the compass and then drive off in a north-westerly direction. As you drive, you have in mind a cognitive map of roughly where you are now, where you want to get to, and the distance between the two. That is, you have a mental representation of the initial problem and of the goal. By driving in a north-westerly direction you are trying to reduce the difference between your current state and the goal. If the road curves away from the goal, to the west for example, you will need to update your current state and change your route accordingly when you have the opportunity. If you follow this procedure faithfully, you should eventually arrive at the goal; and you will have done so not by trying every possible route that you might have taken, but by trying to reduce the difference between where you are now and where you want to be – that is, by successively reducing the difference between the initial problem situation and the goal.

If the solution is successful, it will be used again, so in the example above, the route that is learned will be used again if the same situation re-arises. In many cases of learning, the same problem occurs again many times, and learning is seen not only as finding the solution initially but also as using the solution repeatedly until the problem can be solved automatically without conscious thought. For example, problem solving is a very common activity in learning mathematics. Imagine the situation of a child first learning to multiply, say, 2 by 4 without pencil and paper. How might the child reach the goal of knowing the answer? First, the child has to remember the equation and keep it in mind; that is, the original problem has to be held in working memory. Then he or she must remember that 'multiply 2 by 4' means something like 'four lots of two'. This information too has to be held in memory while the child tries to add up 'four lots of two'. Each time two is added, the partial solution has to be remembered so that the next four can be added to it, and a tally has to be kept of how many twos have been added together so far so that the child knows when the answer is reached. The child has thus taken his or her first steps in learning how to multiply 2 by 4.

As the above description suggests, problem solving can be very demanding when so much information has to be held in memory until the solution is reached. Thus learning also involves finding a way to reduce this load on memory so that the problem can be solved more easily. Such learning occurs with repeated attempts to solve the problem. That is, learning occurs as a result of practice. As the child practises, the mental activities are strengthened and eventually get stored as a single unit (or rule) in long-term memory.

To show what is involved in such learning, consider the example of a child learning how to do the above problem. Initially he or she may learn a rule that says something like:

IF   the goal is to multiply 2 by 4
THEN add 2 to itself 4 times and report the result.

With further practice in this and other multiplication problems, the child also learns a general rule about how to do multiplication:

IF   the goal is to multiply a by b
THEN add a to itself b times and report the result.

The learning of this general rule makes it possible to solve a wider range of problems, including ones that have not been explicitly taught. However, further practice with a specific problem also strengthens the specific rule, a strengthening that causes it to become automatic. Eventually, when the problem has been solved correctly a large number of times, the answer and the problem are linked directly in an even more specific rule, a rule that says:

IF   the problem is '2 times 4'
THEN report the answer '8'.

Now the child can report the answer immediately the problem is encountered, without having to think about how it is solved, and without having to hold information in working memory. Thus, the space in working memory is freed up, allowing new learning to occur by using the newly available space in memory.

This view of learning to do things automatically is based on Anderson's (1983) model of skill acquisition. According to Anderson, skills are learned as a result of practice and they become automatic when highly specific rules that give the solution directly are stored in memory. As we saw above, in the process of acquiring such specific rules, other rules that describe the way the solution is achieved are also stored in memory. These additional rules remain available in memory and can be used when needed. Their strength is determined by the number of times they are used. Anderson calls all these rules *production rules* because they enable actions to be produced in response to problems. These actions may be mental actions as in the example above, or they may be physical actions, as when learning to drive a car. The knowledge that is embedded in production rules is known as *procedural knowledge*; it is knowledge of how to do things like solving mathematical problems, conducting a scientific experiment or driving a car.

We have described two ways in which problem solving results in learning. The first is when the problem is originally solved in working memory: the novel solution means that something new has been learned. We may work this solution out for ourselves or we may be given the solution by an instructor or a teacher. The second is described by Anderson's model of skill learning: repeated use of a successful solution results in its becoming stored in long-term memory as a specific rule. Retrieval of the rule gives the answer immediately whenever the problem is encountered. This automatic retrieval of the solution bypasses working memory altogether, so enabling new learning to occur: working memory is no longer needed for working through the steps of the solution and so new learning can be attempted.

Despite these obvious advantages to problem solving as a form of learning, it also has some inherent dangers. The main one is that a preoccupation with problem solving can lead to a neglect of understanding. The reason why this is a serious problem is that automatic skills learned in the above manner can only be used in the situation in which they were learned. The solution is activated whenever the problem described in the first part of the specific rule is fired. This means that there is no generalization to new situations, unless they are very similar to the original learning situation. Generalization is a very important aspect of learning. It is what enables new learning to be used in novel situations. For good generalization to occur, one needs to understand conceptual principles that underlie a whole range of problems that seem on the surface to be very different. Hence by understanding these principles, the whole range can be tackled in a similar manner. For example, if you know only how to find the solution to a problem, such as finding the square root of a number, but do not understand the mathematical concepts that explain the solution, or the mathematical steps required to reach it, then you will not be able to solve a similar problem in a novel context. Such a situation arises when a person can find the solution using a calculator but is unable to solve the problem when there is no calculator available. A more striking example of such a state of affairs can be illustrated by contrasting the mathematical abilities of Brazilian street children with those of Japanese children who use the abacus for calculation.

Brazilian street children earn a living by selling things on the street (Carraher *et al.*, 1985). They acquire some remarkable arithmetical skills while doing so. For example, to find the price of twelve lemons of $5.00 each, a 9-year-old street vendor counted up by 10 (10, 20, 30, 40, 50, 60) while separating out two lemons at a time. According to Carraher *et al.*, the mathematical abilities of the street vendors reveal a 'solid understanding of the decimal system', and their performance is equivalent to the use of decomposition and regrouping in formal mathematics.

Furthermore, these children show good generalization: they readily adapt their numerical operations to finding the solution to novel problems. Carraher *et al.* tested the children on new problems in the laboratory. The children could solve word problems that involved the same operations they used on the street, even though word problems are normally found to be more difficult than number problems (Carpenter and Moser, 1982). Thus, the Brazilian children could use their street knowledge to solve equivalent equations in the laboratory. Of course, the children could not solve the equivalent problems if they were presented in numerical form (e.g. 5 times 35 = ?) rather than as a verbal description of the situation on the street. The unfamiliar format of the problem failed to activate the knowledge that they typically used in their street transactions. Such difficulty is not surprising since it requires knowledge of formal conventions that need to be specifically taught. However, the children do show a deep understanding of mathematical principles, principles that can be applied in novel situations, such as the experimental laboratory.

Hatano (1988) suggests that the reason these children are so good at mathematics is because they are engaged in an interpersonal exchange that requires semantic transparency to prevent the customer from becoming suspicious. Calculations are performed very quickly, through the use of rich conceptual knowledge. However, there is no great premium on accuracy because errors will easily be spotted by either the vendor or the customer. Such behaviour contrasts markedly with that of Japanese children who use the abacus.

Japanese children who use the abacus perform extremely rapid and accurate calculations. Hatano describes a 9-year-old child who solved 30 multiplication problems, such as 148 times 395, in less than a minute. He suggests that the children have acquired a vast store of specific rules that over time have become merged into general rules for solving equations, a view that is consistent with Anderson's model of skill acquisition. However, the abacus users were unable to solve the same problems using pencil and paper (Amaiwa, 1987). Amaiwa suggests that this is because they did not understand the meaning of the steps used on the abacus and so could not retrieve the relevant knowledge to help solve the pencil-and-paper problems. In other words, they had acquired a set of specific rules that are used to solve equations automatically, but had not gained an understanding of the mathematical concepts that lead to an understanding of how the procedures work.

A preoccupation with problem solving may lead to a neglect of understanding because both require the use of working memory. We saw in the example of a child learning multiplication that problem solving is effortful because of its excessive use of working memory. The search for understanding is also effortful for the same reason. So if you are doing one kind of learning you cannot also be doing the other. Perhaps more worrying is the observation that schoolchildren are more likely to learn mathematics by problem solving than by understanding (Sweller, 1988). Sweller showed that while this focus on problem solving led to the solution of the problem, it did not lead to understanding. That is, it did not lead to a conceptual understanding of the kind that we see in the Brazilian street children. This was because, as we might expect, the problem-solving activities left no spare memory capacity for conceptual understanding. Owen and Sweller (1985) showed this to be the case. They prevented subjects from using problem solving by changing the goal from a specific one, such as 'What speed will the car reach?', to a non-specific one, such as 'Collate the value of as many variables as you can.' When they did this, conceptual understanding, in the form of knowledge of mathematical principles, improved considerably.

Thus there is a basic tension in mathematics teaching (and the teaching of other subjects too) between the need for problem solving and the need for understanding. Repeated practice at problem solving ensures that mathematical rules can be used automatically and that new rules can be learned through the solution of new problems, but it does not help the child to learn general mathematical principles that can be applied in new situations. One possible solution to this problem is to engage in problem solving first, so that fluency in the rule will be attained, but then to reflect on the solution and use it to understand the problem more thoroughly.

Schoenfield (1985) advocates this approach to mathematics learning, but he also claims that it is rarely used in schools, to the detriment of the children's mathematical education. That is, the premium in schools is on fast and accurate performance, so once a solution has been found the student simply moves on to the next problem. There is no pause for reflection, for learning through understanding to take place. For instance, a simple activity that enhances understanding is to go back to the original problem and check that the obtained solution is plausible and makes sense as an answer to the question. Yet students frequently fail to take this step towards understanding. Schoenfield comments that many students do not even notice when they produce an answer that is an implausible solution to the problem. This is probably because to assess the plausibility of the solution requires the deliberate application of high-level processes of understanding. As we saw in the previous section, people find it difficult to make deliberate attempts to evaluate new learning material (in this case the solution to a mathematical problem) in the light of what is already known (in this case the original problem). However, some undergraduate students seem to search for understanding spontaneously, and these students are the ones that are good at mathematics. Good mathematics students, unlike poor ones, tend to pause after solving a problem, apparently to extract generalizable knowledge from the experience (Davis and McNight, 1979).

Overall, therefore, problem solving is a necessary component of learning, but a preoccupation with problem solving runs the risk of sidestepping understanding. When this happens, true learning will not occur, because the opportunity to gain deep conceptual knowledge that can be used in new and different situations will be missed.

Learning as memorization

Memorization is involved whenever a person reads or listens to material with the intention of memorizing it. Typical forms of memorization are rehearsal and repetition of the material. However, also possible are other, more sophisticated techniques that include organizing the material according to some conceptual principle. These involve the integration of the new material with pre-existing knowledge. It is sometimes difficult to distinguish these more sophisticated techniques from processes of understanding, and indeed, processes of memory and of under-standing may form a continuum rather than two distinct sets of activities. Nevertheless, we will maintain the distinction here and say that, in general, memorization results in the accumulation of information in memory. This accumulated information may be added onto existing knowledge if sophisticated techniques are used, or it may simply be added to memory without making con-tact with existing knowledge. In contrast to understanding, memorization does not change or modify either the new material or existing knowledge in any way. Accumulation is the key word, in contrast to adaptation, modification or change. Norman (1978) makes a similar distinction when he talks about learning as the accretion of facts, what we have called memorization, and learn-ing as the reorganization of knowledge, what we have called understanding.

In contrast to popular wisdom, pure rote repetition is not the best way to practise and memorize new information. Some years ago, the British Broadcasting Corporation was required to change the wavelengths on which some of its programmes were broadcast. To prepare the public for the change, the BBC implemented a saturation advertising campaign in which the details of the new wavelengths were presented over and over again at frequent inter-vals. After this campaign, Bekerian and Baddeley (1990) tested a large sample of the listening public on their knowledge of the new wavelengths. Such knowledge was virtually non-existent. And yet according to the amount of time the subjects claimed to listen to the radio and the frequency with which the information was broad-cast, they must have heard the information well over a thousand times.

Repetition alone, therefore, is not a successful memory tech-nique. Rather, what counts is what is done with the material as it is repeated or rehearsed. Learning and memory are improved if subjects can organize the material in some way and integrate it with pre-existing knowledge. An example of this comes from a series of studies by Tulving (1962). In a typical experiment, Tulving had subjects listen to a list of 16 unrelated words and then asked them to recall as many of the words as possible, in any order they wished. After a subject had remembered as many words as possible, the list was presented again, with the words in a different order. This procedure of listening to the list, remembering as many words as possible, then listening to the list again was repeated 16 times, with the words in a different order each time they were presented. In spite of the differing order for each presentation, most subjects tended to recall the same set of words together each time they remembered them. Further, for most subjects, the incidence of this clustering increased systematically from trial to trial. Its effect was dramatic. At the end of the 16 trials, the correlation between the degree of clustering and recall performance was an almost perfect 0.96. In other words, the more the clustering, or subjective organization, the better the recall.

These results show that the more a person tries to organize the information according to some already known principle, the better he or she will remember the information. This view was developed by Craik and Lockhart (1972), who proposed the *levels-of-processing* view of memory. Craik and Lockhart argued that the strength of a memory depended on the level (or depth) of processing carried out on the information. The deeper the processing, the more durable the memory trace. In explaining what they meant by depth of processing, Craik and Lockhart pointed out that perception involves the rapid analysis of input at a number of levels. Early levels are concerned with the analysis of physical features, such as lines, angles, brightness, pitch and loudness. Later stages are more concerned with matching the input against stored knowledge from past learning. That is, later stages are concerned with identifying the input and establishing its meaning. In this hierarchy of processing stages, the greater the depth of processing, the greater the degree of semantic or cognitive analysis.

An important series of experiments was carried out by Craik and Tulving (1975) from a levels-of-processing perspective. In one study, they presented people with a list of 60 target words to memorize and asked the subjects to answer a question about each one. The question preceded each word and the subjects had to answer yes or no to the question after they had seen the word. Twenty of the words were preceded by *structural questions*, for example, 'Is the word written in upper case?'. The subject read the question, then saw the word and answered yes or no. Another twenty words were preceded by *rhyming questions*, for example, 'Does the word rhyme with "money"?'. The remaining twenty words were preceded by *semantic questions*, for example, 'Does the word fit the sentence, "The girl placed the ____ on the table"?'. These three types of question were designed to ensure that the words received different levels of processing, from very shallow to deep. Thus the structural questions induce only a shallow level of processing, since it is not even necessary to read the words to answer the questions; only their shape needs to be considered. Slightly deeper processing is induced by the rhyming questions; in order to answer these, the words have to be processed to the level of their sounds. The semantic questions, on the other hand, induce a deep level of processing; to answer these, it is necessary to grasp the meaning of the target word. After answering the questions about the target words, the subjects were then asked to remember as many of the words as possible.

Craik and Tulving's basic finding, one that has been replicated many times, was that the deeper the level of processing the better the words were remembered. All the words that were preceded by semantic questions were well remembered, while words that were preceded by structural questions were very poorly remembered. Memory for the words preceded by rhyming questions was intermediate between these two extremes. Craik and Tulving also found that the greater the degree of semantic processing, the better the memory. Degree of semantic processing depended on two factors. One was the amount of integration with prior knowledge. This was shown by the fact that words resulting in a yes answer to a question were remembered better than words that led to a no answer. If the answer is yes, the word and the sentence can be integrated into a single unit in memory. But if the answer is no, the word has to be remembered on its own.

The other factor was the extent to which the memory representation of the word was elaborated. This was shown by varying the complexity of the sentence used in the semantic questions. Some sentences were complex (e.g. 'The great bird swooped down and carried off the struggling ____'); others were simple (e.g. 'She cooked the ____'). Craik and Tulving found that memory for the words was best when complex sentences were used. This indicates the importance of an elaborate memory representation, because the complex sentences would have more elaborate representations than simple ones. Thus, the greater the integration with prior knowledge and the more elaborate the memory representation, the better was the memory for a word.

The usual way of doing this kind of experiment is to use an *uninstructed memory task*; that is, the subjects are not told beforehand that they will be asked to remember the words. As far as the subjects are concerned, they are making decisions about a series of words and not taking part in a memory experiment. Hence they are unlikely to be trying deliberately to memorize the words. However, there is another way of doing the experiment. This is to tell the subjects beforehand that they will be asked to remember the words at the end. In these circumstances, we would expect the subjects to try to remember the words as they are presented. The most striking outcome of this changed version of the experiment is that it does not affect the results. Whether the subjects know beforehand that they have to remember the words or not, the results are similar: the words that receive deep semantic processing are remembered best and the words that receive shallow structural processing are remembered poorly, if at all. Craik and Tulving suggest that this is because people do not use optimal learning strategies when deliberately trying to memorize material. For example, they might simply try to repeat the words rather than analyse their meanings.

Despite the fact that the experimental results are very robust, the levels-of-processing viewpoint has been challenged (e.g. Baddeley, 1978, 1982). In particular, Baddeley points to the difficulty of specifying depth of encoding independently of amount remembered. Nevertheless, the work does have two important implications for learning. First, it highlights the importance of deep semantic processing – that is, of integration and elaboration – if the material is to be memorized successfully. Such integration makes it easier for the information to be used again when needed. In particular, it lays the groundwork for learning through understanding. In order to make explicit use of learned material, it has to be easily accessible. Deep processing will make it more accessible. Second, the work highlights the fact that people frequently fail to use optimal learning strategies when they are deliberately trying to memorize material. That is, the focus of memorization is on getting the material into memory and keeping it there, and this may lead to the neglect of integration with prior knowledge.

As was said at the beginning of this section, memorization leads to a concern with the accumulation of information rather than with understanding that information. Specifically, while memorization may involve the use of prior knowledge to interpret new material (as shown in Tulving's clustering experiments), it lacks the evaluative component that is part of understanding and that may lead to extensive revision and reorganization of pre-existing knowledge. Memorization, therefore, is not the best way of trying to learn new material, although it will be satisfactory to the extent that deep semantic processing is used. However, new learning is best achieved through understanding; memorization can then be used to consolidate such learning.

Summary

Learning may be either implicit or explicit. Implicit learning is found in all animal species and occurs without conscious awareness. Through such learning we come to respond to the regularities in the world in consistent ways. The knowledge gained through implicit learning is itself implicit and inaccessible to conscious awareness. We use the knowledge to act in the world, but we cannot describe that knowledge. The ease and rapidity with which we use language and act in the world reveal the extent of our implicit knowledge. Explicit learning is unique to humans and enables us to think deliberately and consciously about what things mean, about how to solve problems and about how to remember things. That is, explicit learning occurs through understanding, problem solving and memorization. Since explicit learning is conscious, it requires the use of working memory and deliberate effort. Understanding is the most difficult form of explicit learning, since it depends on the deliberate use of pre-existing knowledge to interpret and evaluate incoming information, and also on the deliberate use of the incoming information to evaluate and revise pre-existing knowledge. These are both high-level cognitive skills. Understanding is also the most important form of explicit learning, since it is responsible for our ability to generalize what we have learned to new situations. However, because of its difficulty, it is often sidestepped and replaced by problem solving or memorization.

Problem solving results in learning when a novel solution is found to a problem. Further learning occurs when the solution is used repeatedly to solve the problem until it can be retrieved from long-term memory automatically without using working memory. Thus working memory capacity is freed up and becomes available for further learning. The ease and rapidity with which we can drive a car or find the square root of 25 testify to the ease with which we gain automatic skills through repeated practice. These are implicit and so inaccessible to conscious awareness. However, if working memory is occupied by problem-solving activities, it cannot also be used for understanding. One solution to this 'bottle-neck' is to evaluate the plausibility of an answer to a problem, thus searching for understanding once the problem has been solved.

Memorization results in the accumulation of material in long-term memory. The material is best remembered if it is integrated with pre-existing knowledge through the use of deep semantic processing, but memory is poor if the material is simply rehearsed through constant repetition and not integrated with pre-existing knowledge. When people deliberately try to memorize material, they frequently use non-optimal strategies such as repetition rather than engaging in deep semantic processing. This means that memorized material is not readily accessible for use in understanding. However, even when deep semantic processing is involved, deliberate memorization fails to engage in the two-way evaluative process that is the hallmark of understanding. Thus, memorization is not the best way to learn new material, but may be better employed in consolidating material that has already been thoroughly understood.

Now that we have described the nature of learning, implicit and explicit, we turn our attention to the learning of specific subjects: science, reading, mathematics and writing. But before we do that, we will set the discussion in the context of educational policies and practices. It is our belief that policy and practice need to be governed by an understanding of the nature of learning and of how such learning can be facilitated in specific subjects. We start, therefore, with a brief account of the changes in attitudes towards education since the 1960s and of how these changes have led to marked changes in policy and practice. After that we embark on our specific discussions of learning in subsequent chapters. We then return to the issue of policy and practice in Chapter 8, when we review what we have said about learning and apply it more specifically to practice. By doing that we hope to show that learning principles, not *ad hoc* policies, provide the best guide for good practice.

CHAPTER 2

The Educational Context for Learning

Overview

In this chapter we consider the educational context for learning in Britain. In particular, we focus on the primary years of schooling. A variety of influences has made a significant impact upon shifting emphases in both policy and practice in recent years. The most significant influence is, of course, legislation. The Education Act (1944) confirmed the establishment of a working partnership between central government and local education authorities. Within this framework, a great deal of responsibility and autonomy was invested in individual schools and teachers.

The publication of the Plowden Report, *Children and Their Primary Schools* (Plowden, 1967), ranks as another of the most crucial influences on policy and practice in British education over the past few decades. This report gave total support to child-centred learning. It promoted a recognizable philosophy of primary education as well as making specific recommendations about how schools might go about the task of implementing this child-centred philosophy.

More recent years have seen an increasing level of articulated concern about standards in schools and quality of education. Various reports by Her Majesty's Inspectors of Schools during the 1970s and early 1980s commented on such matters as low teacher expectations, uneven standards and lack of adequate or balanced curriculum coverage. In the mid-1980s there was a noticeable shift in emphasis in the educational debate. A long-established focus on approaches to curriculum delivery (*how* knowledge should be taught) was replaced by a new focus on curriculum content *what* should be taught). This new emphasis is reflected in the ~ent legislative context for education in England and Wales; ~ational Curriculum for Schools.

~ and legislation have thus brought about significant

changes in the nature of British educational practice. Alongside such changes, a number of independent studies have been carried out. Their findings relate to such issues as teaching and learning styles, matching teachers' intentions to pupils' activities, and classroom management practices.

Background

The Education Act of 1944 confirmed the idea of a partnership, in which central government and local authorities would share responsibility for the running of schools, and, within each local authority, head teachers and their staffs would implement policy. This partnership gave individual schools and teachers considerable autonomy. Decisions on such matters as design and implementation of the curriculum, school and classroom organization, teaching methodologies and organization of time were generally made by individuals and staffs within schools. This degree of freedom and responsibility awarded to teachers inevitably resulted in experimentation and innovation in the development of methods of organizing both classrooms and approaches to teaching and learning.

Set against this backcloth of teacher autonomy and innovation, the Plowden Committee commenced an enquiry into primary education in England and Wales. The work of this committee spanned the years from 1963 to 1966 and resulted in the publication of the Plowden Report (Plowden, 1967), the most comprehensive study ever published of the early years of schooling and the way young children learn and should be taught. This report unequivocally gave support to child-centred learning.

The Plowden era

CHILD-CENTRED LEARNING

The overall significance of the Plowden Report lay as much in the promotion of 'a recognisable philosophy of primary education' as in the making of its specific recommendations. It promoted the view that children are 'at the centre of the education process'. Its theoretical framework and recommendations for practice are grounded in the assumption that each child is unique. The report

hasizes this uniqueness in terms of development across three
.nensions – physical, intellectual and emotional.

It claims that individual differences between children of the
same age are so great that any school class, however homogeneous
it may seem, must be treated as a group of individual children.
Every member of that group will have specific needs and will
require different attention from the other members. It is a waste
of time to try and teach any child to move forward in any aspect
of learning until he or she is ready to make that particular
advance. Furthermore, it argues that all children develop at different rates and react in different ways. This applies to intellectual,
emotional and physical development, and a teacher needs to know
and take account of a child's 'developmental age' in all three
respects. Plowden articulates the view that the child's physique,
personality and capacity to learn develop as a result of continuous
interaction between his or her environment and genetic
inheritance. Furthermore, the Plowden philosophy promotes the
view that children generally have innate, enquiring, discovery-
oriented natures, which are central to their thinking and reasoning. Because of this nature and the uniqueness of the child, it is
argued that there is a need to individualize the classroom tasks and
activities of children and the nature of teachers' interactions and
involvement with them. Education is a process of enquiry and
discovery with the child at the heart of this process. This is central
to learning and development.

PROGRESSIVISM IN THE CLASSROOM

A cluster of characteristics is associated with Plowden's philosophy
of 'progressivism' and its interpretation in the classroom, as summarized below:

- *child-centred learning.* Emphasis in both teaching and learning
  is on the individual child. A teacher adopting this approach
  will follow an individual's natural curiosities, impulses,
  needs and interests. She or he will encourage free expression,
  and will provide opportunities for the development of experiences and awareness. Knowledge, therefore, may well
  be tentative or incomplete, as it is based on spontaneity.

- *discovery or experiential learning.* The transmission and learn-

29

ing of knowledge is secondary to the process of discovery. Emphasis is on the learner 'doing' things. Learning is through active engagement with ideas or materials. The pupil does not passively receive knowledge, or engage in prescriptive tasks laid down by the teacher. There will be emphasis on originality and diversity in response to classroom experiences; and indeed on enjoyment of learning as a process.

- *process emphasis, rather than product.* The processes of learning – that is, the emphasis on experiences, discovery and skills – are as important as the knowledge or product which results. The learning experience is thus seen to be of great value in its own right. Education is intrinsically worthwhile.

- *integration of knowledge.* A curriculum based on a philosophy of child autonomy, individual interests and experiential learning has (for many teachers) been associated with integration of subject knowledge rather than the teaching of subject-specific content. In primary schools, integration has traditionally been achieved through topic or project work, wherein a central theme (such as water, transport, ourselves) has been developed in a cross-curricular manner.

- *teacher as enabler.* A teacher adopting the philosophy of progressivism will view his or her role as that of a guide, facilitator or enabler of learning. Knowledge is not 'imposed from above'. The teaching task is to provide a rich range of experiences and opportunities for learning by discovery, maximizing each child's potential to develop as an individual. Emphasis will clearly be on individual and smallgroup teaching rather than on whole-class teaching.

PLOWDEN'S RECOMMENDATIONS

The child-centred, discovery-learning philosophy and related recommendations of the Plowden Report had significant implications for classroom practice. Examples of specific recommendations include the following:

> We recommend a combination of individual, group and class work and welcome the trend towards individual learning.

... we welcome unstreaming in the infant school and hope that it will spread through the age groups to the junior school.

It was recommended that learning in primary schools was to be active rather than passive. Practical experiences were to be the overriding priority along the route to theoretical learning. Children were to be shown how to learn rather than told what to learn.

The conclusions of the Plowden Report led to a general acceptance of teaching by discovery methods, of integrating subject matter through topic or project work, and an emphasis on the learning of skills and processes, rather than on the formal teaching of discrete areas of knowledge and understanding. A post-Plowden trend in primary education was to establish a school ethos in which children learn to live first and foremost as individuals, in accordance with the child-centred philosophy and description of an effective school:

> The school sets out ... to devise the right environment for children, to allow them to be themselves and to develop in the way and at the pace appropriate to them. It tries to equalise opportunities and compensate for handicaps. It lays special stress on individual discovery, on first hand experiences, and on opportunities for creative work. It insists that knowledge does not fall into neatly separate compartments and that work and play are not opposite but complementary. (Plowden, 1967)

POST-PLOWDEN CONCERNS

There has been a trend in recent years to blame the Plowden philosophy for low standards of pupil achievement in schools, and for the perceived problems of education in general. Furthermore, the current political concern over strategies for teaching and learning is undoubtedly fuelled by reports of mediocre educational practice. Various HMI reports of the post-Plowden era have reinforced the value of 'integrated' and discovery learning. Yet they also report concerns about uneven standards, problems of differentiating between pupils according to their individual needs, low teacher expectations, and lack of adequate curriculum coverage (e.g. DES, 1978, 1985). Such reports indicate that classroom practices and learning outcomes were not fulfilling the promise of progressivism.

Following on from such concerns, the mid-1980s were characterized by a noticeable shift in emphasis in the educational debate. The emerging crucial issue became definition of curriculum content (*what* knowledge, understanding, concepts and skills should be taught), rather than approaches to curriculum delivery (*how* these components should be taught; that is, by formal, didactic, subject-based teaching or by more progressive, discovery–learning approaches). This changing emphasis was reflected in the Great Education Reform Bill, the Education Reform Act of 1988 and the current National Curriculum for Schools.

The National Curriculum

The National Curriculum with its related assessment arrangements provides the current legislative context for teaching and learning.

Statutory Orders and related curriculum guidance identify a range of subjects and cross-curricular issues which pupils aged 5–16 should be taught in schools (NCC, 1990). Most subjects are divided into separate units or topics, such as 'algebra' and 'shape and space' in mathematics, or 'reading' and 'spelling' in English. These units are called Attainment Targets. Programmes of Study and the Attainment Targets for each subject set out the range of knowledge, skills and understanding that pupils are expected to acquire. These are divided into the four Key Stages of learning, covering the age range 5–16. Key Stage 1 covers 5–7-year-olds, Key Stage 2 is the 7–11 age group; Key Stage 3 is ages 11–14; and Key Stage 4 is ages 14–16. There are ten levels of achievement for each Attainment Target in most subjects. At the end of each Key Stage, when children are 7, 11, 14 or 16, they must take national tests, known as Standard Assessment Tasks. Their scores in these, combined with the teachers' assessments, determine each pupil's level of achievement.

CORE AND FOUNDATION SUBJECTS

The three core (and formally assessed) subjects are:

- English
- mathematics
- science,

to be taught alongside the foundation subjects, these being:

- technology
- history
- geography
- modern foreign language
- art
- music
- physical education (PE).

Together with religious education, and Welsh in Wales, the above range of subjects forms the basic entitlement (and legally required curriculum) of every pupil in school.

CROSS-CURRICULAR ISSUES

Alongside and interwoven with this entitlement are a number of cross-curricular issues that permeate the curriculum as a whole. Such elements are non-statutory but are intended to form an essential part of every child's learning experiences. 'Cross-curricular issues' include three elements which permeate the whole curriculum:

- cross-curricular dimensions
- cross-curricular skills
- cross-curricular themes.

Cross-curricular dimensions include matters such as providing equal opportunities for all pupils and preparing them for life in a multicultural society. National Curriculum Council (NCC) documentation states that these are an essential part of the personal education to which all learners are entitled, and should permeate all aspects of the curriculum (NCC, 1990). This does of course mean that part of a teacher's task is to ensure that all pupils have access to the basic curriculum.

The NCC believes that a number of *cross-curricular skills* are transferable across the curriculum, being independent of content. The documentation states, therefore, that it is considered

> absolutely essential that these skills are fostered across the whole curriculum in a measured and planned way . . . all are transferable, chiefly independent of content and can be developed in different contexts across the whole curriculum. They will be developed from the age of 5 through to 16 and beyond. (NCC, 1990)

The skills that are assumed to be transferable are:

- communication

- numeracy

- study

- problem solving

- personal and social

- information technology.

Five *cross-curricular themes* are included in the curriculum, these being:

- education for economic and industrial understanding

- health education

- careers education and guidance

- environmental education

- education for citizenship

Such themes have clearly identified aims and a suggested content of knowledge, understanding, skills and concepts.

> The themes have in common the ability to foster discussion of questions of values and belief, they add to knowledge and understanding and they rely on practical activities, decision making and the interrelationship of the individual and the community. (NCC, 1990)

In summary, the ten core and foundation subjects form the basic curriculum for all pupils aged 5–16, which in practice will be augmented by:

- religious education

- cross-curricular issues (dimensions, skills, themes)

- additional subjects beyond the ten prescribed areas (perhaps an additional foreign language or economics)

- extra-curricular activities (areas of learning which take place outside class or lesson time and extend beyond the formal school day; for example, outdoor education).

This combination fulfils the requirements of Section 1 of the Education Reform Act (1988) which places statutory responsibility upon schools to provide a broad and balanced curriculum.

Non-statutory guidance suggests that the National Curriculum is intended to be a framework for implementation rather than a straitjacket of subject-specific content. Legislation allows for some freedom of interpretation and delivery of material. Nevertheless, the Attainment Targets and Programmes of Study are precise and specific in their instructions.

For the first time, therefore, educators in England and Wales are provided with clear statements of pupil entitlement, targets and 'benchmark' standards. Teaching and learning objectives for each subject are prescribed. This specificity represents a marked change of emphasis from the philosophy and practice of the Plowden era.

Changing attitudes

The recent upsurge of interest in the content and quality of education in schools has resulted not only in the introduction of the National Curriculum for Schools with related arrangements for assessment, but also in a subsequent concern with classroom organization, teaching methodologies and the training of teachers. Statements associated with policy and legislation (e.g. Clarke, 1991) have signalled the government's intention to make clear

35

recommendations on teaching and learning strategies. Such speeches have included strong messages about classroom practice and teaching methods, school organization, resources and teacher training. They paved the way for the publication of a government discussion paper (Alexander *et al.*, 1992), commissioned by the Secretary of State, which makes recommendations about curriculum organization, teaching methods and school practice that are appropriate to implementing the National Curriculum successfully. These recommendations endorse an acceptance of the framework of the National Curriculum. They call for discussion about standards of teaching and learning and for consideration of the role of the classroom teacher, and make strong statements about the place of subject knowledge. The paper criticizes current teaching quality and standards of achievement, and emphasizes how the task of (primary) teaching has changed dramatically in recent years, largely as a result of the introduction of the National Curriculum for Schools. It promotes discussion on how children can most effectively be taught in order to raise standards of achievement in all pupils.

Concerns raised by Alexander *et al.*, challenge familiar and long-established policy in school classrooms. Together with concerns articulated by HMI they have led to a marked shift in emphasis, from the progressivism of Plowden and the post-Plowden era towards formality and a 'return to basics' or more traditional teaching methods.

We now turn our attention from educational policy to classroom practice as actually observed in schools. We continue with a focus on the primary stages of education and on the findings of a number of substantial studies of classroom life which have been undertaken in the post-Plowden era in the UK. Such studies and their published reports have been completed within the context of the changing policy we have described. Thus they are in no way intended to be comprehensive in terms of reporting global research on classroom practice.

Classroom practices

The changing face of British educational practice at the level of policy and legislation has been accompanied by a number of independent research studies that reveal examples of the kinds of interaction and activity that actually occur in primary school classrooms. The following sub-sections describe some of the significant findings of the major reports.

TEACHING AND LEARNING STYLE

Bennett (1976) conducted a questionnaire survey to investigate teaching methods including classroom organization, pupil seating arrangements, and curriculum organization, and also sought teachers' opinions about education; its aims, issues and methodologies. Using cluster analysis, the teachers in his survey were classified into twelve teacher types or 'styles' of teaching. These teaching styles fall within a general distinction between 'progressive' and 'traditional'. They result in the adoption of distinctive strategies for or approaches to teaching and learning, as listed in Table 2.1, which shows the clusters of attitudes and classroom strategies associated with the basic division of overall style between progressive and traditional. Only one of the 12 styles (9 per cent of the population of 468 teachers studied) identified by the survey was categorized as 'progressive'. Others were described as either mixed or traditional.

Bennett also found that these teaching styles had a marked influence on learning outcomes in all areas of the curriculum tested in his studies. In reading, formally (traditionally) taught pupils and pupils taught in a mixed style made more progress than pupils of informal (progressive) teachers. He found a difference of three to five months' equivalence in performance. In mathematics, pupils of formal teachers performed better than pupils of both mixed and informal teachers; the difference being some four to five months. In English, formally taught pupils again performed better than those of mixed and informal teaching, with a difference in progress measured at three to five months.

The Observational Research and Classroom Learning Evaluation Project (ORACLE – Galton *et al.*, 1980) also focused on teaching styles and pupil behaviour. This project is noted by

Table 2.1 Characteristics of progressive and traditional styles

Progressive	Traditional
Integrated subject matter	Separate subject matter
Teacher as a guide to educational experience	Teacher as distributor of knowledge
Active pupil role	Passive pupil role
Pupils participate in curriculum planning	Pupils have no say in curriculum planning
Learning predominantly by discovery techniques	Accent on memory, practice and rote
External rewards and punishments not necessary	External rewards, such as grades
Intrinsic motivation	Extrinsic motivation
Not concerned with conventional academic standards	Concerned with academic standards
Little testing	Regular testing
Accent on co-operative group work	Accent on competition
Teaching not confined to classroom base	Teaching confined to classroom base
Accent on creative expression	Little emphasis on creative expression

educationalists for its development of systematic classroom observational techniques to investigate interactions in the learning environment. A major objective of the ORACLE project was to study the relative effectiveness of different teaching approaches across the main subject areas of primary-school teaching. Teachers and pupils were observed over a three-year period.

The findings of Galton *et al.* showed that pupils varied considerably in their style of approach to learning activities, and that the prevalence of particular types of pupil activity was interlinked with and influenced by the style adopted by the teacher. Four types of pupils' behaviour in primary classrooms were identified:

1. *Attention seekers* (19.5 per cent of the research sample) engage in task-centred activity or routine work for a substantial part of the school day, and are characterized by a need for direct teacher contact. They often wait for teacher's attention, queuing at the teacher's desk, rather than collaborating with other children.

2. *Intermittent workers* (35.7 per cent of the research sample) spend some 20 per cent of time distracting other children, and avoid teacher contact rather than seek it. They were found to spend some 64 per cent of time on task.

3. *Solitary workers* (32.5 per cent of the research sample) spend the greatest amount of time on task (77.1 per cent), tend to stay at their desk and work quietly without distraction. They do, however, frequently interact with the teacher and other children.

4. *Quiet collaborators* (12.3 per cent of the research sample) tend to interact with the teacher as members of a group rather than as individuals. They rely on teacher support and will wait for this rather than work independently. They spend a large amount of time on task (72.6 per cent).

Four principal teaching styles were identified:

1. *Individual monitors* (22.4 per cent of the research sample) tend to concentrate on individuals rather than interacting with the class as a whole. They are didactic in approach, telling children what to do, rather than initiating problems to be solved. Many 'intermittent workers' are found in classrooms where this teaching style dominates.

2. *Class enquirers* (15.5 per cent of the research sample) concentrate on class teaching and individualized learning. They rely largely on questioning, which is directed by the teacher and involves little interaction with pupils in groups.

3. *Group instructors* (12.1 per cent of the sample) concentrate on working with groups of children rather than the class as a whole. They place emphasis on factual statements and verbal feedback. Researchers found a ratio of seven to one 'quiet collaborators' to 'attention seekers' responding to this style.

4. *Style changers* (50 per cent of the sample) are divided into three sub-groups:

   (a) infrequent changers, who changed teaching style only when it was considered necessary

   (b) rotating changers, who organize their teaching so that pupils rotate through different activities in specific locations and at specified times

   (c) habitual changers, who often make unplanned changes in style, seemingly for no good reason other than to encourage discipline and increase pupils' time on task.

One significant result of the Galton *et al.* research is to demonstrate the importance of matching learning styles and preferred teaching styles. It suggests that the traditional, structured mode of delivery could be totally unsuited (in terms of promoting effective learning), for example, to learners of quiet collaboration style. Furthermore, teaching style has implications for management. For example, it was found that, in practice, teachers utilize probing, higher-order questions and statements largely in whole-class teaching situations, rather than with individuals. In the whole-class situation, teachers can concentrate on such teaching tactics (as 'class enquirers' do). Thus they can focus on the subject matter under discussion with the class as a whole rather than devote time and activity to the management of 30 or more individualized tasks. This suggests that given contemporary class sizes, the Plowden 'progressive' ideology, based essentially on individualization, is impractical.

TEACHERS' INTENTIONS AND PUPILS' ACTIVITIES: A QUESTION OF MATCHING

Bennett *et al.* (1984) examined classroom activities in terms of what the teacher intended children to be doing and what they were in fact doing and achieving. This study investigated the nature and content of classroom tasks designed for 6–7-year-old children, and the factors that influence their choice, delivery, performance and diagnosis. It considered classroom tasks in all aspects of language and number work. For each task assigned to children, researchers asked about:

1. The teacher's intention in assigning the task.

2. How that attention was manifested in the particular task set.

3. The teacher's task instructions, i.e. how it was presented and specified.

4. The pupils perceptions of (3).

5. The materials available for the task.

6. The pupil's task performance, including interactions with the teacher or other pupils.

7. An assessment of short-term learning outcomes, i.e. immediately following the task.

8. An assessment of longer term learning outcomes, i.e. at the end of each term, in order to evaluate development and retention of learning over series of curriculum tasks. (Bennett *et al.*, 1984)

Using direct observation and interviews of teachers and children, a number of striking findings were reported. Understanding and interpretation of these require a knowledge of the classification of five task types identified within the study. These are:

1. *incremental tasks*, which 'involve the process of accretion in the acquisition of new facts, skills, rules or procedures'.

2. *restructuring tasks*, where pupils working with familiar materials are 'required to discover, invent or construct new ways of looking at a problem'.

3. *enrichment tasks*, which 'demand the use of familiar knowledge in unfamiliar contexts'; that is, transfer or application of new knowledge.

4. *practice tasks*, which 'require the repetitive and rapid application of familiar knowledge and skills to familiar settings and problems . . . to speed up and make automatic processes already in the pupils' repertoire'.

5. *revision tasks*, which involve bringing back to children's consciousness material and skills learnt on previous occasions.

Results showed that approximately 40 per cent of tasks were matched to the children's abilities. In 28 per cent of cases, mismatching occurred because the task set was too difficult for the child, while in 26 per cent of cases, mismatching occurred because the task set was too easy. However, these percentages varied according to the attainment level of the child: 41 per cent of all tasks were too easy for high attainers, while 44 per cent of tasks were too difficult for low attainers.

The research also showed that the tasks assigned to children frequently fail to match the teacher's intention (Bennett and Desforges, 1988; Bennett and Kell, 1990). For example, Bennett and Kell studied 4-year-olds in infant classes and found that while teachers often articulated clear ideas of what they wanted to do, the tasks that children were asked to undertake frequently did not match the teachers' intentions. An example is given of a case when a teacher's aim was to teach a child the sound of the letter 'h'. The child was given a series of pictures of things beginning with the letter 'h' and was asked to colour the pictures. The sound of the letter was not mentioned. Thus it was not clear to the child what she or he was expected to learn. The same study found a mismatch between the teacher's stated aims and his or her assessment of whether learning intentions had been achieved successfully. In many instances, results were considered successful simply because a child had completed a task. Learning might or might not have taken place.

In general, mismatching has been found at many different levels. These include (Bennett and Desforges, 1988) mismatches between the attainment level of the task and the difficulty of the task, and between the teacher's intention and the real demands of the task, as in the above example. They also include mismatches between instructions and task demands, between physical resources and task requirements, and between the learning processes assumed (such as restructuring) and those actually used (such as practice).

Bennett and Desforges (1988) provide statistics on matching task type to the balance of types of task. Significant findings include those of 1.3 practice tasks for every 1 incremental task in mathematics, 5 practice tasks for every 1 incremental task in language, a very low incidence of enrichment tasks, and an almost complete absence of restructuring tasks. A significant interpretation of these findings is that teachers have difficulty ensuring interconnectedness, appropriateness, balance and quality when designing and assigning a range of classroom tasks.

Bennett and Desforges (1988) interpret the above findings in terms of a number of interacting classroom processes. Thus they suggest that the following processes lead to mismatching:

- teachers adopting management techniques that permit rapid responses to each child's immediate requests but leave the teacher ignorant of the child's deeper confusions or potential

- teachers' preferences for immediate instruction rather than for the accurate analysis of children's starting points

- teachers' inexperience with and lack of skill in diagnostic work

- teachers' adopting a reinforcement strategy focusing on efforts to deliver concrete products rather than on less tangible evidence of engagement (for example, evidence of thinking)

- students' co-operation in these processes, as evidenced by their happy and industrious efforts to complete tasks by whatever means.

Thus there appears to be a complex relationship between teaching and learning activities and more general classroom management practices and skills of teaching. In the next section we consider management practices in the classroom in more detail.

CLASSROOM MANAGEMENT PRACTICES AND PUPIL PROGRESS

Motimore *et al.* (1988) examined factors which contribute to an effective school. Teaching strategies, classroom management strategies and pupil progress were included in this research agenda, which aimed to investigate 50 of the Inner London Education Authority's (ILEA's) junior schools.

Researchers followed a group of 2,000 pupils through four years of classroom life, from age 7 to 11, in 50 schools selected at random in ILEA. The study as a whole had four formal aims:

1. to produce a detailed description of pupils and teachers, and of the organization and curriculum of the schools

2. to document the progress and development of nearly 2,000 pupils over four years of schooling

3.   to establish whether some schools were more effective than others in promoting pupils' learning and development

4.   to investigate differences in the progress of different groups of pupils.

Data were divided into three categories: measures of the pupil intakes to school and classes; measures of pupils' educational outcomes; and measures of the classroom and school environment.

The study as a whole identified critical findings which help to create educational effectiveness in a school as a whole. We highlight examples which focus on policy variables and management at classroom level.

It was found that there was a strong relationship between sessions in which work covered only one curriculum area and the percentage of teacher time spent interacting with the class as a whole. Teachers who organized pupils so that they all worked within the same subject area also communicated more with the class as a whole. Both of these factors had a positive relationship with pupil progress.

It was found that the teacher's role in ordering activities during the school day is crucial, and is linked to pupil progress and development. The increasing degree of pupil responsibility for managing a programme of work activities over a long period was related negatively to several cognitive outcomes.

In classrooms where teachers provided ample planned work for pupils, progress was enhanced. The provision of plenty of appropriate work is linked to good use of questioning (especially the use of higher-order questions and statements) and to emphasis on praise and positive reinforcement techniques. Successful teaching involves being well organized. For example, it was found that where teachers sequentially planned language work, they were also more likely to keep written language records. Where teachers had a long-term plan for language, teaching sessions were more challenging and pupils demonstrated higher levels of engagement with their tasks.

Some evidence was found that when pupils worked in groups on the same task as other pupils of roughly the same ability, or when all pupils worked within the same curriculum area but on different tasks at their own level, then a positive effect on pupil progress resulted. When all pupils worked on exactly the same task, negative effects on pupil progress were recorded. This reinforces the need for teachers to take account of individual abilities and to organize pupil groupings and tasks accordingly.

One significant result of the Mortimore *et al.* study in its entirety is to illustrate how actual classroom practice is influenced by factors outside the classroom; in particular, aspects of management and communication in the school as a whole. Alexander (1991) draws similar conclusions on school effectiveness in the Primary Needs Independent Evaluation Project, commissioned to evaluate the city of Leeds' four-year Primary Needs Programme. However, he also found a mismatch between the physical layout of the classroom and the kinds of activity undertaken by the pupils. A substantial proportion of classrooms investigated were physically organized for group work while activities and tasks being undertaken within them were designed for and completed by individuals.

MANAGEMENT OF THE CURRICULUM

Alexander (1992) reports findings on the time spent by children and teachers on different areas of the curriculum. Figures for time spent within the curriculum are similar to those of other studies (e.g. Galton *et al.*, 1980) and suggest a fairly consistent pattern, wherein around 33 per cent of pupils' time is spent on language, 20 per cent is spent on mathematics, and all other subjects are far behind this (science 8.5 per cent, art 6.1 per cent, PE 5.4 per cent, topic work 4.5 per cent, environmental studies 1.7 per cent, computing under 1 per cent).

Furthermore, this study found that irrespective of specific tasks set and subject labels used in a classroom, pupils invariably undertake one or more of a small number of 'generic activities' (write, use apparatus, read, listen/look, draw/paint, collaborate, move about, talk to teacher, construct, talk to class) when going about their work. Observers analysed the percentage of time spent by pupils on these generic activities in different areas of the curriculum. The striking finding was that the curriculum was dominated by writing (56 per cent of the time in language, 55 per cent in mathematics, 53 per cent in computer work, 44 per cent in environmental studies, 40 per cent in topic work, 16 per cent in science), followed by reading, the use of apparatus, and listening/ looking. Children were found to be spending far more time on writing than on undertaking any other activity, and over half of their time was spent on reading and writing together.

These findings led Alexander to question the balance of activities within the curriculum as a whole, and within each of its subject areas. He also linked them to implications for subject-based and whole-class teaching. The research report calls both for more sharply focused and rigorously planned topic work and for an increase in single-subject teaching.

Summary

This chapter has outlined a number of the significant influences which have made an impact upon changing emphases in the policy and practice of education in Britain since the Second World War. It has focused in particular on the influential Plowden Report of 1967, its philosophy of 'progressivism', and concerns of the post-Plowden era leading up to the Education Reform Act (1988) and the framework of the current National Curriculum for Schools. Examples of statutory orders have shown that the National Curriculum documentation places emphasis on prescription of curriculum content rather than on a consideration of teaching methodologies and approaches to learning. Clear statements are made about knowledge and understanding to be taught in the core and foundation subjects, and about cross-curricular issues, such as skills that are believed to be transferable across the curriculum, being independent of content.

Alongside changes in legislation and the publication of government reports, educational understanding and thought have been influenced by the findings of a number of independent research studies. These reveal that education as it is currently practised in primary schools is significantly influenced by teachers' attitudes towards and styles of teaching (Bennett, 1976). Furthermore, teaching is affected by the day-to-day working styles of both pupils and teachers (Galton *et al.*, 1980).

Within this context of attitude and natural style preference, learning tasks and activities are designed by teachers and engaged in by pupils. There is a significant degree of mismatch between teachers' intentions for tasks, actual engagement in them and learning outcomes (Bennett *et al.*, 1984; Bennett and Desforges, 1988; Bennett and Kell, 1989).

Pupil progress is linked to classroom management policy and practices. For example, focus on a single curriculum area and teacher communication with a class as a whole are related to positive pupil progress. A teacher's role in ordering pupil activities and in planning is also crucial in terms of maximizing the progress of learners. Research findings indicate the need for teachers to take account of individual abilities and to organize pupil groupings, the classroom and tasks accordingly (Mortimore *et al.*, 1988).

Finally, research findings illuminate issues concerning management of the content of the curriculum. There is an imbalance across the curriculum in terms of percentage of pupils' time spent on particular areas of content. Pupils commonly undertake one or more generic activities when going about classroom tasks, irrespective of the subject matter under consideration. The curriculum as a whole is dominated by writing activities, followed by reading, the use of apparatus, and listening/looking (Alexander, 1991). The curriculum of primary schools does not reflect the overall balance that legislation and non-statutory guidance recommend.

From this general overview of the educational context for teaching and learning, we now turn attention to a more specific focus on the nature of learning in the curriculum's core areas. Chapter 3 discusses the development of scientific literacy, Chapter 4 considers the fundamental skills of learning to read and reading to learn, and Chapter 5 examines learning in mathematics and learning to write.

Towards Scientific Literacy

Overview

This chapter provides a focus on the nature of science, scientific knowledge and scientific processes, in order to illuminate aspects of the ways in which students may be helped to develop scientific literacy. Successful learning in this area incorporates the development of appropriate knowledge, skills and attitudes. Four classroom case-study situations are used to illustrate the range of components of scientific literacy and different ways in which teaching and learning may be approached. Three key questions are then considered: what is the nature of scientific knowledge and how is it acquired? What role does prior knowledge play in the acquisition and use of knowledge? How do misconceptions or naive theories affect learning in science? Discussion of these questions focuses on the key role of teaching in helping students to construct ideas and meaning and to extend their existing knowledge repertoire.

The nature of science

Scientific literacy is an essential part of life in our modern world, a world characterized by a complex intermingling of diversity and order. Science enables us to explore and to question observations in the universe; to find hidden order; to analyse and interpret findings.

The view of science commonly embodied in curricula, including the National Curriculum for Schools, is that it should be an essential part of a whole curriculum that is broad, balanced, relevant and differentiated. It should be directed towards effective learning. This means ensuring that all pupils are eager to participate in science, are stimulated by interest and curiosity, and can see relevance in what they are learning for their own lives. If this is achieved, then pupils should acquire scientific knowledge and understanding, develop skills of investigation and experimentation and have wide-ranging opportunities for communication about science. Within the philosophy and framework of the documentation for science as a core area of the National Curriculum, approaches to teaching and learning parallel the procedures and attitudes used by scientists. Teachers are expected to pose questions, provide appropriate challenges and experiences, and offer learners possibilities for new ways of thinking. The student's role is that of investigator. Understanding of the world is developed by existing ideas and concepts that are available; also by processes by which these ideas are used and then tested in new situations. A learner's knowledge and understanding of scientific ideas and his or her ability in problem solving should progressively increase as new experiences with objects and situations are encountered and as skills of investigation and exploration are mastered and developed.

Closer scrutiny of the nature of science, scientific knowledge and scientific processes will help our understanding of aspects of the complex process of developing scientific literacy. Physicist John Rigden (1983) emphasizes two key characteristics in the nature of science: its empirical character and its analytical nature. Progress in scientific literacy requires engagement with the empirical aspects of the universe; that is, those that can be observed or experienced directly. Students of science need to observe, explore, investigate and describe objects and situations, leading to an appreciation of both diversity and order in our biophysical surroundings. Only analytical activities such as experimentation and investigatory procedures can lead to the discovery of hidden patterns or laws, meanings and explanations. This interaction between empirical and analytical foci accounts for most of the activities that could be described as 'science'. The development of scientific literacy requires engagement with both. As empirical experiences lead to greater knowledge and understanding, so conceptual frameworks, explanations and theories require further empirical confirmation and application.

Investigating scientific phenomena involves interrelationships among scientific products, process and attitudes. *Scientific products*, otherwise termed scientific knowledge, comprise facts, concepts, generalizations, principles, theories and laws. This knowledge has been established as the result of the empirical and analytic activities of scientists through time. Scientific facts, or objectively confirmed statements about objects and events, such as that ice melts when it is heated and apples fall to the ground if severed from a tree, are the results or products of empirical activities. Generalizations, concepts, principles, theories and laws are the products of analytic tasks. Together they make possible the understanding and prediction of a wide range of behaviours, reactions and events in the world. They are what is *known* in science.

Students who are engaged in successful learning of scientific knowledge will almost certainly be learning to apply related methods of investigation and analysis, which may be termed *scientific processes*. Only by continued practice in employing a range of scientific processes will the learner develop the ability to separate inferences from evidence systematically and accurately. Table 3.1 provides a summary of scientific processes or enquiry skills that are fundamental to the learning of science in school programmes.

Alongside the gaining of knowledge and understanding, and the development of the skills and processes of scientific exploration, a number of *attitudes* or predispositions characterize the work of scientists. In particular, the attitudes of curiosity, respect for evidence, willingness to tolerate uncertainty, critical reflection, perseverance, open-mindedness, sensitivity to the living and non-living environment and co-operation with others are significant. Good programmes of science education will help students to learn and demonstrate these predispositions, leading to higher levels of motivation and an increased willingness to participate in exploration and learning.

Approaches to teaching and learning

In order to illustrate a range of the components of science literacy so far identified, we turn to four classroom situations in which pupils in schools are learning science.

CLASSROOM A

A group of mixed infant-age children are engrossed in the classroom play house. In their world of domestic role play, it is washing

Table 3.1 Scientific processes or enquiry skills

Process or enquiry skill	Definition
Classifying	Arranging or distributing objects, events, or information representing objects or events in classes according to some method or system
Creating models	Displaying information by means of graphic illustrations or other multisensory representations
Formulating hypotheses	Constructing a statement that is tentative and testable about what is thought likely to be true based on reasoning
Generalizing Identifying variables	Drawing general conclusions from particulars
	Recognizing the characteristics of objects or factors in events that are constant or change under different conditions
Inferring	Making a conclusion based on reasoning to explain an observation
Interpreting data	Analysing data that has been obtained and organized by determining apparent patterns or relationships in the data
Making decisions	Identifying alternatives and choosing a course of action from among the alternatives after basing the judgement for the selection on justifiable reasons
Manipulating materials	Handling or treating materials and equipment skilfully and effectively
Measuring	Making quantitative observations by comparing to a conventional (or non-conventional) standard

Table 3.1 *continued*

Observing	Becoming aware of an object or event by using any of the senses (or extensions of the senses) to identify properties
Predicting	Making a forecast of future events or conditions expected to exist
Recording data	Collecting bits of information about objects and events that illustrate a specific situation
Replicating	Performing acts that duplicate demonstrated symbols, patterns, or procedures
Using numbers	Applying mathematical rules or formulas to calculate quantities or determine relationships from basic measurements

Source: New York State Education Department, 1985.

day. Interesting questions are raised about preparing the washing (undressing the dolls to remove their clothes), getting the water and soap powder ready, washing, rinsing and drying it (the house has a clothes line). Then it is time to get ready for lunch. Some go to fetch the children from school while others stay and set the table. One by one the jobs are discussed and done, and a complex series of ordered tasks is completed. The teacher aims to capitalize on this everyday activity to develop basic scientific skills of ordering, sequencing, classifying and fair testing.

Rachel: Come on, everybody. It's Monday. Monday is washing day. Time to have a good clean up.
Paula: Sam – take Jo to get all the dirty clothes and put them in the big washing basket. A big, big basket.
William: I'll get the water ready.
Jo: Come on, Sam.
Sam: Right.
Rachel: Make sure the water's really hot, William.
William: Why?

Rachel: 'Cos mummy says it needs to be like that to get all the dirt out. It must be hot – hot.

William: Won't cold water do?

Paula: No. But don't make it too hot or we'll burn our hands. And don't forget the soap powder.

William: All right.

Teacher: Do you have all the things you need?

William: No, the babies are still dressed.

Jo: Help me undress the babies. Come here, Sam. I'll take their clothes off and you put them in the basket. Ready?

Sam: Yes.

Jo: Let's get their jumpers and pullovers off. Here you are. Where's the basket? Right.

Sam: They're a bit mucky, aren't they?

Jo: Yes, but we'll soon have them clean again. Shirts and blouses next . . . and dresses and trousers. . . .

Sam: Yes. Pass 'em over.

Jo: Vests and pants . . . got them?

Sam: Yes. Is that everything? What about the babies? They'll get cold with no clothes on.

Jo: Just a few pairs of socks, that's all.

Sam: Help me carry the basket back to the kitchen. It's too heavy. What a lot to wash.

Jo: Come on, then. You can't leave the babies lying there. Pick them up. Here, put them on the bed.

William: Water's ready.

Paula: Not too hot, is it?

William: No. I put my hand in. Just OK.

Rachel: Have you remembered the washing powder?

William: Yes – how much do we need?

Paula: My mum usually puts two or three lots of powder in. She gets it with a plastic scoop thing. We haven't got one.

Rachel: Use a big spoon instead.

Sam: Right, pass it over.

Jo: Wait a minute, Sam – we can't just dump everything in at once.

Sam: Why not?

Rachel: There's too much clothes for one wash. We'll have to do two or three lots.

Paula: That's what my mummy does. She sorts them into different piles.

William: What sort of piles?

Paula: Well, she puts jumpers in one pile, and the tee-shirts in another . . .

Rachel: And the vests and socks in another. Some things are dirtier than others. Dirty things will make clean things dirty.

Paula: But we are going to clean everything.

Jo: You don't wash everything the same way.

Rachel: Some things are harder to wash than others.

Paula: My mum uses a washing machine, and it washes different clothes. You push buttons, one for jumpers, one for socks . . . they're made of different things.

Teacher: So it depends what they're made of, then? How can you tell?

Rachel: Easy. Read a label. It tells you on there, I think.

William: Is that right, Jo?

Jo: Yes. Help me sort the dolls' clothes out, will you?

William: Right. Well, these are all woolly things, so I'll put them over here.

Jo: The pants can go here.

Sam: What are these socks made of, miss? What does it say on the label?

Teacher: Nylon, Sam.

Sam: So we need another pile over there.

Jo: Right. That should be enough.

William: We're ready, now . . .

Paula: What shall we start with?

Rachel: My mummy usually starts with the white things. She leaves the woollies till last, so she won't get any bits on the other clothes.

Sam: Let's do that, then. Pass them over . . .

Paula: Right, that's the last pile done.

Rachel: We need to rinse them and hang them out to dry.

William: Why can't we hang them up here, then?

Jo: 'Cos they're still full of soap and dirty water. We have to get rid of all that first. Go and fetch some clean water, Sam.

Sam: Right. Come on, William, you can help me.

Jo: My mom has a spin drier.

Rachel: So has mine.

Paula: Wish we had one. Still, we can squeeze the water out when we've rinsed all the clothes. It hurts my hands.

William: There! We've got most of the water out.

Sam: So we're ready to dry them now.

William: Where shall we put them?

Rachel: My mom says the best place is on the washing line out in the sun.

Paula: If it's really hot, they'll be dry soon.

William: What if there's no sun? It might be raining, silly.

Rachel: We can put them out as long as it doesn't rain.

Jo: But they will take longer to dry if there's no sun, 'cos the sun isn't there to take the water out.

Paula: Yes. The wind is very good for drying clothes, too. It helps to blow them dry.

Rachel: My mummy says it's not worth hanging the clothes out if it's dark. She likes it sunshiny or windy.

Sam: But what if it's raining?

Rachel: We'll have to dry them indoors.

Jo: We need to put them somewhere warm – like by the radiator . . .

Paula: Or a fire. No fire.

Rachel: My mummy's spin drier gets most of the water out. Then she puts them in the airing cupboard to dry off.

Teacher: Let's see where the clothes dry best, shall we? We haven't got a spin drier, but it's sunny outside . . . well, it is at the moment. So we can hang some out in the sun, and some in the shade.

William: And leave some by the radiator.

Teacher: Yes, fine, then we can wait and see which are dry first.

Sam: We'd better share the clothes out first, or it won't be fair.

Paula: What do you mean?

Teacher: Yes, Sam's right. The woollies are thicker, so they'll be wetter. They'll take longer to dry. We ought to put one woolly in each place, and share out the other things too.

Rachel: All right. You and William put the clothes line up outside while we get them ready.

(The children proceed with placing the washing out to dry.)

Paula: Look at the clock. Soon be dinner time.

William: What's for dinner. I'm starving!

Rachel: Beans on toast.

William: My favourite!

Rachel: Time to fetch the children from school.

Jo: Sam and me will go. Come on.

Sam: OK.

Paula: We'll set the table. You can help us, William.

William: Do I have to?
Paula: If you want any dinner, yes.
William: You're just like my mum. All right, what do we need?
Rachel: Plates.
Paula: And a knife and fork for everybody.
Rachel: We'll need the teapot, and the sugar bowl. And the milk jug.
Paula: And cups and saucers. And teaspoons.
William: Hang on, I can only do one job at once!
Rachel: Don't worry, we're coming to help you.
William: Come on, then. They'll be back in a minute . . .
Teacher: We have jelly for dessert, today.
William: Oh, great. Beans and jelly.
Teacher: What shall we eat it with?
Paula: We haven't got enough forks.
Teacher: Do you think a fork is the best thing to use for jelly?
Rachel: No, we need spoons. I'll get the spoons.

CLASSROOM B

Children aged 5 and 6 have set up an experiment in the context of a topic on soil, to investigate what happens when autumn leaves are buried in the soil. In pairs, they have selected a dead leaf, drawn around it on squared paper to observe its shape and size, then buried it in damp soil in a plastic bag. That was six weeks ago, and they are now engrossed in opening the bags to see what has happened to the leaves and compare findings. Each pair of children carefully tip out the contents of the bag on to some paper and search for their leaf.

Teacher: Right, children. Time to open your bags of soil carefully, and see what you can find.
Peter: Hurry up, Rosie.
Rosie: Hold the paper still while I pour it all out.
Peter: I'll spread the soil out. It's messy. It's smelly.
Teacher: Found anything yet?
Sue: Not yet, miss. Keep looking, David. Look at the colour of your fingers.
David: Think I've got something.
Maxine: Me too, miss. Look, Julia.
Julia: What is it?
Maxine: I think it's a piece of leaf, 'cos it's got a bit of green left in it.

Sue: We've found some leaf, too. But there's holes in the middle. It feels slimy.

David: Where's the rest of it? It was a bigger leaf when we buried it.

Sue: It's turned all brown and scrunchy.

Maxine: So's ours – there's bits broken off the edges. See, it's gone smaller, and it's all broken up.

Julia: I'll try to pick it up. It feels all crumbly. Yuk!

David: Look, there's the middle bit of it. It looks like a tree does in winter with its branches all bare.

Peter: I can't find anything in our soil. I think our leaf has all gone. It can't have gone.

Rosie: Are you sure, Peter? Let me have a look.

Peter: It's not fair. The others have still got some left.

Teacher: Let's work out how much is left of each leaf, shall we?

Peter: But where's my leaf?

David: How do we do that, miss?

Teacher: Listen carefully, children, and I'll tell you. Do you remember when we drew round those leaves before we buried them?

Maxine: Yes, miss.

Teacher: Well, if you find as much of the leaf as you can, we can put it on top of the leaf shape we drew, and that will show us how much is missing.

Julia: Right.

Sue: We'll have to be careful, though. There's only a few bits left, and they're all fiddly and small. I can't pick them up.

Maxine: You take the bits out, Julia, and I'll put them on the paper.

David: It's not easy, miss. They're ever so easy to break.

Sue: These thin bits look just like a spider's legs, miss. All skinny . . .

David: And twiggy.

Teacher: When you've put all the bits of leaf on your shape, see if you can tell how much is missing.

Peter: How can we do that?

Teacher: Think of how we counted squares before. Remember the biscuits?

Maxine: I know, miss. We can count how much squares we haven't covered up.

Teacher: That's right, Maxine. Well done. I wonder which of you will have the most leaf left.

Peter: It won't be ours, miss. The soil's eaten it. Well, it's gone somewhere. Unless someone climbed in the bag and stole it, the soil ate it.

CLASSROOM C

Two groups of Key Stage 2 children are setting up an experiment to observe the germination and growth of seeds. The seeds are the same variety in each case, in order to make it a fair experiment. The intention is that some will be grown in a light place and some in the dark, to see which grow best, so other variables need to be the same. The children are preparing the seed trays, filling them with soil and discussing how to make sure it is a fair experiment.

Teacher: So, children, let's check that we know what we're doing before we start. What are we trying to find out?

Nasreen: Whether seeds will grow best in a light place or a dark place.

Teacher: That's right. The only difference between all your seeds is that some will be put in daylight, and some in the dark. Everything else has to be the same.

Kate: Everything, miss?

Teacher: Yes.

James: So we ought to start with everybody planting the same seeds.

Sarah: Why?

James: 'Cos if they're different, some might take longer to grow than others.

Nasreen: Or some might need more watering than others.

James: And if they're all different, it wouldn't be a fair test. It would all end up a mess.

Kate: What seeds shall we use?

Sarah: Sunflower seeds. They're really nice. They're big.

Teacher: Yes, we have plenty of those. Here. Take some and pass them on to the others. Each group should have the same number of seeds, remember.

Sarah: What shall we plant them in?

Teacher: Think about whether these seed trays are a good idea.

Nasreen: Are they all the same size, Kate?

Kate: I think so. Why?

Nasreen: Well, if they're different sizes, some of the seeds won't have as much room to grow in as others.

James: And some might be planted deeper than others. That means they might take longer to grow up to the top.

Kate: So we need . . .

Sarah: All the seed trays to be the same size.

Nasreen: What about the soil, then?

Kate: What about it?

Nasreen: Well, it will have to be the same for all of them. It won't be fair otherwise.

Kate: Why not? You can't make soil the same. It's all different.

Nasreen: If some soil is full of stones, the seeds won't grow so well. You wouldn't grow if you had big stones on top of you.

James: We'd better get them out before we start planting.

Sarah: How can we do that, miss?

Teacher: Try these sieves, Sarah. Take one and pass the others on.

James: Wait a minute, Sarah.

Sarah: What for?

James: Well, just look at them – they're all different sizes. That's no good at all.

Sarah: So they are.

Kate: How do you mean?

Nasreen: The holes are all different sizes. See? This one's got much bigger holes than the others.

Sarah: If one of us uses this, their soil will have bigger lumps in it than the others . . .

James: Or more stones.

Sarah: So their seeds won't grow so well.

Kate: We've all got to use the same size sieve, then.

Nasreen: Yes. Let's use this one – it'll let the little soil through and keep out all the stones and other bits.

James: Right, let's get started.

Teacher: Is everything equal now? Count the seeds.

Kate: Should be – we're using the same bag of soil, the same kind of seeds . . .

Nasreen: The same size seed trays, and the same size sieve.

Kate: As long as we remember to fill all the trays with the same amount of soil, and water them the same way.

Teacher: Then it should be a fair test.

CLASSROOM D

Form 7B enter the laboratory for Tuesday's science lesson. Apparatus and clearly presented workcards are meticulously arranged, and Mr Joyne, an experienced secondary-school physics teacher, provides a clear explanation of what is to be done. The students set about their tasks in small groups with enthusiasm, familiar with the clarity of projects such as the one in hand.

Joanne appears to be the leader of the group on the front line of workbenches. She reads the list of what is needed.

Joanne: A small bottle with a screw-on top
A plastic drinking straw
A pair of scissors
Plasticine
A pin
Some drops of blue ink
A bowl of hot water

The group checks and is reassured to see that all items are on hand apart from the water, to which they have easy access.

Jayne begins the tasks in hand, reading step-by-step instructions from the workcard. She takes the top off the bottle, and makes a hole in it with the pointed ends of the scissors. She then half fills it with cold water. Lynn adds a few drops of ink to the water and, according to instructions, screws the top on and inserts the straw through the hole. Joanne presses plasticine around the join of the straw and the top to seal it. A small plug of plasticine is then inserted in the end of the straw, and a small hole is pierced in this with the pin. Jayne then places the bottle in the bowl and Lynn is despatched by Joanne to fetch hot water to fill up the bowl. The girls sit back, pleased with their achievement, and wait with anticipation. They are not disappointed. After a few minutes (they time the wait), their fountain begins to work and a gentle shower of water cascades from the hole in the top of the straw. Mr Joyne takes great interest in the result and congratulates the group. While waiting for other groups to complete the task, the girls begin to write up an account of their investigation. When the whole class has completed the practical work, Mr Joyne leads a discussion on what has been achieved. He elicits accurate responses from his pupils through careful questioning.

Mr Joyne: What effect does the hot water have on the contents of the bottle?

Ian: It warms it sir.

Mr Joyne: OK. What is inside the bottle that gets warmer?

Sue: Air and water.

Mr Joyne: So can you tell me more about what happens to the air when it gets warmer?

Lynn: It expands sir. So it pushes the water up the straw and it flows out of the top.

At the end of the lesson, there is little doubt that all pupils can explain why their fountain works.

In each of these classroom learning situations, a range of scientific processes – that is, a variety of empirical and analytic procedures – is inseparably linked to the acquisition of scientific knowledge and development of attitudes. In each of the scenes, science education is taking place alongside familiar, everyday activities, objects and experiences. Natural curiosity and existing subject knowledge underpin the structured development of knowledge, understanding and processes of science.

In *Classroom A*, everyday happenings are organized into a range of activities that will promote skill and concept development. Key concepts such as order and sequence are discussed and have relevance and importance: preparing the water, adding the soap powder, sequencing the order of washing and drying, etc. Classification skills are at the forefront of the task as woollies and cottons, jumpers and socks, vests and tee-shirts are considered and sorted. The teacher intervenes as and when necessary in order to structure investigatory methods and scientific understanding – for example, by suggesting a test of putting some wet washing in the sun and some in the shade. Thus during this pretend day, key concepts are discovered, discussed and seen to have importance, even though this is an imaginative situation. Order and sequence are noticed and logically reasoned.

The need for selection of materials is another key aspect of science education essential to this 'play'. Water of appropriate temperature is provided, and the cutlery and crockery necessary for the task of eating beans on toast and jelly for lunch is identified. As the session ends, a lengthy and complex series of tasks has been accomplished, introducing and reinforcing a wide range of science considered appropriate for the children's stage of learning. The classroom teacher recognizes that her task involves attempting to give structure to and to expand the ordinary everyday experiences of the young learners, while promoting attitudes of curiosity and co-operation.

In *Classroom B*, we see organization through a topic which clearly has science as a discernible core. It is easy to identify and extract the science content; for example, that dead leaves decompose in soil.

Alongside the learning of facts, skills of detailed observation and investigation are essential to the task being undertaken. Natural processes of the environment are discovered and discussed. The children's motivation for learning is engaged in the context of familiar objects from the world around them. Learning here involves making connections between objects and events, discovering outcomes and testing ideas.

In *Classroom C*, we see a situation wherein the children's tasks and learning are organized to introduce the subject matter of science itself alongside the development of scientific processes. Experiments are taking place to investigate the growth of seeds maintained in different conditions. A key concept being taught is that of fair testing. As in the other scenarios, the teacher's task involves facilitating learning while guiding its development by the designing of appropriate tasks; in this instance, investigation and experimentation. Learning arises as a result of the organization of practical experiences, upon making connections, and through logical testing of these experiences.

Finally, in *Classroom D*, the students are again organized to accomplish tasks aimed at teaching the subject matter of science. They are actively engaged in practical work involving experimentation. The scene could be interpreted as one closely resembling Classroom C in terms of its aims and organization. Yet we point out a substantial difference: in Classroom D, the practical activities are designed and set out in a highly structured way by the teacher. The role of the learner in this laboratory is to follow step-by-step instructions, to copy a method, and see it through to its conclusion. The aim of the teacher seems to be to ensure that the lesson's scientific content is 'learnt' or received in a foolproof way. He is successful. At the end of the lesson all pupils have accomplished the tasks set out for them and can explain the results of their practical work.

62

We identify a subtle difference between the activity-based learning of this schoolroom and the more 'active' learning of Classroom C, whose occupants have far more involvement in initiating, designing and organizing their investigations. Classroom C learners decide for themselves that everyone should plant the same seeds; they choose the seed variety, and work out other variables that can be controlled in the experiment. They have much greater personal involvement in both method and results of their science, and indeed of their learning. More will be said about teaching and learning styles and approaches to task design and classroom organization in Chapter 7; at this stage we highlight the distinction between activity-based learning of science, which may well be a passive or transmission form of learning, and genuinely active learning, in which students have far greater ownership of and responsibility for their decisions and actions.

So far this chapter has identified the major components of scientific literacy and has illustrated a variety of ways in which teachers may go about engaging students in learning in this area. All of these ways represent, albeit to a greater or lesser extent, approaches to the various domains of science education.

McCormack and Yager (1989) define these as: knowing and understanding (scientific processes), imagining and creating (creative), feeling and valuing (attitudinal) and using and applying (applications and connections). A teacher's theoretical understanding of how pupils think and learn in science is fundamental to success in these domains, alongside more practical considerations such as teaching and learning styles, and curriculum and classroom management. Such theoretical understanding incorporates three key questions:

1. what is the nature of (scientific) knowledge and how is it acquired?

2. what role does prior knowledge play in the acquisition and use of knowledge?

3. how do misconceptions or naive theories affect learning in science?

SCIENTIFIC KNOWLEDGE

Knowledge may be viewed as consisting of complex networks of products and processes. It may be classified as either declarative knowledge or procedural knowledge.

Declarative knowledge is that which concerns facts, concepts, principles, laws and theories. It can be communicated to others. An example of declarative knowledge in science is knowledge about the facts of tree classification. This would include the fact that trees may be classified as broadleaf or conifer, that other common habits are associated with these categories (such as evergreen and deciduous), and that trees in each category display a range of other characteristics (relating to leaf size and shape, and the nature of their fruits) which assist the biologist with identification and classification.

Procedural knowledge is a knowledge of how to execute a range of intellectual and practical tasks. It is knowledge that can be used in interpreting new situations, in solving problems and reasoning, and that is often learned by using and applying declarative knowledge. It may involve making inferences, generalizations or constructing classifications. To extend the above example, knowing how to use knowledge about the deciduous habit to explain the difference between the appearance of temperate woodlands and tropical forests at different times of the year is using procedural knowledge in a scientific context.

PRIOR KNOWLEDGE

No discussion of the acquisition of knowledge in science can ignore the importance of existing or prior knowledge. What students bring 'in their minds' to learning experiences critically affects how their learning will proceed and what will be learnt. Champagne and Hornig (1987) report that when students observed science demonstrations, their reported findings of these more closely aligned with their existing views and knowledge than with what actually happened in the demonstrations.

What, then, do we know about students' prior knowledge and assumptions in the field of science? Driver *et al.* (1988) document the conceptions that have been uncovered in pupils aged 10–16, in different physical domains, and indicate the importance of these for teachers and others concerned with science education. They emphasize how children come to a science class with ideas and interpretations concerning the phenomena they are studying, even if they have not received systematic instruction in these areas of study: 'Children form these ideas and interpretations as a result of everyday experiences in all aspects of their lives: through practical physical activities, talking with other people around them and through the media' (Driver *et al.*, 1988).

This research also draws attention to a number of general findings about the characteristics of children's ideas – their personal nature, their coherence and their stability. First it is suggested that pupils' existing ideas are personal in the sense that when individuals write about the same experiment, they will give various different interpretations of the same phenomena or events. A parallel situation is reading a book – a number of students reading the same text will not necessarily gain the same information from it or retain the same points: 'Individuals internalise their experience in a way which is at least partially their own; they construct their own meanings. These personal "ideas" influence the manner in which information is acquired' (Driver *et al.*, 1988). Furthermore, this personal manner of approaching phenomena is also found in the way in which scientific knowledge is generated. Observations of events are influenced by the theoretical frameworks of the observer: the observations children make and their interpretations of them are influenced by their ideas and expectations too (Driver, 1983). The personal nature of ideas does not of course mean that others may not share them, and research demonstrates (Driver *et al.*, 1988) that pupils in different countries may have the same ideas, or the same interpretations of similar scientific phenomena.

A second key point to emerge from this research is that a pupil's individual ideas may seem incoherent. Often in science lessons, individuals will propose different and contradictory interpretations of phenomena. Various explanations may be given for the same sequence of events.

The need for coherence, and the criteria for coherence, as perceived by the student are not the same as those of the scientist: the student does not possess any unique model unifying a range of phenomena that the scientist considers as equivalent. Nor does the student necessarily see the need for a coherent view, since ad hoc interpretations and predictions about natural events may appear to work quite well in practice. (Driver *et al.*, 1988)

Thirdly, this research concludes that children's ideas are stable. Even after being taught, they may not modify their ideas in spite of attempts by a teacher to challenge them by offering counter-evidence. If such counter-evidence is considered, it may be interpreted in terms of existing ideas held.

Other researchers document evidence which demonstrates that students bring to the classroom or laboratory many ideas derived from their everyday experiences, which are not in accord with accepted scientific knowledge. Paulu and Martin (1991) report examples of sixth-grade students' misconceptions; for example, 'Fossils are bones that animals are through wearing.' Philips (1991) reports misconceptions commonly held by students of earth science, and points out that misconceptions held by adults may also be held by children and vice versa; for example, 'Rain comes from holes in the clouds' and 'Clouds are made of cotton wool or smoke' (reported from school-age pupils), 'The oxygen we breathe does not come from plants' (reported from adults). Palmer (1993) reports misconceptions held by 4-year-old children as they enter formal schooling; for example, that if the temperature rises at the North Pole the snow will go away to live with Santa Claus, that melting snow goes to heaven, and that trees 'hurt' when they are chopped down.

MISCONCEPTIONS

Other researchers confirm the view of Driver *et al.* that personal theories and misconceptions are hard to give up. Roth (1987) reports research on children's conceptions of photosynthesis, demonstrating that they have many ideas, including erroneous ones, about the concept. Misconceptions include the belief that plants obtain food from the soil through their roots. Such misconceptions have been arrived at through pupils' personal experiences; for example, they may have added 'plant food' to the soil of their houseplants. Such explanations are thus plausible and persist in the learners' minds, even into adult life.

Research studies show (Driver *et al.*, 1988; Roth, 1987) that learners' misconceptions must be changed before more accurate concepts can successfully be learned. Roth (1987) argues that for conceptual change to occur, students need to realize and accept that their theories and beliefs are not congruent with accepted scientific beliefs. This involves understanding that their personal theories may be incomplete or at variance with accepted evidence. Furthermore, scientific evidence is more persuasive than their own explanations. This transition inevitably takes time. Students will need to engage in repeated tasks which focus their minds on the inconsistencies between accepted theories and their own beliefs. They will need to modify their existing ideas, and make appropriate links between these and accepted scientific concepts.

A key issue for teachers to consider is of course the need to ascertain the nature and extent of pupils' misconceptions, a topic addressed in Chapter 7. Furthermore, teachers themselves will need an adequate grasp of the subject matter – a knowledge of science – in order to help others learn it.

THE CONSTRUCTION OF MEANING

Developing scientific literacy thus involves both the changing of existing misconceptions and the extending of accurate knowledge. It incorporates interaction between the learners' experiences and their ideas or mental 'schemes' which are used to interpret and give meaning to these experiences. This view of learning is based on the belief that information is stored in memory in the form of schemes. Learning input from experiences or input from existing knowledge stored in long-term memory is the stimulus for thinking and developing understanding. Research (Keig, 1989) on memory facts and concepts suggests that memory links involved in schemata (activation of key ideas and spreading of them to linked concepts in order to recall or retrieve facts and concepts) are made best when:

- information is emphasized or presented in 'memorable' rather than incidental ways

- items are linked together logically or occur together in space and time

- information is meaningful to the learner.

As already discussed, meaning must be constructed by the learner: it is not inherent in a learning situation. Meaning is constructed by the association of new information with prior knowledge and experiences. The teacher's role, therefore, is to enable pupils to make such links. Teaching in science thus involves engaging students in tasks which assist the construction of ideas and meaning; that is, through active participation in empirical and analytic activities. Such activities provide challenging situations for the learner to apply and extend existing knowledge. They will also assist in the development of metacognitive strategies. Learning will be enhanced when cognitive efforts are considered, controlled and regulated through strategic approaches. A crucial goal of all science educators should therefore be to enable learners to develop autonomy or self-regulation of learning processes.

Summary

The acquisition of scientific literacy involves the development of knowledge and understanding as well as a range of process or enquiry skills. It also incorporates the adoption of a number of attitudes or predispositions that characterize the work of scientists.

There are a number of ways in which teaching and learning in science may be approached and organized. Hopefully, natural curiosity and existing subject knowledge will underpin pupils' structured development of knowledge, understanding and processes. A teacher's theoretical understanding of how pupils think and learn in science is fundamental to all domains of science education. This theoretical base incorporates a recognition of the key role of prior knowledge in the acquisition and use of scientific knowledge and processes; also an understanding of how misconceptions affect learning in science. A key goal for science teachers is to engage students in tasks which assist in the construction of ideas and meaning through participation in empirical and analytic activities. Related to this is the need to enable learners to develop autonomy or self-regulation of learning processes.

CHAPTER 4

Learning to Read and Reading to Learn

Overview

The ability to read is a remarkable human achievement. To start with, it is not a 'natural' skill. We do not learn to read spontaneously the way that we learn to talk. When we learn to talk, we are biologically prepared for the task that confronts us. Through evolution, our brains are specially adapted to enable us to speak and to listen to others. But this is not the case with written language. Written language is a human invention; that is, it is a product of cultural rather than biological evolution, so we are unlikely to have brains that are specially adapted to dealing with it. Reading, therefore, generally needs to be specifically taught. In spite of this, the process of learning to read has only lately been understood. We discuss these recent advances in the first part of this chapter.

Once we have learned to read, we gain a new and very powerful learning tool – we can learn many things about the world that we did not know before. The use of reading for learning is a topic of much current research, which has important implications for education. What is more, this research tells us a great deal about the nature of learning itself. We therefore devote the second part of the chapter to a discussion of reading to learn. In the course of this discussion, we will come face to face with one of the high points of human activity: how we can improve our own learning.

Components of reading

Reading is a complex cognitive activity, consisting of a set of inter-related processes. We can associate one set of processes with word recognition, another with sentence comprehension, and a third with text comprehension:

- *word recognition*: Traditionally, work on learning to read has concentrated on word recognition, a set of complex perceptual activities that enable us to identity each word on the page and to determine its meaning. We will follow this tradition in our own discussion.

- *sentence comprehension*: Sentence comprehension processes are those that we use to understand each sentence as it is read. They consist of linguistic and cognitive skills that are also used in listening. They therefore do not have to be learned all over again when learning to read; instead, we only have to learn to apply them to the written rather than the spoken word.

- *text comprehension*: Text comprehension processes allow us to understand the sequence of sentences that makes up a text. These are the processes that allow us to learn from reading. Like sentence comprehension processes, they also use linguistic and cognitive skills that can be used in listening. However, writing, unlike speaking, leaves a permanent record and so we can go back and reread a part of the text. Because of this, many text comprehension processes may only be used in reading, thus giving reading a key role in learning.

Learning to read: word recognition

When we want to think about the way that something is learned, a good place to start is with the mature skill. We will therefore begin by discussing how adults recognize printed words. After that, we will return to our main concern of how children learn to read. Then we will comment on the methods used to teach children to read.

WORD RECOGNITION: MATURE PERFORMANCE

What happens when mature readers go from print to meaning? That is to say, how do mature readers see a group of letters on a page and immediately recognize it as a word? And how do they find the meaning of that word? Psychological research provides us with answers to these questions.

The visual route to meaning   Mature readers generally use a direct *visual* route from print to meaning (see e.g. Ellis, 1984). That is, after lengthy exposure to reading, mature readers come to store the representations of familiar written words in memory. Because the words have become so familiar, these word representations are automatically activated when letter strings are encountered and, in turn, the representations activate the meanings of the words. Thus, mature readers recognize the printed words on a page 'by sight': the visual pattern activates the word's representation in memory, and that, in turn, activates the word's meaning.

Kolers (1966) has obtained some very compelling evidence to support this idea. He asked bilingual subjects to read aloud passages made up of haphazardly alternating English and French words, such as: 'His horse, followed by deux bassets, faisait la terre resonner under its even tread. Des goutes . . .' Kolers found that the subjects frequently continued using one language after the text had switched to the other. Thus, 'deux bassets' might be read aloud as 'two hounds', and so on. Such errors could only happen if readers recognized, say, the French word 'bassets' visually, activated its meaning, and then used the wrong (English) word, 'hounds', to name this meaning when reading aloud.

The phonic route to meaning   An alternative *phonic* route to meaning may also be used when a reader is faced with an unfamiliar word. This alternative route makes use of spelling-to-sound rules to convert letters or groups of letters into sounds. Then the sound is used to activate the word's meaning in the same way as the spoken word does in the mind of the listener. Ellis and Young (1988) suggest that mature readers only use this route when faced with unfamiliar words, such as 'rantipole' or 'skiagrapher'. However, others have argued that the phonic route is always used during reading (e.g. Gough, 1972; Rubenstein *et al.*, 1971). In general, though, the evidence fails to support this idea. Take the case of people who have become dyslexic through brain damage, but who were skilled readers before their injury. Some of these dyslexics suffer from an inability to pronounce even very simple non-words, such as 'Pib' or 'Zub'. That is, they seem to lose the ability to use the phonic route that uses spelling-to-sound rules to pronounce a string of letters. Despite this loss, the patients are able to pronounce and understand almost any familiar real word, such as 'book' or 'house' (Patterson, 1982; Funnell, 1983). This finding indicates that the phonic route is not necessary for reading familiar words, contrary to the claims of Gough and of Rubenstein *et al.*, since the dyslexics have no phonic route but can still read familiar words. It therefore seems that mature readers use a visual route when assigning meanings to familiar words, but they may fall back on a phonics route when reading unfamiliar words.

LEARNING TO RECOGNIZE WORDS

A plausible strategy for learning to read would be to make use of familiar processes that are already used for spoken language. That is, the best strategy would be to convert the words to sounds and then 'listen' to those sounds as if they were spoken words, to find their meaning. We will see that such a strategy is used by children, but only at certain points in development. These stages of development have been mapped out by Marsh *et al.* (1981).

Stage One In the first stage, which emerges when children are perhaps 4 or 5 years of age, reading is characterized by rote learning. Children remember the association between a visual string of letters (the word) and a spoken response. The small set of words that is read in this way makes up what is called the child's *sight vocabulary*. When reading, a child at this stage will recognize words in his or her sight vocabulary and make a guess at other words. The guess will be based on what would make sense in the context. For example, when presented with 'The cat sat on the chair' a child in Stage One may guess the more familiar 'The cat sat on the mat'.

Stage Two The second stage is an elaboration of Stage One, in which children seem to read a word by deciding which word in their known reading vocabulary is the one that has been presented. Even though the word may be one that is outside the known vocabulary, or even a non-word, children behave as if these possibilities are to be ignored. The job seems to be to collect just enough information about the letter string to be able to distinguish the printed word from all the other words that the child can read. Word length is one source of information used to decide what the word is. For example, one of the children in a study by Seymour and Elder (1985) read 'television' as 'children' and, when asked why, said that he knew the word was 'children' because 'children' is a long word. Another source of information is the presence of particular letters. Other children in Seymour and Elder's study read any letter string containing *k* (such as 'likes', 'bkaacl' or 'pjoek') as 'black'. In this stage, children's guesses are more constrained than they were: in Stage One, guesses are only constrained to be syntactically and semantically plausible, but in Stage Two, they are also constrained by information in the word, such as its length or the presence of a particular letter. Thus, on encountering the sentence 'The cat sat on the chair', the Stage Two child may guess 'The cat sat on the carpet', since it shares the initial letter *c* with the actual word.

Stage Three In Stage Three, signs that the children are using letter-to-sound rules begin to appear. The spoken response is no longer selected only from the reading vocabulary, but may be a word that has never been used in reading before, or even a non-word. Furthermore, the number of words that can be correctly read aloud now expands very rapidly. All this suggests that the child is beginning to use a phonic route to reading. Doctor and Coltheart (1980) carried out an experiment that supported this conclusion. They asked children aged from 6 to 10 years to decide whether a sequence of words made sense or not. Some of the sequences were meaningful sentences, others not. Two different kinds of meaningless sentence were included, one sounding like meaningful sentences (e.g. 'Tell me wear he went') and the other kind neither looking nor sounding so (e.g. 'Tell me new he went'). Doctor and Coltheart found that the 6-year-old children said that almost 70 per cent of the meaningless sentences that sounded meaningful made sense, but that only 29 per cent of the sentences that neither looked nor sounded meaningful made sense. These results suggest that the 6-year-olds were relying very heavily on a phonic route, since sentences that sounded meaningful were judged to make sense even though the spelling indicated that they were meaningless.

Stage Four In Stage Four, the use of the phonic route begins to decline and the direct visual route is used more frequently. No doubt this is because the words have become familiar and so are stored as whole units in memory. Thus they can be recognized as wholes without the need for a letter-by-letter analysis. Evidence for this stage also comes from Doctor and Coltheart (1980): 10-year-old children were much less likely than the 6-year-olds to say that the sentences that sounded meaningful made sense, thus indicating a lessening of the reliance on the phonics route.

Two new abilities are seen at this stage that also support the idea that a visual route is being used. One is the use of context to determine the pronunciation of letters. The context that is used may be that of the surrounding letter in the word. For example, a hard *c* is used if it occurs at the beginning of a word, as in 'cake', but a soft *c* if it occurs before an *e*, as in 'nice'. Alternatively, the context may be that of the surrounding words, which are needed to recognize that *homophones* have different meanings. Homophones are words that sound alike but are spelled differently (e.g. 'bow' and 'bough'), and so can only be recognized by using the visual route. The two sentences below show how the other words in the sentence are needed to decide which pronunciation and hence which meaning is intended with the use of the word 'tear':

Maria wiped a tear from her eye.
Maria noticed a tear in the dress.

The second new ability is the use of an *analogy strategy*, which is now used more and more for the successful reading of new words. New words are pronounced not strictly according to letter-to-sound conversion rules but by analogy with particular existing words. For example, on encountering the word 'bough' for the first time, it might be pronounced 'buff' by analogy with the word 'rough'. Both of these abilities show that children at Stage Four are using the visual route more and more. With extensive practice and experience reading an ever wider range of books, Stage Four children eventually recognize words with the same speed and fluency as adults.

Overall, during the period from 6 years to 10 years, there is a transition from using a rote visual route to using a phonic route to using a direct visual route. The distinction between Stage Three and Stage Four is one between using the *sounds* of words to activate their meanings and using the way the words are *spelled* to determine their meanings. What is more, these stages can be observed in children taught by a mixture of methods, so they do not simply reflect the way that children are taught to read (Harris and Coltheart, 1986). Instead, the stages can be said to reflect what the children learn during this period of development. Nevertheless, teaching will facilitate these developments, and so we turn our attention now to the teaching of reading.

THE TEACHING OF READING

Teaching methods   There are two main methods of teaching reading, which reflect two contrasting philosophies and that have been the subject of much debate:

- the *look-and-say* or *whole word method* encourages children to associate the visual pattern of the word with its meaning, without systematic teaching on letter–sound correspondences. The walls of classrooms in which look-and-say is emphasized will be covered with pictures of familiar objects, each paired with the appropriate word.

- the *phonic method* encourages children to learn the typical sounds of letters and groups of letters. Stringing these sounds together produces the sound of the word, which can then be recognized in the same way as a spoken word. The walls of classrooms in which phonics is emphasized will be decorated with the letters of the alphabet, each letter paired with a picture of a familiar object to illustrate its sound. For example, the letter *A* may be paired with a picture of an apple, *B* with a picture of a bee, and so on.

These two methods correspond to the two routes to reading that were described above and, as we saw, children use both during the development of reading. This correspondence between learning stages and teaching methods suggests that each method may be useful at a different stage of development, an idea that has been put forward by Chall (1969) to explain the complex findings relating reading performance to teaching methods. Indeed, many teachers do use a combination of both methods rather than sticking exclusively to one (e.g. Chall, 1967; Harris and Coltheart, 1986). Unfortunately, such peaceful co-existence of methods has not prevented heated debate about which is the best (see e.g. Chall, 1967, 1979).

So is there a 'best' method? The answer to that question seems to be a cautious 'yes'. A number of people have tried to evaluate the different methods of teaching (e.g. Adams, 1990; Anderson *et al.*, 1985; Chall, 1967). There are difficulties in interpreting these findings, because the pure use of a particular method occurs so rarely in practice. Nevertheless, the overwhelming conclusion of most researchers is that the phonics method is superior to look-and-say. In particular, it appears that when phonics is used to foster the recognition of spelling patterns, learning is enhanced (Adams, 1990). Practice in identifying the sounds of groups of letters, even when they do not form words, improves both the speed and accuracy of word recognition (Beck and Roth, cited by Beck and Carpenter, 1986). Indeed, Chall (1967) observed that the teaching of phonics was best when the children practised with sub-components of words rather than with whole words. It is as if the use of whole words inhibits the attention to letter–sound correspondences, knowledge of which is crucial for the recognition of new words that are not already part of the reading vocabulary.

Why should phonics and the learning of letter-to-sound correspondences lead to better learning outcomes than look-and-say methods? After all, according to Marsh *et al.* (1981), children begin to read by recognizing whole words, and the final stage of reading is marked by an increasing dependence on the visual route. The most likely answer is that it is through using phonics that children are first able to identify new words that have not been read before. Once identified, each new word can be stored as a whole in memory and eventually recognized as a single unit by means of its spelling pattern. Phonics, therefore, is needed to identify new words initially so that they can later be recognized by the visual route.

PRACTICE, AND THE IMPORTANCE OF PARENTAL INVOLVEMENT

The method of teaching is only one aspect of reading development. Another is the strong association between reading test scores and family background. Chall (1979) suggests that this may be because the amount of exposure to reading that is available in the classroom is insufficient to enable children to become fluent readers. To explain why this is so requires an understanding of how fluency is achieved.

We have seen how, in the course of development, the painful sounding out of individual letters gives way to the sounding out of groups of letters that are recognized as units, and that sounding out of these units eventually gives way to the recognition of whole words. In addition, all of these processes speed up during development, so that the slow and hesitating progress of a beginning reader is replaced by the rapid, automatic skills of the fluent reader. This learning process can be seen as an example of learning through problem solving, as discussed in Chapter 1. Learning to read a previously unknown word is the result of initial problem solving, while constant repetition and practice result in the learned solution becoming automatic. The processes involved in learning to do things fluently and automatically can be seen most dramatically in learning to drive. Initially, a learner driver executes each movement individually. To change gear, for example, requires a series of separate actions: engaging the clutch, releasing the accelerator, moving the gear lever and so on. As learning proceeds, these actions come to be 'chunked' together, so that engaging the clutch and releasing the accelerator, say, are treated as a single action. Eventually, all the needed actions are combined into a single smooth action that is executed automatically without conscious thought. The processes involved in word recognition can be thought of as mental actions that are learned in an analogous manner (see e.g. LaBerge and Samuels, 1974). At first, the sound of each letter is identified separately, then groups of letters that frequently occur together are chunked into a single unit. Then whole words are identified as units, and eventually a word is recognized automatically without conscious thought.

As we saw in Chapter 1, a major element in the development of such automatic skills is practice, which ensures that word recognition processes are repeated often enough for chunking and fluency to occur. The need for practice is emphasized by the observation that speed of word recognition seems to lie at the heart of good reading. Perfetti and Hogoboam (1975) have shown that good readers – that is, readers who are good on comprehension tests – are consistently faster at pronouncing words than are less skilled readers. Indeed, it seems that slow word recognition may underlie poor reading in adults as well as in children: Perfetti (1985) found that skilled adult readers could pronounce words faster than less skilled adults. Thus, adults too may be unable to perform the more complex feats of comprehension if their word recognition skills are not sufficiently developed. These results and other similar ones suggest that the more automatic word recognition has become, the better is the overall reading performance.

Thus it is important that children gain sufficient practice for word recognition to become highly automatic. One implication of this is that what goes on at home may be as important as what goes on at school. Chall (1979) has pointed out the home background is crucial for providing the opportunity to read many familiar books – familiar because the stories are familiar, the subjects are so, or the structure is so, as in fairy tales and myths. As Chall argues, the greater the amount of practice and the greater the immersion in reading, the greater the chance of developing automatic word recognition skills and a general fluency with print.

In support of this idea, Chomsky (1978) had backward readers listen to an audio-tape while silently reading the recorded stories. When the child was sufficiently familiar with the story, the audio input was discontinued. This simple practice procedure produced a noticeable improvement in the children's reading skills. Attempts by schools to encourage parents to listen to their children reading at home have led to similar reading gains. In addition, the enjoyment and emotional satisfaction that children can gain from sharing such activities with their mothers or fathers encourages the likelihood that reading will be pursued. Unfortunately, this need for extensive reading outside the classroom means that children can lose much needed time for practice if their parents cannot afford to buy books or if the patterns of recreation and work in the home do not include borrowing books or magazines from a library. Such a state of affairs may well account for the fact that large-scale learning interventions for deprived children are only successful if the parents are actively involved in the programme.

Furthermore, early reading is facilitated at all stages by a large vocabulary and an expanding understanding of the world. Children are likely to benefit most from phonics teaching if the word they are learning is already familiar from spoken language. The word that is recognized from combining its constituent sounds will only activate its meaning if the child has *heard* the word before. If the word is unfamiliar, then as well as learning the letter–sound correspondences, the child must also learn a new meaning to associate with the word. In fact, up until the age of about 9 years, what is learned during reading is mainly concerned with relating print to speech; that is, with relating print to words and ideas that the child already knows (Chall, 1979). If parents do not read regularly to the child, then language development may be slower and so impede such developments. For all these reasons, teaching programmes that involve the parents in the teaching and encouragement of reading are most likely to be successful.

In summary, the phonics method has been found to be superior to look-and-say for teaching reading. However, in addition to the use of phonics, Chall (1979) points out that it has been consistently found that there is a strong association between reading skill and family background. This association reflects the need for practice that extends beyond what is possible in the classroom, as well as for experience with personally and emotionally rewarding reading activities, and for a good general knowledge and large vocabulary. All these requirements are fostered in a home where there are lots of books, where reading is a familiar and encouraged activity, and where general knowledge is enriched by the kinds of activity and conversation that take place. On the other hand, they are inhibited in homes where books are not needed and so reading is not a familiar activity, and where the day-to-day concerns and activities focus on issues that do not lead to gains in general knowledge. These requirements point to the need to engage parents in reading interventions and may explain why only programmes that do involve parents are successful. By these means, children begin to recognize words fluently and automatically. Once word recognition is automatic, the child's cognitive resources become available for more complex skills of comprehension and interpretation. We turn to a discussion of these skills in the next section.

Reading to learn: comprehension strategies

The stages of reading proposed by Marsh *et al.* (1981) are concerned only with learning to recognize words, not with the more complex aspects of reading that involve the comprehension of sentences and texts. A full-blown model of learning to read would need to include the learning of these high-level processes. Such a model has been proposed by Chall (1979, 1983). It consists of five reading stages and a pre-reading stage. The first three (including the pre-reading stage) cover the same period of learning as Marsh *et al.*'s; the second three concern the learning of comprehension processes and the use of reading to gain new knowledge.

CHALL'S STAGES OF READING DEVELOPMENT

Stage 0 This is the pre-reading stage, lasting from birth to approximately 6 years of age. During this period, a number of skills develop that are important for future reading development. They include visual, visual-motor and auditory perceptual skills that are necessary for beginning reading. They include an increasing knowledge of language; for example, that spoken words may be segmented, that some parts of words sound the same (i.e. they rhyme), and that parts of words can be blended to form whole words. And they include a knowledge of literacy itself: the way that books are used in a literate culture, and (in most languages) the use of an alphabetic system of writing. All these aspects of knowledge, and more besides, begin to develop long before a child learns to read. This stage probably includes Stage One of Marsh *et al.*'s, in which children rote learn whole words before they can analyse individual letters and their sounds.

Stage 1 This is the initial reading stage. It spans the ages 6 to 7 and corresponds approximately to Marsh *et al.*'s Stages Two and Three. According to Chall (1979), the essential aspect of this stage is the learning of arbitrary sets of letters and the association of them with the corresponding parts of spoken words. The transition from Stage 0 to Stage 1 occurs when insight is gained into the nature of the spelling system, and the reader gains a new understanding about the relationship between spelling and reading.

Stage 2   This is a stage of confirmation, spanning the ages 7 to 8 years. Activities consolidate what was learned in Stage 1 and increase the store of whole words that can be recognized as a unit. It corresponds approximately to Marsh *et al.*'s Stage Four. Reading in Stage 2 is used to confirm what is already known to the reader. This familiarity with the content of what is read means that the reader's attention can focus on the printed words – their spellings and sounds – to increase the range of learned words. Also, since the basic decoding skills were learned in Stage 1, the reader can use pre-existing knowledge to recognize and match what is in the text. At this stage, as long as there is sufficient extensive practice with reading about familiar things, the child gains in fluency and speed of reading.

Stage 3   This is the stage at which reading for learning new things about the world first occurs. It spans the ages of 9 to approximately 13, and represents a change from learning about the relationship between print and speech to learning about the relationship between print and ideas. Before Stage 3, listening and watching are the main ways in which new things are learned about the world. But during the course of this stage, reading as a means of learning gradually comes to equal and may even surpass these other ways of learning. Stage 3 is also characterized by the growing importance of using pre-existing knowledge to facilitate comprehension. Finally, according to Chall, the learning that occurs during Stage 3 is from one viewpoint only. That is, reading at this stage is essentially for facts, concepts, and how to do things. Any reading for nuance or different perspectives probably occurs only during the reading of fiction. Chall suggests therefore that the time taken to progress from Stage 3 to Stage 4 depends on the time it takes to acquire knowledge in the many areas needed to read and understand the multiple viewpoints that will be encountered in Stage 4.

Stage 4   As has just been indicated, this concerns multiple viewpoints; for example, a school textbook at this level in, say, history requires dealing with a variety of points of view. Stage 4 depends on formal education, on the reading of mature fiction, and on the free reading of books, newspapers and magazines. Through dealing with more than one set of facts, with various theories, and with multiple viewpoints, practice is gained in learning ever more difficult concepts and in learning how to gain new concepts and new points of view through reading.

Stage 5 This is the most mature stage and is reached from 18 years and above. It often requires higher education and, according to Chall, is normally reached during the college years. In characterizing Stage 5 reading, Chall makes use of the work of Perry (1970) on intellectual development during the college years. Perry found that people differ in their epistemological standards; that is, in their view of the nature of knowledge. Some people have a dualistic orientation and others a relativistic one:

- *dualistic orientation*: the belief that something is either right or wrong. Students with this orientation agree with such statements as 'If professors would stick more to the facts and do less theorizing, one could get more out of college.'

- *relativistic orientation*: the belief that knowledge is a theory, a coherent set of beliefs, that is used to interpret situations in the world. Students with a relativistic orientation disagree with statements like the one above.

During the college years, there is a shift from a dualistic orientation, in which knowledge is conceived of as a set of discrete truths, to a relativistic orientation, in which knowledge is assessed in relation to its context. It is this that characterizes Chall's Stage 5, since the change in orientation leads to a change in the way that people read. Someone with a dualistic orientation reads to obtain the 'truth' – that is, the facts about a subject – while someone with a relativistic orientation reads to gain new insights into how to understand the subject matter. However, it is possible that not all people reach Stage 5, even after three or four years of college (Chall, 1979).

Thus, Chall's last three stages identify increasingly advanced skills of comprehension. They reveal the lengthy developmental period that is involved where these high-level cognitive activities are concerned. Furthermore, there is ample evidence to suggest that people of whatever age may fail to learn these activities or learn them only with considerable difficulty. We will now examine this evidence, consider why these difficulties might arise, and indicate how the hurdles to such learning might be overcome.

At the beginning of the chapter, we distinguished between sentence comprehension and text comprehension. Our concern in this section is with *text comprehension*, since it is at the textual level that high-level strategies can be used to gain new knowledge from texts. The strategies are used to integrate the information in each sentence with pre-existing knowledge about the subject matter and to integrate the information from different sentences. By these means readers are able to establish what the text is about and what information it conveys. Other strategies are even more sophisticated. They go beyond integration and use pre-existing knowledge to evaluate the information in the text, which they use to evaluate and revise pre-existing knowledge. In other words, text comprehension involves understanding, one of the three kinds of learning that were described in Chapter 1. A person who integrates pre-existing knowledge with information in the text, and who integrates the information in different portions of the text, attempts to go beyond the text itself to grasp a body of knowledge about the subject matter in question. Thus learning is achieved.

Understanding and memorizing   Recall from Chapter 1 that understanding is a more successful method of learning than is memorization, since it involves updating one's current ideas about the subject matter rather than accumulating new facts. However, it is sometimes difficult to distinguish between understanding and memorization. We can characterize the difference by saying that when studying a text for purposes of understanding, one is not interested in retaining a memory of the text itself. Instead one is interested in using the information in the text as part of a more general effort to construct a mental representation of the subject matter. For this purpose, it makes sense to integrate the text information with what one already knows and then forget about the text

83

itself. However, if one is interested in memorizing the material, it may seem better to memorize the text itself or key parts of it, since this avoids the effort required for integration. Further, some strategies or activities that help us to remember (e.g. rehearsal and repetition) are of little help in understanding. Conversely, some strategies that help us to understand (e.g. looking up unfamiliar words in a dictionary) can be of relatively little help in remembering.

Despite these differences, some of the processes of understanding overlap with processes of remembering. In both cases, the basic processes of reading and of the comprehension of sentence meaning are involved. Because of this overlap, children (and adults too on some occasions) find it difficult to distinguish between memorization and understanding and to realize that each has its own distinct characteristics. To make matters worse, what is said to be a comprehension strategy for children may be regarded as a memorization strategy when used by an adult. This is because children are not able to use the sophisticated comprehension strategies that adults use. Instead, they need to use whatever strategies are within their grasp. Thus, there may really be a continuum, the strategies at one end being pure memorization and those at the other being very high-level comprehension.

High-level comprehension strategies used by adults include assessing the new information and prior information in relation to each other, looking for logical relationships in the text, identifying the important ideas, and taking a critical attitude towards the material by relating it to one's own beliefs, emotions and experience, and by thinking about how the material can be used. Strategies that children use for comprehension include skimming, reviewing, paraphrasing and summarizing. These are commonly viewed as memorization strategies when used by adults. Memorization strategies include rehearsal, repetition, categorization, and integration with prior knowledge. These last two look rather like simple comprehension strategies and indeed could probably be classed as such when used by very young children.

Lovett and Flavell (1990) showed that the distinction between understanding and memorization was a difficult one for young children to make. They asked their subjects to choose a particular audio-tape to help them identify the referents of words (an understanding task) or to help them remember a list of words (a memorization task). They found that when 8–10-year-olds and undergraduates were required to point to the pictorial referents of a series of words, they chose to hear a tape defining the meanings of the words. When required to memorize the words they chose to listen to a tape that repeated the words over and over again. However, 7-year-old children were no better than chance at choosing the tape that matched the task; in other words, they were unable to distinguish between understanding and memorizing.

When high-level strategies are examined, college students have comparable difficulties. Students do not invariably read for understanding but frequently engage in memorization activities instead. Spring (1985) presented evidence to support these claims. He asked two groups of college freshmen (first-year students), identified as good and poor readers, to complete a reading strategy questionnaire that consisted of statements describing study strategies and ones describing comprehension strategies. (Spring's study strategies correspond to what we have called memorization strategies.) The students were asked to indicate on a scale from 1 to 3 whether or not they used each strategy, where 1 indicated 'I do not use the strategy', 2 indicated 'I sometimes use the strategy' and 3 indicated 'I frequently use the strategy'. Table 4.1 shows the statements used and indicates whether they were classified as study strategies or comprehension strategies.

As can be seen from the table, there were three groups of memorization strategies: a *verbal rehearsal* group, so called because the statements describe rehearsal techniques for memorizing; a *written rehearsal* group, consisting of statements that describe rehearsal techniques like those in the first group but that also involve writing; and a *figural rehearsal* group, consisting of a statement describing the use of diagrams. There were two groups of comprehension strategies: an *understanding* group, consisting of statements describing strategies that relate textual information to prior knowledge (item 9) or that relate information from different sentences (items 10 and 11); and a *critical reading* group, consisting of statements describing the reader's personal reaction to the text by relating the text to beliefs, experiences and emotions in a critical manner (items 12, 14 and 15) and by identifying possible uses of the text material (item 13).

Table 4.1 Questionnaire items used by Spring (1985)

Study strategies
Verbal rehearsal
1. Reread some of the material.
2. Underline or highlight the main ideas.
3. Ask myself questions to test my understanding or memory of the material.
4. Restate the material in my own words.

Written rehearsal
5. Take notes.
6. Make an outline of the material.
7. Summarize the material.

Figural rehearsal
8. Draw diagrams or pictures related to the material.

Comprehension strategies
Understanding
9. Relate the material to what I already know.
10. Look for logical relations within the material.
11. Mentally identify the most important ideas.

Critical reading
12. Relate the material to my own beliefs and attitudes.
13. Think about how the material could be used.
14. Relate the material to my own experience.
15. Think about my emotional or critical reaction to the material.

The results showed that both good and poor readers reported using all the study strategies equally often. However, there was a marked difference in their use of the first group of comprehension strategies, those concerned with understanding. The good readers reported a much greater use of these than did the poor ones. Thus it appears that what distinguishes good and poor readers at college level is not the reported use of study strategies but that of comprehension strategies that facilitate understanding. This suggests that poor readers may be using study strategies on imperfectly understood material. Spring found no differences in the reported use of the second group of comprehension strategies, those concerned with critical thinking. As Spring suggests, this is probably because even the good readers reported using these only occasionally. Spring comments that these critical reading strategies characterize Chall's fifth and last stage of reading development described above. Since this stage is only reached sometime during the college years, it is likely that the habit of critical reading had not yet reached full development in either group.

One of the major implications of Spring's results is that there is an important distinction between study strategies and comprehension strategies, and that the use of the former but not the latter is what marks good readers off from poor readers. Further, even good readers in the early college years do not seem to engage in the comprehension strategies concerned with critical reading. As Spring suggests, therefore, there may well be a need for continued instruction in comprehension rather than study strategies. A second implication of the study is that many readers fail to engage in the strategies needed to ensure successful learning. Poor readers may neglect them altogether, while good readers may fail to employ the full range of strategies available, possibly because they have not attained Chall's final stage of reading. This failure to employ comprehension strategies applies at all ages, as reviews of the research show. Bransford *et al.* (1989) and Brown *et al.* (1981) review the research on children, and Baker (1989) reviews the work on comprehension difficulties experienced by adults.

As we will see in the next section, another important feature of comprehension strategies is that people do not use them in an all-or-none manner; instead, people seem to use them on some occasions but not on others. In particular, people will use strategies with easy or intermediate texts but then fail to use them with difficult texts. In other words, the situations where comprehension strategies are most needed are the ones where they are least likely to be used.

So why are comprehension strategies so hard to use when they are needed? It is becoming increasingly clear that a major reason is the failure to engage in *metacognitive activities*. These involve the ability to reflect on one's own thought processes, to think about how one is thinking. Metacognition is an important component of learning, since it is apparently needed if comprehension strategies are to be successfully employed.

Metacognition

We use the term 'metacognition' to refer to two related abilities. One concerns having *explicit knowledge* of learning strategies and of one's own learning processes (Flavell, 1970, 1976); the other concerns the ability to *use* comprehension strategies by monitoring and controlling one's own thinking and learning (Brown, 1977). Restricting our understanding of metacognition to either knowledge alone or use alone would not do justice to the richness of the concept. If the term were restricted to knowledge alone, then it would fail to consider how that knowledge is used; if to use alone, then we would overlook a considerable body of research results indicating the importance of explicit knowledge of one's own learning processes.

METACOGNITIVE KNOWLEDGE

Paris *et al.* (1983) proposed that adept learners have three sorts of knowledge about strategies:

1. *knowledge of what strategy to use.* For example, good learners know that a rereading strategy will help when comprehension difficulties are encountered (e.g. Baker and Anderson, 1982).

2. *knowledge of how to use a strategy.* For example, good learners know how to skim a text and use key words to locate the relevant portions to be reread when a comprehension difficulty is encountered (Garner, 1990).

3. *knowledge of when to use a strategy.* Some strategies depend on the task requirements. Thus, older and better readers vary their reading strategy depending on the task. They know when to skim a text to find a particular piece of information, and when to read for study and when for fun (Forrest-Pressley and Waller, 1984). Strategies may also depend on the subject matter: as Bransford and Heldmeyer (1983) have noted, it is important to allocate extra attention to numerals in mathematics and perhaps in history, but it is unimportant in most literature. Indeed, subject matter probably determines most of the important strategies that help learning.

This has led a number of people to argue that strategies can only be taught effectively as part of the teaching of specific subjects, so that strategies specific to the subject can be learned in conjunction with learning subject content (e.g. Bransford *et al.* 1989).

Evidence for the importance of explicit knowledge comes from studies showing that reading ability is related to the things people can report about their reading activities. One example comes from Spring (1985), described earlier; another is that students who report using strategies in response to comprehension difficulties are better readers than those who report no such use (Fischer and Mandl, 1984). Similar results have been reported with children: Forrest-Pressley and Waller (1984) found that good readers but not poor readers could describe how they assessed their level of comprehension. They also found that good readers could report the strategies that they used when faced with comprehension difficulties. Comparable results reveal the important relation between metacognitive knowledge and performance in non-academic environments. Mikulecky and his colleagues examined the influence of metacognitive aspects of literacy on the job performance of nurses (Mikulecky and Winchester, 1983) and electronics technicians (Mikulecky and Ehlinger, 1985). They found that metacognitive awareness and reported use of metacognitive strategies, such as self-questioning, focusing on key ideas, and setting purposes, were more common among workers considered superior at their jobs than among those considered adequate performers. Thus, knowledge of strategies seems to be an important component of metacognition and needs to be borne in mind when attempting to foster the use of such strategies. It is worth adding here that as strategies are learned and used repeatedly, use of them probably becomes automatic over time. Once one becomes automatic and so no longer needs conscious attention, cognitive resources become available for learning new and even more sophisticated strategies.

Explicit knowledge of strategies, therefore, appears to be crucial for the employment of comprehension strategies. However, just knowing about something is no guarantee that the knowledge will be used. As far back as 1929, Whitehead talked about *inert knowledge*, knowledge that people possess but that they seldom if ever use in circumstances that call for it. Rothkopf (1988) has painted a vivid picture of this state of affairs as it applies to metacognitive knowledge. He pointed out that strategies involve knowing and translating knowledge into action just as, for example, manners and dietary information do. Yet, just as tube travellers who stare at an older pregnant woman with a broken leg know that they should offer her their seats but do not, and dieters at the dinner table can count calories but still overeat, learners involved in a task may know that they should use strategies but do not. Thus, knowledge alone will not ensure that strategies are used. What is needed as well is the ability to monitor and control (or regulate) one's own performance. This is the second ability referred to by the term 'metacognition', the one that has been emphasized by Brown (e.g. 1977).

METACOGNITIVE MONITORING AND CONTROL

Monitoring refers to the ability to assess one's own comprehension level, while *control* refers to the ability to regulate one's use of a strategy. Such regulation includes checking that a strategy has been implemented successfully and being able to apply it in those situations that call for it, but not in those that do not. A good example of the importance of monitoring and control comes from Brown and Day's work on summarizing skills.

Summarizing uses comprehension strategies that are quite hard to learn, so Brown and her colleagues attempted to teach them to students. In order to do that, Brown needed to be able to say explicitly what the strategies are. Hence Brown and Day (1983) studied students and experts while they were reading and constructing summaries of what had been read. This allowed the researchers to identify the strategies that good summarizers use. Six were identified in this manner, and are shown in Table 4.2.

Brown and Day (1983) examined the use of these strategies by fifth graders (approximately 11 years old), seventh graders (approximately 13 years old), tenth graders (approximately 16 years old) and college students, and they found clear developmental differences in the ability to use them. Deletion strategies were the easiest and were used by all the subjects. The use of substitution strategies increased with age, as did topic selection

Table 4.2 The six summarizing rules identified by Brown and Day (1983)

Deletion:

Two rules delete material. One deletes trivial material and the other material that is important but redundant.

Substitution:

Two rules involve the substitution of a superordinate term. One replaces lists of items; for example, a list such as 'cats, dogs, horses and snakes' can be replaced by the term 'animals'. The other replaces a sequence of actions by a single action, such as 'Jane went to school'.

Topic identification:

Two rules are used to find the topic of a text. One selects a topic sentence, if there is one, from the paragraph being summarized. The other is used when there is no topic sentence: invent your own.

---

and topic invention. The last of these was particularly difficult: it was rarely used by the fifth or seventh graders, and even college students used it only 50 per cent of the time.

Thus, students do not always use good summarizing strategies, particularly that of inventing a topic sentence. Consequently, Brown *et al.* (1981) tried to teach students how to use these. When carrying out the study, Brown *et al.* used three different teaching methods. The first told the students what to do but not how to do it, while the second included instructions about how to summarize. However, the third method also gave instructions on how to gain metacognitive control of learning. These three methods are outlined below:

1. *'blind' instruction*: The students were told *what* to do. That is, they were given general encouragement to produce a good summary, to capture the main ideas and to dispense with trivia and all unnecessary words, but they were not told any rules for how to achieve this.

2. *informed instruction*: The students were told not only what to do, but *how* to do it as well. This method was the same as (1) except that the six rules for achieving these ends were also provided and practice was given in how to use them.

3. *self-control* learning: This was the same as (2) but explicit training was given in how to monitor and control those rules. Students were shown how to check that all redundancies and trivia had been deleted, that any lists of items had been replaced by superordinates, that they had a topic sentence for each paragraph, and whether they needed to invent topic sentences. Thus, they were taught how to monitor and assess their own ongoing performance and how to regulate and control their performance by tailoring their strategies in the light of those assessments.

The results showed that with all three teaching methods students improved their ability to select and invent topic sentences. However, the self-control techniques were particularly effective with less proficient students and with more difficult texts. In other words, a good (metacognitive) grasp of how to monitor and regulate the strategies seems to be particularly important when people are having difficulty in comprehending and learning. Thus, it should not surprise us to learn that many people, adults as well as children, fail to monitor their comprehension and regulate their strategies accordingly. Indeed, Garner (1990) has suggested that one of the main reasons why strategies are not used is because of poor cognitive monitoring. If children and adults do not notice that they are not learning, they are unlikely to seek a strategic remedy. As Brown and Day's results suggest, these problems are most likely to arise with difficult texts; that is, texts requiring the reader to understand new material. Because of the seriousness of these problems, we will take a closer look at the metacognitive processes of monitoring and control.

COMPREHENSION MONITORING

The ability to assess one's level of comprehension has received considerable attention with both children and college students (e.g. Markman, 1979; Scardamalia and Bereiter, 1984; Baker and Anderson, 1982). Many of these studies gave subjects texts to read that contained inconsistencies, and then asked the subjects if they noticed them. In general, the results show that both children (Markman, 1979) and adults (Baker, 1989) fail to report the inconsistencies. For example, Markman (1979) gave children texts to read like those shown in Table 4.3. Each paragraph contains an item of information intended to be inconsistent. In the 'fish' passage, the statement that fish at the bottom of the sea know their food by its colour contradicts the preceding statement that there is absolutely no light there. In the 'ice cream' passage, the statement that Baked Alaska is made by putting ice cream in a hot oven clashes with everyday knowledge about the tendency for ice cream to melt.

Markman's study revealed striking deficiencies in evaluating comprehension among children and early adolescents. A subsequent study by Scardamalia and Bereiter (1984), using the two passages in Table 4.3, showed that these deficiencies were mainly confined to the 'fish' passage. That is, children find it particularly hard to monitor their understanding of the relationship between different sentences, suggesting that the children have failed to integrate the information in the different sentences. By contrast, they find it relatively easy to monitor their comprehension of each sentence by assessing it in relation to prior knowledge, suggesting that very familiar knowledge is more readily used to evaluate the information in a text.

Table 4.3 Examples of materials used by Markman (1979)

'Fish' passage:

Many different kinds of fish live in the sea. Some fish have heads that make them look like alligators and some fish have heads that make them look like cats. Fish live in different parts of the ocean. Some fish live near the surface of the water. Some fish live at the bottom of the oceans. There's absolutely no light at the bottom of the ocean. Some fish that live at the bottom of the ocean know their food by its colour.

'Ice cream' passage:

Lots of different kinds of desserts can be made with ice cream. Some fancy restaurants serve a special dessert made out of ice cream called Baked Alaska. To make it, they bake the ice cream. As soon as it is finished baking they cut it into pieces with a knife and serve it right away. One of the things children like to eat everywhere in the world is ice cream. Some ice cream stores sell many different flavours of ice cream, but the most popular flavours are chocolate and vanilla.

Undergraduate students also find it difficult to detect comprehension failures, and like the children described above, they find textual contradictions harder to notice than prior knowledge violations. Baker (1985) presented students with passages of text adapted from college-level textbooks and asked them to underline anything that they found problematic. The texts were modified to contain three different kinds of confusion. These confusions were either: (1) *lexical* – nonsense words occurred instead of real ones; (2) *externally inconsistent* – prior knowledge was violated; or (3) *internally inconsistent* – prior textual information was contradicted. The results showed that lexical confusions were most likely to be identified, prior knowledge violations much less so, and contradictions even less so. Indeed, the external and internal inconsistencies were unlikely to be noticed at all if the subjects were not told beforehand that the text contained some confusions. In addition, as is usually the case, the inconsistencies were most likely to be noticed by good readers.

THE CONTROL OF COMPREHENSION

When a comprehension failure is detected, what can the reader do about it? The ability to apply a strategy to put right a comprehension failure is what is meant by *control* (or *regulation*). And it seems that the ability to respond to comprehension difficulties is one of the main things that distinguishes good from poor readers. Since such difficulties are most likely to arise with difficult tasks, Kletzien (1988) gave high-school students texts of differing levels of difficulty and asked them to carry out cloze tasks on the texts. In a *cloze task*, a word or phrase is deleted from a text and the reader has to supply the missing information from knowledge of the text. Kletzien found that when the passages were of easy or intermediate levels of difficulty, good and poor readers alike reported using the same small set of strategies (rereading previous text, using prior knowledge, making inferences and using key vocabulary). However, on difficult passages, the non-achieving readers seemed to give up trying and used few, if any, strategies, while the achieving readers persisted in their efforts to understand.

Fischer and Mandl (1984) reported similar differences between good and poor readers in response to comprehension failures.

Biology students were asked to read a psychology passage in preparation for free recall and multiple choice tests. After taking the tests, the students were interviewed about how they had prepared for them. Good and poor readers did not differ in whether or not they monitored their comprehension and learning, but they did differ in how they responded to difficulties. The poor learners showed negative feelings about themselves as learners and their ability to learn and they saw comprehension failures as confirmation of their poor ability. Since they believed they were not very good, they also believed that they would not be able to do anything about a comprehension failure and so they made no effort to cope with their difficulties. By contrast, the good readers used the information they acquired through self-assessment in a much more functional manner. They regulated their progress by using strategies to overcome their difficulties. Comparable findings on the way beliefs about oneself affect learning have been obtained with schoolchildren by Dweck and Leggett (1988).

The above are important studies because they highlight the significant role of motivation in learning and in the use of comprehension strategies. One of the main points about Whitehead's discussions of inert knowledge and Rothkopf's pessimistic comments about the gulf between knowledge and action is that without the motivation to apply learned knowledge it will remain inert and unused. Lack of motivation is the problem for the poor achievers and readers in the studies mentioned above. If people believe that they cannot improve their performance and that comprehension failures reflect their own incompetence, then they are unlikely to expend the effort required to engage in comprehension strategies. Why spend all that time trying to do something when you believe you are going to fail? This motivational issue is such an important aspect of learning that we will devote a large part of Chapter 6 to discussing it.

However, to return to the main theme of this chapter, we have seen that metacognitive knowledge and control are crucial components of learning from texts. Perhaps the best way to summarize their importance is to describe a study by Chi *et al.* (1989) on good and poor physics students. They asked their subjects to study four chapters of a physics text and solve a series of problems after each chapter. Analysis of the students' verbal reports revealed that the good students tended to study example problems by explaining and justifying each step in the problem, and by relating their explanations to the principles outlined in the text. This resulted in an increase in their knowledge of the principles concerned. Good students also successfully monitored their comprehension successes and failures while studying the examples. Their ability to detect comprehension failures led them to formulate specific questions that they could not answer and then return to the text to find the answers. By contrast, poor students rarely explained the example problems to themselves. They were also less accurate at detecting comprehension failures, and when they did, they seemed unable to use specific strategies to help them.

Thus, the good students used a powerful comprehension strategy of explaining and justifying the steps in the problems, and relating the steps to their conceptual knowledge. This powerful strategy made it obvious when they did not understand, and so their comprehension monitoring was correspondingly good as well. When comprehension failure occurred, the good students used a strategy of formulating questions and searching for the answers in the text. The good students, therefore, were good strategy users: they used the metacognitive skills of monitoring and controlling their comprehension.

Summary

Learning to read is mainly concerned with the beginning stages of reading, when children learn to recognize words. Most adults are very adept at this task, using the visual pattern to activate the meaning of a word directly. But children go through several learning stages before they reach the same level of proficiency as adults. First, they recognize a few whole words by rote, then they start to use features of the words, such as their length, to distinguish between the words that they know. Next they learn to use spelling-to-sound rules to recognize unfamiliar words, and finally they learn to recognize words directly by using spelling patterns to activate their meanings and to identify unfamiliar words that have familiar spelling patterns. Research indicates that the phonics teaching method is more successful than look-and-say. Phonics ensures that new words can be readily learned by applying spelling-to-sound rules. Once learned, the words can then be recognized as units by means of their spelling patterns.

Reading to learn concerns comprehension processes at the text level. These processes integrate the information in the text with pre-existing knowledge, and integrate the information from different sentences. They also use pre-existing knowledge to evaluate the consistency of new information in the text, and the information in the text to evaluate and revise pre-existing knowledge. Such strategies are to be distinguished from memorization by their emphasis on understanding and integration, although the distinction is not clear cut: the comprehension strategies of younger readers become the study strategies of older readers who use more sophisticated strategies. However, comprehension strategies are hard to learn, and people frequently fail to apply them where they are most needed: when reading a text that is difficult to understand. One reason why these strategies are so difficult is that they also require metacognitive skills: explicit knowledge of the strategies and how to use them and the ability to monitor and control their use.

CHAPTER 5

Learning Mathematics and Learning to Write

Overview

Children in school are expected to become skilled readers, skilled writers and skilled mathematicians. In this chapter we consider what is involved in becoming skilled in mathematics and writing. Our discussion of mathematics begins with a discussion of the context of learning and how this can influence what is learned. We focus specifically on the arbitrary nature of school learning and the way this impedes learning. We then discuss mathematics in the classroom and illustrate some approaches to its teaching that try to facilitate understanding rather than problem solving. After that we discuss writing. First we consider how children initially learn to write. Then we discuss what is needed to write coherent and continuous prose. Finally we describe two writing strategies, one in which the goal is problem solving and the other in which it is understanding. We regard writing as a particularly important skill because it is the tool *par excellence* that can facilitate explicit learning.

Learning mathematics

In Chapter 1, mention was made of the fact that much of the mathematics that is learned in schools concentrates on problem solving to the neglect of conceptual understanding. Indeed, there is a wealth of rather pessimistic research evidence to support such a view, and to suggest that the mathematical procedures that are taught in school are not used elsewhere. For example, Fitzgerald *et al.* (1981) have found that mathematical methods taught in school are rarely used in the workplace. In addition, Sewell (1981) has found that most adults have either forgotten their school mathematics or lack the confidence to use it in real life situations. Finally, it has been found that both children (Hart, 1981) and adults (Sewell, 1981) use a wide variety of methods to solve practical mathematical problems that are different from the procedures they were taught in school. All in all, school mathematics seems not to generalize to situations outside the school, and it is easily forgotten. We begin our account, therefore, with a discussion of research that tries to explain why school mathematics is so difficult to learn. This research shows that mathematics can be learned very easily outside the classroom, and it focuses on notions of *practical intelligence* and *situated learning* to explain this surprising observation.

PRACTICAL INTELLIGENCE

Practical intelligence refers to the ability of individuals to become expert in a domain without formal teaching. Studies on the topic have demonstrated some impressive feats of cognition, such as mathematical thinking by people doing supermarket shopping (Lave *et al.*, 1984), sophisticated statistical reasoning by tipsters when working out the odds for a bet on a horse race (Ceci and Liker, 1988), three-dimensional mathematical and spatial reasoning by dairy workers skilled at stacking crates (Scribner, 1988), the sophisticated practices of the Brazilian street children described in Chapter 1 (Carraher *et al.*, 1985), and complex navigational skills in pre-literate Micronesian islanders (Oatley, 1977). These studies provide spectacular evidence for people's abilities to acquire complex mathematical knowledge in the absence of formal training or, in the case of some of the cross-cultural studies, in the absence of any formal schooling at all.

Consider the study by Lave *et al.* (1984). They found that housewives make highly sophisticated calculations based on quantity and cost when choosing among similar items in a supermarket. They are able, that is, to use mental arithmetic to equate items of different sizes and different costs. For example, they will rapidly work out which packet of breakfast cereal is cheapest when faced with a 225 g pack at 63 p, a 450 g pack at £1.10, and a 500 g pack at £1.40. However, they are unable to solve problems using the same arithmetical operations if the problems are expressed in formal mathematical terms. Thus, the subjects could not retrieve and use the formal mathematical knowledge that is taught in school, yet they had learned ways of making comparable calculations in practical situations. The mathematical abilities of the Brazilian street children, described in Chapter 1, also demonstrate practical intelligence, since these children gain their knowledge and understanding in earning a living on the street.

The study by Ceci and Liker (1986) is even more striking. They showed that expert racing tipsters make sophisticated judgements about interactions between up to six different variables concerning the characteristics of the horse and those of the jockey in order to place a bet. Yet there was no relationship between expertise in picking a winner by these methods and measured intelligence. Specifically, an expert tipster with a measured IQ of 80 exhibited far more cognitive complexity when betting than did a non-expert with a measured IQ of 130. These observations suggest that learning through understanding occurs with considerably less effort outside school than it does inside. To explain such ease of learning in everyday practical situations, people have proposed the idea of situated learning.

SITUATED LEARNING

Brown *et al.* (1989) argue from observations on practical intelligence, such as those above, that learning is facilitated if it is situated. The notion of situated learning is rooted in the belief that learning is equivalent to *enculturation*; that is, to the acquisition of beliefs and practices that are specific to a particular culture, whether that culture be the one of contemporary Western thought, of an inner city, of professional mathematicians or of a school. The school culture fosters a set of beliefs about the nature of knowledge and the nature of learning that are probably firmly entrenched in our technological Western culture. According to Brown *et al.*, children are quick to learn features of the school culture, a good example being their rapidly gained ability to learn arbitrary knowledge in order to pass exams.

Brown *et al.* also point to the differences between situated learning, which occurs in everyday practical contexts, and school learning, which occurs in the classroom. Situated learning is said to be *natural learning*; that is, it is trouble tree. In contrast, school learning is said to be *arbitrary learning*; that is, it is effortful and difficult.

According to this view, it is the arbitrary nature of knowledge that is learned in schools that accounts for why it is rarely used outside them.

To explain why school learning is arbitrary, Brown *et al.* argue that the formal knowledge that is taught in schools comes originally from a different culture (the culture of mathematics, say) but it is taught to the students as if it were independent of the original cultural context in which it is normally acquired and used. Mathematics, for example, is taught in school as if it consisted solely of a set of procedures that are divorced from the goals and activities that make up the culture of being a mathematician. In other words, the knowledge that is taught lacks the significance it would gain if the goals of learning were the same as those of mathematicians when they require and use such knowledge. Instead, the goals of learning within a mathematical culture have been stripped away and replaced by those of the school culture. Thus the set of beliefs that the learners acquire in the school culture is likely to include the belief that knowledge is abstract and arbitrary and bears little relation to the practical world. This view is compatible with the observations of Schoenfield (1985). He found that many school experiences of mathematics lead students to see it as an abstract system that is known only by experts and that does not apply to practical problems (see also Chapter 6).

The distinction between situated learning and arbitrary learning, therefore, is an important one and seems to characterize the distinction between relatively painless, practical, everyday learning and considerably more painful school learning. An additional point made by Brown *et al.* probably lies at the heart of the difference: in everyday situations, learning occurs in the context in which the knowledge will be used, therefore the goals of the activity that are important in its use are transparent from the very beginning of learning. Lave *et al.*'s shoppers, for example, were guided by the need to obtain value for money when making their calculations of unit costs, while the Brazilian street vendors studied by Carraher *et al.* are guided by the need to demonstrate their honesty to the customer. By contrast, learning in schools takes place in the absence of any indication of the purposes to which the acquired knowledge will be put. Hence the learning is arbitrary and difficult. Indeed, it has been found that generalization based on an understanding of underlying conceptual principles is considerably facilitated if the goals of the task are known (Holyoak and Speelman, 1993; Keane, 1990).

Overall, therefore, the learning of mathematics in school seems fraught with difficulties when compared with comparable learning in practical situations. School learning does not seem to transfer to these practical situations, suggesting that deep conceptual understanding has not been gained. One reason for this seems to be that school mathematics is arbitrary: it is taken out of its natural context and the practical goals of learning are absent. In the light of this discussion, we will now turn to an examination of school learning and consider some of the attempts that have been made to facilitate in children a deep conceptual understanding of mathematics.

MATHEMATICS IN THE CLASSROOM

Good practice in teaching mathematics at the primary level, particularly practice that is derived from Piagetian ideas, is often described as follows: 'Proceed from the known to the unknown. Make everything concrete. Don't force abstraction on children at an early age' (Shuard *et al.*, 1991). These sound like very reasonable rules of thumb for familiarizing children with mathematical concepts, and for removing some of the seeming arbitrariness of school mathematics. However, it turns out that when learning outcomes are examined in children taught according to these procedures, the results are far from satisfactory. They suggest, for example, that the emphasis stays firmly on problem-solving skills and the practice of mathematical procedures, and neglects conceptual understanding. Yet as we saw in Chapter 1, it is only through conceptual understanding that generalization becomes possible. For instance, Hart (1989) found that despite explicit teaching, children were unable to see the connection between doing subtraction using straws or other concrete materials and using the formal algorithm (Resnick, 1981, cites similar examples from the American school system). Hart (1989) also investigated the teaching and learning of the equivalence of fractions, where the teaching was designed to instruct the children in using formal equations to express equivalence. She interviewed children before and after they were taught the new information and found that the only ones who were consistently successful three months after teaching were those who had revealed an understanding of equivalent fractions prior to teaching. This suggests that as long as the concepts were available to the children, they could learn the formal notation, but if the children did not have them, the teaching they received did not enable those concepts to be learned.

The schemes of work used by the teachers also revealed the focus on problem-solving procedures. In these schemes, teachers' statements of prerequisite knowledge referred to procedures and notation, not to concepts. That is, they described what things children should already be able to *do* before embarking on the next stage, but they did not describe what children should already *understand*. For example, one entry said, 'Ability to record two-digit numbers, some knowledge of addition with carrying' (Hart, 1989). The reason why the use of concrete materials does not alter the situation is that the children are primarily shown how to subtract (for example) one set of materials from another, thus ensuring that problem solving rather than understanding is pursued. Concrete materials are only helpful if they are used to foster understanding, which can then be transferred to the formal domain. The difficulties children encounter are exacerbated when the formal notation is introduced, since teaching continues to focus on procedures, showing how these procedures are formally expressed.

In an attempt to overcome the learning difficulties that children face in the classroom, a series of teaching initiatives has recently been implemented in a sample of British primary schools. One of these is discussed in the next section.

RECENT INITIATIVES IN PRIMARY MATHEMATICS

The Primary Initiatives in Mathematics Education (Shuard *et al.*, 1990) attempt to address some of the learning difficulties outlined above. One of these initiatives is the Calculator-aware Number Curriculum (or CAN), which aims to remove the difficulty associated with the teaching of formal notation. Teachers involved in the project were asked to refrain from teaching the standard notation but to create a climate in the classroom whereby all methods of calculation – mental, calculator or idiosyncratic written – were valued equally. Although it is still too early for a full evaluation, many aspects of this project appear to be successful (Shuard *et al.*, 1991). We will describe some of the activities carried out by the children and then comment on what we see as the merits and drawbacks of the project so far.

The children, aged 7 years and upwards, took readily to using calculators and gradually came to use them to answer sums they had not worked out for themselves. Such practices brought the children painlessly into contact with large numbers, complex sums, and ways to test their understanding. A striking feature of the classroom activities encouraged in the project is the way they facilitated exploration of the number system in ways that made sense to the children rather than were dictated by teachers. Such engagement of the children's pre-existing knowledge is borne out by the notations they used in their pencil-and-paper calculations. Two examples of children's methods of subtraction are given in Table 5.1.

As shown in the table, children's own notations and procedures frequently differ from formal ones by being written across the page from left to right rather than vertically in columns, and by starting at the left-hand side of the sum, in the hundreds column, rather than at the right-hand side, in the units column. These personal notations have the advantage of being more semantically trans-

Table 5.1 Procedures used by two 8-year-old children in the CAN project (from Shuard *et al.*)

---

549 − 331 = 218:
5 take away 3 = 2 (and you make it into hundreds)
so that is 200 and you add 40 → 240
−30 and it comes to 210 + 9 = 219
−1 = 218

135 − 72 = 63:
First I take 70 away from 100.
That leaves me with 30.
Then I add the other 30 back.
That makes 60.
Then I take 2 from 5 that left 3
so the answer is 63.

---

parent than the formal ones, and they allow the children to use their pre-existing knowledge of number so that new learning can be assimilated and integrated with it. This is in contrast to the children taught by more formal methods. In these cases, pre-existing knowledge is often by-passed so that new information cannot be related to it, but instead is treated as isolated equations and procedures that have to be memorized.

The use of calculators also triggered reflective processes by revealing inconsistencies in knowledge. The following dispute between two children over a number displayed by the calculator is an example:

'It says ten thousand.'
'No, it's a hundred thousand.'
'TEN thousand. Look – divide by two. What do you get?'
'Oh . . . five thousand. You're right.' (Shuard *et al.*, 1991)

Thus, some of the merits of this project can be readily appreciated. First, it encourages the children to bring their own pre-existing knowledge to the learning situation. Engagement of pre-existing knowledge may fail to take place in more formal teaching arenas where all the information comes from the teacher, because the teacher may not point out how the new information links with what the children already know. Indeed, the only sure way of enabling such links to be established is to allow the children to make active contributions to learning, so that their prior knowledge can be accurately identified and built upon. As we have seen in the preceding chapters, activation of prior knowledge is important for understanding because it makes the knowledge available for conscious scrutiny, so that it can be revised and updated as a result of the new learning. A second merit of the project is that it encourages learning through understanding rather than through problem solving, because the children's activities are open-ended rather than focused on specific problem-solving goals. Recall from Chapter 1 that Owen and Sweller (1985) found that solving problems without specific goals resulted in the students gaining conceptual knowledge; on the other hand, solving problems that had specific goals (the more usual educational state of affairs) did not lead to conceptual understanding, since in these circumstances problem-solving activities were triggered instead.

However, the project does have some drawbacks too. One is that the environment is very unstructured. This allows learning through understanding to occur, should the occasion arise, but it does not deliberately foster the search for understanding through structured activities. One way in which understanding could be fostered is through the use of group discussions to reveal the different ways in which different children understand a problem. For example, children could be encouraged to explain their own mathematical notations (such as those in Table 5.1) to the rest of the class or group. Then they would discover that there is more than one way of doing calculations and so be forced to reflect on the fact that there is more than one way of thinking about and using numbers, and that different notations may be useful for different purposes. Such activity could also form the basis of introducing and explaining the formal notation to the children so that they are conversant with it before they arrive in the secondary-school system. The main point, though, is that given the effort involved in learning through understanding, it is probably not sufficient to leave its occurrence to chance. Chance occurrences of such understanding are unlikely to give sufficiently frequent experiences of its benefits to encourage the children to engage in it deliberately themselves.

A second possible drawback of the CAN project is also due to its lack of structure: the emphasis on the children's own activities, including the uses of idiosyncratic notations, could result in a failure to practise needed skills. Even though we are emphasizing the importance of conceptual understanding, we do not wish to convey the idea that extensive practice in using the mathematical procedures is unnecessary. On the contrary, practice is essential to make needed skills automatic and so leave working memory available for new learning. Understanding is a prerequisite for mathematical learning, but successful learning also requires the acquisition of a large stock of procedures that have become automatic through extensive practice. Unstructured activities are rarely likely to lead to such practice, and so it needs to be fostered deliberately by the teacher.

A better approach to mathematics teaching, therefore, is to structure the learning environment in ways that specifically encourage understanding and at the same time provide sufficient opportunity to practise mathematical procedures. Schoenfield's (1985) attempts to teach mathematics to American college students exemplify such an approach. We therefore conclude our discussion of mathematics teaching and learning with an account of Schoenfield's work.

SCHOENFIELD'S STUDIES IN MATHEMATICS LEARNING

Schoenfield (1985) deliberately tries to facilitate understanding rather than problem solving. He does this in a number of ways. First, he addresses the preconceived beliefs about mathematics and about learning that students frequently bring to the learning situation. Second, he structures the learning in such a way that problem solving is turned into understanding.

Students' preconceived beliefs Schoenfield has identified a number of beliefs about mathematics that are typically held by students. These beliefs, he argues, are engendered as a result of their learning experiences at school. He also argues that many of these beliefs can seriously impede learning, since they determine the way that it will proceed. One is that mathematics is very difficult and can be learned only by a very few; hence, learning is confined to memorization and problem solving, since students believe that any efforts to understand would not be worthwhile. In addition, when difficulties arise and a student cannot solve a problem, there are minimal attempts to deal with the difficulty, since the student typically assumes that the problem is just too difficult for him or her.

To counteract such deep-rooted beliefs about learning mathematics, Schoenfield begins a topic by giving students problems that they cannot solve. He then introduces them to new strategies that enable them to solve the problems. The students are also encouraged to participate in the solutions as much as they can, and soon learn to solve the problems successfully. Through this process, Schoenfield shows the students that failure to solve problems can be used to indicate the need for further learning, and so turned into success. He therefore tries to counteract a prevailing experience with school mathematics in which failure is seen as a lack of ability rather than of the relevant skills and knowledge.

107

Students also hold beliefs about what it takes to be a good mathematician. Given the emphasis on speed and accuracy in school, the students come to believe that expert mathematicians are expert problem solvers, people who solve routine problems rapidly and accurately. Such a belief, of course, does not match to the reality, in which mathematicians use what they know to gain new knowledge and understanding of the subject. To counter this belief, therefore, Schoenfield challenges the students to bring him difficult problems that he attempts to solve at the beginning of the class. Occasionally the problems are hard enough for the students to see him flounder in the face of real difficulties. Thus the students are encouraged to view expert mathematicians as people who have to solve problems that are difficult for them and that involve serious learning, and not as people who are simply rapid and accurate problem solvers.

Turning problem solving into understanding Although Schoenfield takes problem solving seriously, that is not all that he does. While he uses problems to motivate the students and as a forum for demonstrating new and more sophisticated mathematical methods, he also shows how the learning of mathematics does not stop when the solution to a problem is found. This contrasts markedly with the traditional approach to mathematics teaching, where finding the correct answer indicates proficiency in the relevant techniques and learning is deemed to be complete. Instead, Schoenfield encourages students to pursue the implications of a solution and so gain further insights. As an example, students in a class were required to solve the magic square problem. That is, they were required to place the digits one to nine in a three-by-three square so that the sum of the digits along each row, each column and each diagonal is the same. The completed box is the magic square. Collaborative activity and analysis while reaching the solution helped the students to recognize that the strategies they used were instances of more general and more powerful mathematical ideas. For example, when discussing whether nine can go into the centre of the square, they developed the idea of exploiting extreme cases, and more importantly, they saw the relevance of doing so. Finding the solution in this way helps the students to understand and discover new strategies for solving difficult problems.

Once the solution is found however, learning does not stop. Instead, the class explores other magic squares and so discovers general principles, such as an algebraic form for describing squares, as well as mathematical strategies that are less often seen in classroom practice. Schoenfield also ensures that these strategies are illustrated in action and does not formally instruct the students in them. The belief system of mathematics is acquired through practice, not through being told. Hence it is readily assimilated into the students' pre-existing knowledge and used to extend and clarify understanding. Schoenfield (1991) gives a lively account of the learning achieved through solving the magic square problem.

Schoenfield's programme can be seen as an example of situated learning. First, difficult problems become the stimulus for learning and are not treated as evidence of failure. Second, the goals of the expert are revealed in their true colours: experts too engage in difficult and painful learning processes and are not simply people who are adept at solving problems. Third, Schoenfield ensures that sophisticated mathematical strategies are learned as a result of the efforts at understanding that occur once a problem has been solved. In Schoenfield's classes the real learning does not begin until the problem has been solved and the implications of the solution are pursued. In brief, the overall learning experience is designed to foster a set of beliefs that facilitate learning: expertise is not presented as fast and accurate problem solving, and new strategies and concepts are learned in a context that turns failure into success. Although Schoenfield's work is with undergraduates, his ideas are applicable to learning at all ages, particularly his view of learning as consisting of problem solving followed by a search for understanding.

Overall, then, learning failures in mathematics can be attributed to a concentration on problem solving. Furthermore, the mathematical knowledge that is taught in school is often arbitrary, being shorn of its natural purposes. Thus the learner fails to appreciate how such knowledge is normally used by the expert. The CAN project in Britain begins to address these issues by providing an environment in which children bring their pre-existing beliefs out into the open, where they can be explicitly evaluated. In particular, the project avoids the pursuit of specific goals that encourage problem solving. However, it fails to provide an environment that is sufficiently structured to ensure that understanding is deliberately pursued. That is, the goals of understanding are not made explicit. Schoenfield provides such an environment and in so doing highlights the difference between problem solving and understanding, and shows, moreover, how understanding can be combined with problem solving.

Learning to write

Writing has both motor and cognitive components: the co-ordination of hand and finger movements to write the words on a page, and the co-ordination of plans to construct a coherent text. However, we will focus here on the cognitive components. We begin with a description of the way that writing is learned initially and then turn to an examination of how continuous discourse is produced. The goals of writing are described and two writing strategies are discussed, the knowledge-telling and the knowledge-transforming. The first of these treats writing as problem solving: the problem of how to put one's thought on paper. The second treats writing as a tool for learning through understanding: the demands of communication are used to help clarify and develop one's thoughts.

BASIC WRITING SKILLS

A number of people have observed that children need to grasp the basic insight that writing can be used for communication (e.g. Donaldson, 1984; Vygotsky, 1962). Once this insight is grasped, writing begins to develop. The insight is gained quite early – sometime during the third year according to Jones (1990). Jones's evidence suggests that before this insight, children either fail to write at all or, if asked to label a picture, may scribble over it or try to colour it in. But they do not seem to understand the difference between drawing and writing, and when asked, will not claim to have written anything. After the insight about communication is gained, children's scribbles remain unchanged but the children now claim quite confidently that they have written something. Shortly after this, writing is visibly distinguished from drawing as well. For example, they may produce zigzags when asked to write something, or discrete squiggles that begin to look like real letters. Later still, recognizable letters and numbers appear either alone or in combination with idiosyncratic signs, and the children now believe that their 'writing' says what they want it to say, although their spoken translation is not easy to discern in their written messages. Eventually, children begin to write phonetically and understand that each letter stands for a sound in a word.

Learning to write phonetically continues for many years. While these abilities are developing, a number of other complex cognitive skills are also being acquired, which are needed to turn writing into something more than just putting words on paper. They are the skills needed to produce coherent continuous prose.

An initial impetus to the writing of extended discourse is the analogy between writing and speaking. Since children are already fluent speakers when they learn to write, it makes sense to exploit this fluency when writing. Such an approach can be termed the *conversational analogy*, use of which treats writing as if it were conversation written down. It is a very powerful analogy for learning because spoken conversation is the principle way in which people communicate with each other, so it is already a familiar activity for the children, and hence it seems natural to use it as an analogy through which the skills specific to writing can be learned. However, this analogy cannot be taken too far, since there are many differences between spoken and written language. Perera (1984) has documented some of these, showing how writing is not simply a translation from the spoken to the written word. Speech has many features such as intonation, stress and pause patterns that all help to convey the intended message. Writing may make use of punctuation for these purposes, but compared to the nuances of speech, it is a very blunt tool. It is not easy, for example, to convey emotion in writing: compare the use of tone of voice, facial expression, whispering or shouting, all of which can accompany speech and help to make the message intelligible. Thus learning to write requires learning specific skills of written communication that are not derived from spoken skills.

Another difference between speech and writing is the degree of contextual support that is available. Speech occurs in a specific context, so the words can be seen to refer to objects or people that are known to both the speaker and the hearer. The context is not just the physical one, but also the common knowledge of the situation that is shared by the participants in the conversation. There is, therefore, a wealth of shared knowledge that can be assumed in conversation (see, for example, the contributions in Smith, 1983). However, writing does not have these contextual benefits. It is divorced from the person making the communication and from the shared context. Consequently the writer has to make special efforts to create a context for the reader. This demands the ability to take other people's perspectives into consideration and not to take for granted all the things that are normally taken for granted in a conversation. The cost is a great deal of hard work that continues for many years – if it ever stops at all (see e.g. Bartlett, 1982).

Despite these differences between speaking and writing, young children do exploit their knowledge of speaking when they first learn to write. However, while there are benefits to such a strategy, there are also drawbacks due to the differences between writing and talking. Scardamalia *et al.* (1982) identify one of these, pointing out that one of the problems with children's early writing is its low quantity. Children aged approximately 10 and 12 years may produce opinion essays that are only 32 words long (Hidi and Hildyard, 1980); indeed, their essays may even be as short as 18 words (Scardamalia and Bereiter, 1979). Scardamalia *et al.* suggest that such brevity is a consequence of the spoken-language model. In a spoken conversation, each person takes a turn and waits for a response. Similarly, in the written essays it is as if the writer takes a conversational turn and then waits for a response. Since no response is forthcoming, the essay terminates there.

Scardamalia *et al.* (1982) found that simply prompting children to write some more when they had apparently finished increased both the quality and quantity of their essays. They argued that the prompt acts in place of the contextual supports of conversation and so enables the writer to continue writing in the absence of a conversational partner. The resulting increased length of compositions ensures that practice in writing long texts starts as early as possible, so that an alternative writing schema (or model) can replace the conversational one that the children start with. Once children are producing essays of a reasonable length, the real work of writing can begin. Such writing requires that the different goals of writing are all pursued and integrated.

There are two kinds of goal involved in writing: rhetorical and substantive.

Substantive goals concern the information that the writer wishes to convey. These ideas will be rich and coherent if the writer's knowledge is rich and coherent, but sketchy and incomplete if the writer's knowledge is so. If the writer attempts to elaborate on the ideas to be conveyed, additional information is retrieved from long-term memory. However, if the writer attempts to evaluate those ideas and pursue their implications, then further learning may also occur.

Rhetorical goals concern the way in which the writer chooses to communicate his or her intended message. They include both low-level and high-level goals, some of which are listed below. Low-level rhetorical goals include:

- punctuation
- spelling
- word choice
- sentence structure
- how much to write
- how to construct a sentence
- how to make each sentence follow sensibly from the previous one.

High-level goals include:

- planning the overall content and each successive segment
- planning the content of each successive sentence in accordance with the plan for the segment
- ensuring that the text as a whole is coherent
- checking that statements are not presented without justification

113

- checking that the implications of the statements are spelled out

- checking that there are no inconsistent statements

- ensuring that most space is devoted to the most important points.

As was the case with reading, learning to write requires extensive practice in numerous activities that make up the activities needed to fulfil the goals of writing. Many of these activities, particularly those associated with the low-level rhetorical goals, may become automatic over time, although writing is never completely automatic. In addition, though, writing also involves high-level cognitive activities that combine and integrate the different goals. In this section we focus on these high-level processes. This is not because the activities needed to meet the goals themselves are unimportant: far from it. Such things as spelling, sentence structure, checking and revising these aspects of the text are essential components of the process. However, it is only through a consideration of the high-level integrative processes that we can come to appreciate the way that writing can be used for learning.

INTEGRATING SUBSTANTIVE AND RHETORICAL GOALS

The novice writer needs to learn how to co-ordinate the different and complex demands of rhetorical (both high- and low-level) and substantive goals. That is, he or she needs to be able to move quickly and fluently from concentrating on a low-level goal, such as checking that a word is spelled correctly, to concentrating on a high-level goal, such as checking that the current paragraph is coherent and fits into the writer's overall plan. Further, the writer also needs to co-ordinate these rhetorical goals with the substantive goals of writing. To explain how the integration of substantive and rhetorical goals occurs, Scardamalia and Bereiter (1985) characterize writing as taking place within two problem spaces in the mind of the writer: the rhetorical space and the substantive space. In the *rhetorical space* rhetorical goals are pursued, while in the *substantive space* substantive goals are pursued. To give an example, if you are asked to write an opinion essay on, say, euthanasia and you have not thought very much about this topic, a great deal of your effort will be concentrated within the substantive space. It will be concerned with working out a view on the topic and bringing in relevant knowledge, experience, emotional reactions, relations to other values one holds and so on. Apart from these substantive problems, however, there is also that of producing a successful essay that accomplishes the purpose of convincing the readers of the validity of your position, or possibly of inducing the reader to share your doubts and perplexities about the issue.

Scardamalia and Bereiter characterize two writing strategies that use these two problem spaces differently. One is the *knowledge-telling strategy*, in which information is passed from the substantive space to the rhetorical space and then written down according to the rhetorical goals. This is mainly used by novice writers and is governed primarily by problem-solving principles. The writer has a certain amount of knowledge about a topic and the goal is to put that knowledge onto paper, usually in response to a writing assignment. The other is the *knowledge-transforming strategy*, in which there is a two-way flow of information between the substantive and the rhetorical spaces. Thus, the current goals of the two spaces place constraints on each other. This strategy is used by expert writers and it can bring about new learning and understanding.

To clarify what we mean by using writing for learning, here are some examples from Scardamalia and Bereiter (1985) of the way that information from the rhetorical space leads to further developments of the content:

- a consideration of why readers might object to, or misunderstand, or have no interest in what has been written can lead to the discovery of inadequacies in its content

- demands of the genre influence content: for example, a research report needs to have a search for citations, to have the purpose and method stated, to deal with qualifications in the conclusion and so on; the writer of a business letter needs to think out the next step or to suggest a resolution of the issue raised in the letter

- searching for elements needed in the text, such as examples, definitions and additional reasons, often forces the writer to develop the content further

- the need to write more about a major point to establish its importance in the mind of the reader may lead the writer to further development and elaboration of ideas

- the rhetorical need to delete material or rearrange it may force a reconsideration of priorities in the content.

Scardamalia and Bereiter argue that many school activities encourage the use of the knowledge-telling rather than the knowledge-transforming strategy. Writing, in these circumstances, remains a mechanical problem-solving strategy in which the goal is to put one's thought onto paper. Thus the use of writing for further learning is ignored.

Writing to learn, by means of the knowledge-transforming strategy, is a hard-won skill that takes much explicit reflection and effort. In the remainder of the chapter, we will examine each of these strategies, consider some of the many ways in which writers avoid the use of writing for further learning, and discuss some of the ways that teachers might encourage the learning function of writing.

THE KNOWLEDGE-TELLING STRATEGY

In the knowledge-telling strategy, substantive goals are pursued in activities carried out before the process of writing begins. The knowledge gained through such pre-writing activities is then communicated by means of the strategy, which is therefore mainly a reporting of thoughts. Writers simply spill out everything they know about a topic onto the page and generate text content in a straight-ahead fashion, by using memory cues drawn from the topic, from knowledge of text structure, and from text already generated. This means that texts generated by this strategy tend to reflect the order in which things were thought of, rather than an order imposed on the content as a result of planning (Flower, 1979; Scardamalia and Bereiter, 1987). When people who use the knowledge-telling strategy are asked to think aloud while writing, the resulting verbal reports are relatively devoid of thoughts about goals or main ideas. In particular, the reports show no signs of reflection – of reconsidering previous ideas or decisions (e.g. Bereiter *et al.*, 1988). In this strategy, although information is

116

passed from the substantive to the rhetorical space, there is no two-way interaction between the spaces: information is not passed back from the rhetorical to the substantive space for clarification or development of the content.

The knowledge-telling strategy uses mainly low-level rhetorical goals, such as how much to write, how to construct a sentence and how to make a sentence follow sensibly from the previous one. High-level goals are largely neglected, such as ensuring that the text as a whole is coherent, that statements are not presented without justification, that the implications of the statements are spelled out, and that there are no inconsistent statements. Someone engaged in such writing can appear very skilled. He or she writes quickly and fluently because the preoccupation with low-level rhetorical concerns means that difficult writing problems are minimized. However, if one's knowledge of a topic is scanty or even intermediate, then the knowledge-telling strategy will not generate good texts, because gaps in knowledge or in arguments will be exposed. Poor writing, therefore, may be due to a lack of specific knowledge about the topic or to failures to retrieve the relevant knowledge. Furthermore, gaps in the text are not noticed by the writer, because the knowledge needed to do so is not available and because the concentration on low-level rhetorical goals does not require any major shifts in the way the writer views the subject matter being conveyed.

On the other hand, use of the knowledge-telling strategy will probably generate good text if one's knowledge of a topic is rich, well circumscribed and coherently organized. But generating such a text will not improve one's knowledge and so is not the mark of a true expert. For writing to influence thought beyond a rudimentary level of searching for additional information to fill up the space, it is necessary to confront and resolve recurring conflicts between substantive and rhetorical demands. To bring such resolution about, students must somehow be brought into confrontation with, and must persist in attempting to solve, rhetorical problems of the kinds that have substantive implications. According to Scardamalia and Bereiter (1986, 1991), successful confrontations require the use of the knowledge-transforming strategy.

THE KNOWLEDGE-TRANSFORMING STRATEGY

The knowledge-transforming strategy resolves the conflicts between the rhetorical and substantive demands of writing by making changes to the ideas being expressed and to the ways chosen to express them. As we have seen, Scardamalia and Bereiter characterize these two components of writing as two problem spaces in the mind of the writer: the rhetorical and the substantive space. Thus rhetorical demands and attempted solutions occupy the rhetorical space while the retrieved ideas and their elaboration, evaluation, and revision occupy the substantive. The two-way interaction between these two spaces underlies the understanding process and results in the joint evolution of the composition and the writer's understanding of what he or she is trying to say. This interaction between existing content knowledge and rhetorical goals is a specific instance of the more general account of understanding given in Chapter 1. Recall from there that understanding involved the two-way interaction between pre-existing knowledge and new material. In the context of writing, pre-existing knowledge consists of the ideas that make up the substance of the text, while the new material is the text being written in accordance with rhetorical demands. The interaction means that content is used to guide the choice of high-level rhetorical ploys, while attention to specific rhetorical needs forces a reconsideration or development of the substantive content.

To take a simple example, the rhetorical problem of constraining length may lead to a search in the substantive space for brief labels for complicated concepts. The use of such a label may produce a further rhetorical need to define the concept so labelled. A search through the substantive space for a way to define the concept may lead in turn to the realization that the writer does not in fact have a clear concept in mind, and so a major reanalysis of the point being made may occur, with a consequent reassessment of the rhetorical goals of the text. There are many other high-level rhetorical demands that force a reconsideration of the conceptual content, of which we have already listed some. Given the importance of using high-level rhetorical goals to develop and elaborate on the ideas being expressed, some additional rhetorical demands are listed below:

- length constraints may force a reconsideration of the relative importance of the arguments

- the need to make explicit links between sub-topics may lead to the discovery of previously unrecognized relationships

- the need to justify a position may lead to the discovery of previously ignored facts or the realization that the belief being put forward is unwarranted

- the need to make a text more interesting may lead to questioning about what makes an argument interesting, and this may bring new insights to light.

In each of these cases, the reorganization of conceptual content produces new rhetorical problems to be solved, and so the learning process is maintained (Scardamalia and Bereiter, 1985, 1991).

Scardamalia and Bereiter argue that the learning process involves a real tension between rhetorical and substantive concerns. If one concern predominates wholly, there will not be sufficient tension to lead to new learning. The writer wholly concerned with rhetorical demands and willing to alter substance in any way to meet them is condemned to produce a series of empty phrases. These are probably the preoccupations of political speech writers and other publicity merchants. However, many students and novice writers have the opposing preoccupation. Knowledge tends to predominate, and problems of rhetoric are either not recognized or are solved through ploys that leave the substance unchanged. This emphasis is encouraged by the knowledge-telling strategy.

In their studies of writing, Scardamalia and Bereiter have questioned students about their writing, listened to them composing aloud, or presented them with special rhetorical problems to wrestle with. From their observations, they have gleaned a rather formidable list of the ways in which writers manage to avoid the rhetorical problems that foster learning. As Scardamalia and Bereiter point out, these attitudes and strategies no doubt have a variety of causes and are not deliberately intended to avoid learning. Nevertheless, such avoidance is one of their major outcomes. As will be seen below, learning is most likely avoided because of the effort involved in revising and updating the substance of the text. Some examples of avoidant activities (from Scardamalia and Bereiter, 1985) are listed below.

- *a take-it-or-leave-it attitude towards the audience*. Students can frequently anticipate audience reactions, but do not recognize it as their responsibility to do anything about them. They assume that someone is bound to disagree with an expressed opinion and so you might as well leave them to it. Thus the effort needed to revise a text to avoid objections is not made.

- *willingness to put up with recognized weaknesses in structure or content*. Such a perfunctory attitude may well be due to the amount of effort required for revision and to the fears associated with making major changes to something that seems almost complete. It may well be implicitly encouraged, however, when essay writing is seen as a means of assessment rather than of new learning.

- *satisfaction with superficial connections*. Students tend to rely on superficial connections between sentences that involve little semantic constraint. They therefore fail to search for a substantive connection between one idea and another, a search that is a powerful device for forcing a deeper analysis of the content. Again, the effort required for such a deep analysis may prevent its occurrence.

- *use of the knowledge-telling strategy*. This is the most pervasive method of avoiding confrontation. This strategy, which seems to be pervasive in writing, ignores high-level rhetorical goals completely and typically concentrates on a few low-level problems of style. Here too the question of the effort required for considering high-level goals that lead to knowledge transformation may be crucial.

Overall, therefore, as we saw with reading, the real block to learning through understanding is the considerable effort it entails, effort of a kind that is not always encouraged in the classroom. As we also saw when discussing reading for learning, for someone to put in the kind of effort that is required, he or she needs to believe that it will be rewarding, and this is largely a motivational issue. Motivation will be discussed in Chapter 6, but for the moment we will consider some of the ways in which classroom practices may encourage or inhibit the desired motivation.

One difficulty that is encountered in the classroom is that writing assignments are used to assess specific knowledge of a subject. Thus, marks are obtained for knowing the facts, not for the learning and understanding that has been achieved. In other words, such assessments emphasize knowledge telling at the expense of knowledge transforming. If essays are used for assessment, and yet knowledge transforming is required, then the goals of assessment need to be clear; that is, that the clarity of the thoughts and the quality of the arguments are being assessed and not the sheer amount of knowledge that is conveyed.

Another problem is that many of the learning methods that are used to encourage writing encourage knowledge telling rather than knowledge transforming. For example, pre-writing activities are often used in the classroom, including discussion, films, readings, drawings, outings and the like. Such methods are designed to help students generate and develop ideas *before* deciding how to express them on paper. Their common function is to provide a stimulus to thought. Such activities are certainly worthwhile, since they facilitate the generation of ideas. They may even trigger (but not sustain) reflective processes if they force the learners to confront inconsistencies in their thinking. But their problem lies in the pervasive commitment to the knowledge-telling strategy, so that they are seen as the only way to stimulate and develop thought, with the use of writing itself for such a purpose being neglected. Thus activities in the substantive space are completed first, and the resulting content is then transferred to the rhetorical space, where it is transformed into text. Such pre-writing activities, therefore, encourage transmission of information from the substantive space to the rhetorical space, but not the return trip. Without engagement of a two-way process, the knowledge-transforming strategy will not be acquired and the opportunity to use writing to bring about new learning will be lost.

Yet another problem is that when writing is taught, it is as a skill that is independent of the learning of content. Thus, writing is only explicitly taught as an activity in the English curriculum, not in the curricula of specific subjects, such as history or science or geography. Indeed, learning to write in different genres, such as narratives, scripts, essays and newspaper articles, is all part of the National Curriculum for English, but not of the curricula for specific subjects. Thus writing an essay on, say, what happens to trees in winter is unlikely to include learning how to use writing to develop biological ideas. It is hardly surprising, therefore, that writing that is done in biology (or other subjects) generally reports what is known or observed and is rarely subjected to procedures that might foster further learning through understanding. In other words, for knowledge transforming to be learned as a strategy, it needs to be encouraged explicitly in classes on specific subjects.

Alexander (1992) has pointed to what he seems to regard as the excessive use of writing and reading in all curriculum areas. However, his concern may be only partly justified. Writing and reading are the main ways in which learning through understanding can be encouraged, and so their role in the curriculum needs to reflect their importance. With firm guidance, both reading and writing can facilitate important learning skills that foster understanding. Of course, Alexander's concern may be justified if the time spent in these activities is used in other ways and not for the purpose of understanding. And we have already seen that writing for learning can be subverted in a number of ways that allow students to avoid the effort of learning through understanding.

Scardamalia and Bereiter have conducted a number of studies investigating ways in which the knowledge-transformation strategy can be encouraged. In one series of studies, they introduced cues to stimulate self-questioning on the part of writers and to force writers to evaluate their thinking in response to rhetorical demands (e.g. Bereiter and Scardamalia, 1982; Scardamalia *et al.*, 1984; Scardamalia and Bereiter, 1985). To give one example, Scardamalia and Bereiter (1985) point out that children find it very difficult to revise their texts spontaneously, although they are often able to carry out quite extensive revisions and rewritings with the help of peer feedback (e.g. Graves, 1979). To try to encourage spontaneous revision, therefore, Scardamalia and Bereiter gave children diagnostic cues to help them evaluate and revise their compositions without external feedback. They asked students aged approximately 12 and 18 years to diagnose problems in their own and other people's essays. First the students were instructed to mark the places in each essay where inadequacies were detected. Then they were asked to diagnose each problem. Half the students (the experimental group) were given 13 diagnostic cues to help them identify the problems, while the remaining students (the control group) received no additional support. Each cue was a phrase designed to describe a writing problem. The phrases are shown in Table 5.2.

The experimental students were asked to consider each cue in turn and to judge whether it applied to the essay and, if so, whether it applied to the text as a whole or to a specific, identified part. At the end of the experimental period, all the students were given another essay and asked to identify and diagnose its deficiencies without the use of cues. The results showed that performance improved following practice with the cues, but only with the older students. However, in a subsequent study using more precisely organized cues in more prolonged and more structured activities, 12-years-old also showed improved performance (Scardamalia *et al.*, 1984). Both the experimental and the control subjects made more diagnoses directed towards the sentence, paragraph or text levels than are normally observed in American school students (as

Table 5.2 Thirteen phrases used as diagnostic cues to aid experimental subjects in text analysis (Scardamalia and Bereiter, 1985)

Choppy – ideas aren't connected to each other very well.
Hard to tell what the main point is.
Too much space given to an unimportant point.
The writer ignores an obvious point someone would bring up against what they are saying.
Doesn't give the reader reason to take the idea seriously.
Part of the essay doesn't belong with the rest.
Incomplete idea.
Says something that's not believable.
Says the idea in a clumsy way.
The reader will have already thought of this.
Weak reason.
Too few ideas.
Example doesn't help to explain the ideas.

indicated by National Assessment of Educational Progress, 1977).

Taken together, these results suggest that the use of cues may facilitate spontaneous learning processes in writing. Furthermore, it seems likely that such spontaneous processes are most likely to be triggered when the writer is confronted by internally generated inconsistencies. This is because the studies described above also indicated that simply placing a mark in the margin where inadequacies were detected encouraged the use of high-level rhetorical goals at both age levels. Setting such tasks for children, therefore, may be one way in which classroom practices may encourage writing activities that foster learning through understanding.

Summary

In this chapter we have discussed the learning of mathematics and the learning of writing. In both cases, there is a tension between learning through problem solving and through understanding. Unfortunately, this often means that understanding may be neglected altogether. There seem to be a number of reasons why this should happen in mathematics, to do with the nature of school mathematics and with the beliefs students hold about the subject. Much of school mathematics suffers from being arbitrary. It is stripped of its normal purposes and so seen as abstract knowledge that is required mainly for the purposes of passing examinations. Because of its arbitrary nature, students believe that the subject is difficult and can only be understood by experts. They also fail to integrate their learning with pre-existing knowledge and to engage in the two-way evaluative process of understanding. Thus students rely on memorization and problem solving, since understanding is thought to be out of their reach. However, the work on practical intelligence reveals that such a belief is misleading, since complex mathematical skills seem to be easily acquired in practical situations where the goals of learning are clear. Schools also encourage the use of problem solving (and memorization) by their emphasis on speed and accuracy, thus fostering the belief that mathematics is about fast and accurate problem solving and not about understanding.

An examination of mathematics in primary schools shows how the emphasis on learning procedures for solving problems leads to a failure of understanding. The Calculator-aware Number Curriculum, part of the Primary Initiatives in Mathematics Education, is designed to encourage understanding of mathematics. It does this by enabling the children to bring their pre-existing knowledge to bear on learning and by encouraging open-ended activities that are not geared towards finding a specific mathematical solution. However, the project may not be sufficiently structured to ensure that learning through understanding takes place. In addition, its unstructured nature may push the balance between problem solving and understanding too far the other way by failing to provide sufficient opportunities for practice. Schoenfield's attempts to teach mathematics to undergraduates provide a good example of how such a balance might be maintained. He tries to change the students' beliefs about mathematics by showing how difficult problems can be a stimulus for learning and by showing that experts too spend time and effort in understanding. He also goes beyond problem solving by pursuing the implications of a solution once it has been found. For Schoenfield, therefore, real learning (that is, understanding) takes place at the point where problem solving stops.

Writing is a complex skill in its own right. But it can also be used in other subjects, either to show what has been learned or to develop one's understanding of the subject. Initial learning takes place over a number of years, during which children's writing changes from unidentifiable scribbles to clearly identifiable letters and words. Writing continuous prose requires an understanding of the way that rhetorical and substantive writing goals can be fulfilled. At first, the use of a conversational analogy prevents such learning, since what is written corresponds to a single conversational turn. This means that long essays involving continuous prose are not produced. It is not until long essays are produced that the writer can begin to co-ordinate substantive and rhetorical goals.

These two sets of goals can be combined in two different ways. One results in the knowledge-telling strategy, mainly concerned with problem solving: how to fill up the page with what is already known. When using this strategy, matters of content in the substantive problem space are passed to the rhetorical problem space, where they are converted into sentences. Thus, there is a one-way relationship between substantive and rhetorical goals. The second way in which these goals can be combined is through the use of the knowledge-transforming strategy, mainly concerned with learning through understanding: rhetorical goals are fed back to the substantive space and may trigger a search for deeper understanding of the content. Thus, when using this strategy, there is a two-way interaction between the substantive and the rhetorical spaces that characterizes learning through understanding. With this strategy, writing is more than a means of conveying thoughts; it is a powerful tool for new learning.

CHAPTER 6
Prior Knowledge, Learning and Motivation

Overview

In this chapter, we examine some of the negative effects that pre-existing knowledge may have on learning. It is generally assumed that prior knowledge of a topic facilitates the learning of that topic, and in many instances, that is the case. However, prior knowledge will have a negative effect whenever it conflicts with the new information to be learned. In these circumstances, the pre-existing, inconsistent knowledge turns out to be remarkably resistant to change. Worse still, it seriously interferes with the new learning.

People hold a range of intuitive beliefs about the world that have probably been learned implicitly and have become deeply embedded in their system of knowledge. Some of these beliefs concern the physical world and may interfere with explicit learning and instruction in physics and other sciences. Others, as we illustrate in the case of mathematics, are about the domain itself: the nature of its practices and its relevance to the learner. Intuitive beliefs such as these will impede learning if they are contrary to the actual practices of subject experts. Yet other beliefs are about human nature itself: what is meant by intelligence and what we believe about our own abilities. Beliefs such as these may influence motivation, emotion and action, and so determine the desire to learn, feelings of self-worth and the amount of effort expended in learning.

These preconceived beliefs are often called *intuitive theories*; they make up a personal belief system that explains the things that happen in the world. Intuitive theories have such far-reaching consequences for learning that the importance of understanding them cannot be over-emphasized. Once they are recognized and understood, then they are amenable to change.

Intuitive theories of content domains

INTUITIVE THEORIES OF MECHANICS

When a person walks forward and drops a ball while moving, where on the ground will the ball land? Straight down? Or does it move forward as it falls? Or backward? If you answered straight down, you would be in agreement with over half of the college students tested by McCloskey *et al.* (1983). In fact, the correct answer is that the ball will fall in an arc, striking the ground a few feet forward of the point where it was dropped. However, only 45 per cent of the college students gave this, the correct answer. In a series of experiments, McCloskey and his colleagues revealed a range of misconceptions that students have about motion. The results suggest that most people hold an intuitive theory of motion that is inconsistent with Newtonian principles of mechanics.

Newtonian mechanics holds that just as no force is needed to keep an object at rest, so no force is required to keep an object in motion. In the absence of an applied force, an object at rest remains stationary while an object in motion keeps going at constant speed and in a straight line. The key concept in Newtonian mechanics is acceleration. If an object is not accelerating, it is deemed to be in a neutral state that requires no explanation. In particular, constant motion is no different from being at rest. From the perspective of Newtonian physics, when a constant force is applied to an object it produces a constant acceleration in the direction of the force. This model, expressed in the equation $F = ma$, is a theoretical primitive in the sense that it is a prerequisite for learning many higher-order principles in physics.

Peoples' intuitive theories of physics take a different view. McCloskey and Kargon (1988) refer to this view as the *intuitive impetus theory*. People holding this view of physics have a cluster of beliefs that converge on the idea that motion, even at constant velocity, is a result of an influence in the direction of motion that imparts an internal impetus to the object. These influences are particularly common in explanations of motion that continues in the face of an obvious opposing force. For example, when an object moves upwards, an influence, such as the push from a hand, is said to overcome the force of gravity that pulls the ball down. Thus objects have internal impetus as a consequence of invented influences. The belief that a carried object will fall straight down, as in the example of the ball above, is also related to the view that motion requires impetus. Subjects who hold this belief apparently believe that whereas an object that is actively thrown or pushed acquires impetus, an object that is passively carried does not. Thus, when it is dropped the only influence acting upon it is gravity, which causes it to drop straight down.

McCloskey and Kargon point out that for the most part, an impetus theory functions quite well for predicting and explaining motions. However, in some instances, such as dropping bombs from an aircraft so that they hit the target, the assumptions can lead to strikingly incorrect predictions. The intuitive model arises because in the real world, where friction is present, one must push an object to keep it moving. Friction is often not recognized by the beginner as a force, and so observations of motion in the real world lead to the view that a force or impetus is required to keep something moving. The discrepancy arises because the physicists' view is an abstraction from reality, assuming an ideal world in which friction is not present. However, such abstractions are not visible to the naive observer, so an impetus theory is constructed on the basis of experience. Such intuitive theories, therefore, are reasonable ones for people without formal tuition in physics to hold. Indeed, not all intuitive theories are misconceived; there may also be intuitive theories that can be built upon in new learning (diSessa, 1983). Misconceived theories are most likely to arise in domains where the observable evidence is invisible or ambiguous, as is the case with observations of movement in the physical world.

Intuitive theories that are misconceived can have serious consequences. It turns out that explicit knowledge, such as that produced by formal training in physics, often fails to increase the accuracy of predictions (e.g. Proffitt *et al.*, 1990). For example, persistent misconceptions about Newtonian mechanics have been observed in third-year engineering students after two years of physics and calculus courses (Clement, 1983). These studies show that students can learn to use fairly meaningless routines for manipulating formulas without understanding the principles underlying those formulas. Clement (1991) suggests that this may be because teachers and students are in a hurry to use the most compact formalisms available for expressing the content of the subject. However, studies of misconceptions suggest that in addition to abstract formalisms, conceptual understanding at a qualitative level should also be emphasized.

Chapter 3 described some of the misconceptions that children bring with them to their learning of science. The work described above indicates that such misconceptions are not confined to young children. They will persist at all ages if these pre-existing beliefs are not engaged during the course of formal teaching and learning. This is because problem solving and memorizing are not sufficient to eradicate erroneous beliefs. For such eradication, understanding is needed. Champagne *et al.* (1980) argue that misconceived intuitive theories are resistant to change because novices have loose knowledge structures with little interconnectedness, so they can accommodate any new information locally without having to reorganize the whole system. Armed with intuitive theories, a novice can 'learn' new information without any new reconceptualization. To bring about real learning, a real reorganization of knowledge, understanding is needed. As Clement (1983) points out, learning requires that the students become aware of their intuitive theories and evaluate them explicitly by comparing them with accepted scientific explanations and with convincing empirical observations. As we have seen in previous chapters, such understanding, with its reorganization of knowledge, requires considerable effort and the use of sophisticated metacognitive strategies. Hence, it is frequently side-stepped, leading to a preoccupation with problem solving and memorization instead. This means that new information is simply added to existing, but conflicting, knowledge, thus ensuring that erroneous beliefs persist.

INTUITIVE THEORIES ABOUT MATHEMATICS

A number of people have recognized that beliefs about a domain can affect learning. For example, Pressley *et al.* (1989) report some common beliefs that they have encountered in their research on learning. They found that many learners believe that rewriting destroys the creative liveliness of writing. Such a belief will have negative effects on the desire to learn through writing. On the other hand, they also found learners who believed that good writing often occurs over long intervals and is accomplished through extensive rewritings. This belief is likely to have positive effects on learning.

The domain that has been most extensively studied in terms of beliefs is mathematics, where Schoenfield (1985) has reviewed some typical student beliefs and their effects. Schoenfield has also spelled out how these beliefs might come about as a result of classroom teaching. For example, he documents the way that students tackle a novel geometry problem. While expert mathematicians derive the information they lack through the use of geometric proofs, students try to draw the answer using compass and ruler, and stop when the diagram looks right. That is, students fail to use their knowledge of mathematical proofs, even when they have the relevant knowledge at hand. Schoenfield argues that this is because students hold certain beliefs about the nature of mathematical proofs, derived from activities observed in the classroom. He suggests that students come to believe that proof has a very specialized role in mathematics, since it is taught in very specific circumstances. First, it may be used to prove something that the students have known for several years, such as that 'The base angles of an isosceles triangle are equal'. Schoenfield notes that long before they take a geometry course, students know that the base angles of an isosceles triangle are equal, and they will claim that it is obvious just by looking at such a triangle. From the students' perspective, therefore, this proof and many others like it merely serve as formal confirmations of a fact that is patently obvious. The proof, therefore, seems redundant and superfluous. Second, a proof may also be used to verify something that the students are told is true. Thus, the proof is simply an exercise to be completed, a problem to be solved, and not a tool for exploration and understanding, for determining the truth of something not yet understood. The things being proven, therefore, are of little interest to the students, and the proofs remain a set of formalisms to be memorized.

In the schools that he visited, Schoenfield observed that memorization was often stressed. So too was the degree of speed and precision that the students would need to develop in order to pass their examinations. The emphasis on speed and accuracy

131

resulted in extensive practice of exercises that were easily solved. Schoenfield notes that students complete thousands of such exercises during their mathematical education, all of which can be solved in just a few minutes, as long as the students know the right procedures. Rarely, if ever, do students see problems of any other kind. Thus, they never experience making slow progress on complicated problems over periods of time. They therefore never learn to expect that progress of this kind is possible and rewarding, but rather come to expect that all of the mathematical problems they will encounter will be solvable either in a few minutes or not at all. Confronted with difficult problems, they act accordingly: after only a few minutes of unsuccessful attempts, they give up. Schoenfield argues that under these circumstances, students are hardly likely to discover the usefulness of mathematical strategies or the need to apply them in different circumstances. In other words, the focus on drill and practice results in a set of beliefs that prevents the learning of powerful mathematical strategies and underlying mathematical principles.

In general, the evidence suggests that intuitive theories and beliefs can interfere with learning and may be resistant to change through explicit tuition. However, as if this were not serious enough, it seems that intuitive theories can have more far-reaching consequences than those discussed above. People also hold intuitive theories of intelligence, and these seem to determine the goals that people set themselves, the way they interpret their own actions and the views they hold of themselves and of others. In short, intuitive theories may underlie people's self-concepts in a way that determines their motivation to learn and the likelihood that they will attempt to learn at all. We turn, therefore, to the motivational consequences of intuitive theories.

Intuitive theories and motivation

Motivation, as the word itself implies, is concerned with *motive*. The term refers to the reason or purpose that lies behind a person's actions and that influences the initiation, direction, intensity and persistence of behaviour (Evans, 1989). Motivation can be thought of as consisting of two components: goal setting and self-regulatory activities (Kanfer, 1990); that is, it consists of deciding what to do and working out how to do it. With both of these components, it is becoming increasingly clear that beliefs, attitudes and emotions are also involved. Self-attributions concerning ability and general feelings of self-worth all influence the goals people choose and how much effort they will expend in attaining those goals.

We have mentioned several times in preceding chapters that motivation is a major determinant of learning. In particular, we have argued that the search for understanding is more difficult than problem solving and memorization, the other forms of explicit learning. Not only does understanding require a large degree of attention, and hence easily overloads working memory, it also requires the use of sophisticated and difficult metacognitive skills. The rest of this chapter, therefore, is devoted to motivational issues. In particular, we show how a person's motivation depends upon his or her intuitive beliefs about intelligence and ability.

Intuitive theories of intelligence

According to Dweck and Leggett (1988), a person's basic goal orientation is the result of an intuitive theory of intelligence. They base their conclusions on a number of studies of children asked to complete easy and difficult tasks. When the children were given difficult tasks, Dweck and her colleagues found that the children displayed one of two distinct patterns of cognition, affect and behaviour. One they called the *helpless pattern*. It involves the avoidance of challenge and a deterioration of performance. That is, it involves low motivation and results in poor performance. The other they called the *mastery-oriented pattern*. It involves the seeking of challenging tasks and the maintenance of effective striving under failure. That is, it involves high motivation and results in good performance. Dweck and Leggett argue that these two response patterns result from differing intuitive theories of intelligence that determine what goals learners will choose for themselves. The two response patterns are described below. There then follows a discussion of how these two result from intuitive theories of intelligence.

133

HELPLESS VERSUS MASTERY-ORIENTED RESPONSE PATTERNS

The cognitive, affective and behavioural response patterns of helpless and mastery-oriented children were first documented by Diener and Dweck (1978, 1980). They identified children as either helpless or mastery-oriented by presenting them with a set of problems, the first eight of which could be solved successfully. However, the children were given a further four problems that were too difficult for children of their age (10 to 11 years) to solve. It was found that when the children moved from success on the first eight problems to failure on the next four, their response patterns fell into two distinct groups: helplessness and mastery-orientation. What is more, the children did not differ in the ease with which they solved the first eight problems or the strategies they used to solve them. Thus, their initial performance was equivalent. However, the children were strikingly different in their responses to failure. The two response patterns are described below.

Helpless children showed:

- *negative self-attributions*. They quickly began to report negative thoughts about themselves. They attributed failure to personal inadequacy, such as deficient intelligence, memory or problem-solving ability. This was accompanied by a complete absence of any positive prognosis and seemed to fly in the face of the fact that only minutes before their ability had yielded consistent success.

- *emotional responses*. Helpless children began to express pronounced negative feelings. They said that they disliked doing the problems, that they were bored with the problems, or that they were worried about their performance. Once again this was in the face of the fact that shortly before they had been quite pleased with their performance.

- *avoidant behaviour*. More than two-thirds of the helpless children started talking about things other than the task. For example, they talked of talents in other domains, and some boasted of unusual wealth and possessions, presumably in a defensive attempt to direct attention away from their present performance and towards more successful or praiseworthy attributes.

- *Performance decrements*. Helpless children showed marked decrements in performance over the failure trials. Over 60 per cent of them lapsed into ineffective strategies, despite the fact that they had previously demonstrated their ability to employ sophisticated and helpful ones.

When the mastery-oriented children were confronted with the difficult problems, their response patterns were in striking contrast to those described above:

- *self-attributions*. Mastery-oriented children did not offer attributions for their failure. Rather, they appeared to view the unsolved problems as challenges to be mastered through effort, and they engaged in extensive self-instructions and self-monitoring to meet those challenges. They not only planned specific strategies to use and with which to monitor their performance, they also instructed themselves to exert effort or to concentrate, and then monitored their level of effort or attention. Thus their self-instructions and self-monitoring referred to both cognitive and motivational aspects of their performance.

- *emotional responses*. Rather than becoming negative about the task, the mastery-oriented children seemed to maintain an unflagging optimism that their efforts would pay off. For example, they said such things as 'I did it before, I can do it again'. Furthermore, many of them gave evidence of enjoying the challenge and relishing it.

- *lack of avoidant behaviour*. None of the mastery-oriented children diverted his or her attention from the task by talking of other things.

- *performance increments*. Unlike the helpless children, mastery-oriented children clearly benefited from their attempts to solve the difficult problems. Eighty per cent of them maintained their problem-solving strategies at or above their pre-failure levels, with over 25 per cent increasing the level of their strategy. In other words, these children taught themselves new, more sophisticated hypothesis-testing strategies over the four failure trials.

In short, in the face of difficulty, helpless children had negative thoughts about themselves, had negative feelings about the task, engaged in task-irrelevant defensive manoeuvres, and seemed to view further effort as futile. The result was a marked deterioration in performance. By contrast, in the same situations, the mastery-oriented children increased their efforts in both cognitive and motivational domains, and maintained a belief that the problems were solvable. As a result, they maintained and even improved their learning strategies.

Despite the fact that the children had all received identical tasks and earned identical task outcomes, helpless children and mastery-oriented children interpreted and responded to the situation in entirely different ways. As Dweck and Leggett point out, these patterns have also been well documented in adults (e.g. Brunsen and Matthews, 1981). The question is, therefore, how do these two different response patterns arise? According to Dweck and Leggett, they result from a chain of processes that begin with different theories about intelligence and represent a person's self-concept. These self-concepts guide the choice of goals that people set themselves, and guide their self-attributions in the face of needed effort or failure.

INTUITIVE THEORIES OF INTELLIGENCE AND CHOICE OF GOALS

Bandura and Dweck (1985) identified children who endorsed either an *entity theory* of intelligence or an *incremental theory*. They asked children questions like, 'What makes people smart?'. Entity theorists said things like: 'You can learn new things, but how smart you are stays pretty much the same.' Incremental theorists said things like, 'Smartness is something you can increase as much as you want to.' Thus, we can characterize the two theories as follows:

- *entity theory*: Intelligence is regarded as a fixed entity or uncontrollable characteristic, a thing that never changes.

- *incremental theory*: Intelligence is regarded as a malleable, changeable, improvable and controllable characteristic.

Having identified these two groups according to their beliefs about intelligence, Dweck and her colleagues then went on to examine

136

ngs of self-worth? In general, self-esteem is fostered by out-
.mes that indicate high ability. Thus, these individuals will strive
to display high ability by tackling problems they can solve successfully. But they will avoid situations of failure, since these will indicate low ability and so will lead to lowered self-esteem. In other
words, for these individuals, the pursuit of performance goals will
generate and maintain self-esteem.

Consider now a person who believes that the self is a collection
of changeable characteristics that can be improved over time.
What must this person do in order to generate self-esteem? For
such individuals, outcomes that indicate high ability are those that
result from successful attempts to improve that ability. Therefore,
these individuals will strive to succeed at difficult tasks because of
the opportunities these offer for improvement. But they are likely
to avoid easy tasks, or lose interest in them, since these offer no
opportunity for mastery or improvement. In other words, for
these individuals, the pursuit of learning goals will generate and
maintain self-esteem.

Thus, for the entity theorist, self-esteem is channelled through
performance goals. Outcomes indicating the adequacy of one's
abilities will raise and maintain self-esteem. However, for an
incremental theorist, self-esteem will depend on learning goals.
Pursuit of learning goals leading to progress with and mastery
of challenging tasks will raise and maintain self-esteem. Results
reported by Dweck and Bempechat (1983) support these ideas.
Children were told, 'Sometimes kids feel smart in school, sometimes not. When do you feel smart?'. Children who had endorsed
an entity theory reported that they felt smart when their work was
correct, when it was better than that of their peers, or when the
work was easy for them. Children who had endorsed an incremental theory reported that they felt smart when they worked
on hard tasks and when they personally mastered their challenges.
Thus the theories and their allied goals can be seen as two distinct
self-systems.

Overall, Dweck and Leggett (1988) spell out different intuitive
theories that individuals hold about intelligence and that lead them
to value their abilities in different ways. These differing beliefs and
values lead different individuals to set different goals, which either
display or develop 'smartness'. Thus, Dweck and Leggett spell

out a chain of processes that start with people's beliefs about intelligence and their own abilities, and lead to characteristic self-concepts, which, in turn, lead to different ways of generating and maintaining self-esteem. People who hold an entity theory maintain self-esteem by adopting performance goals so that they can demonstrate their ability; people who hold an incremental theory maintain self-esteem by adopting learning goals so that they can demonstrate mastery and progress. Furthermore, these two different self-systems will lead to different self-perceptions in the face of effort or failure. For people who see intelligence as fixed, the need for effort leads to a belief that their ability is low, and they suffer a blow to self-esteem when faced with failure. Thus such situations will be avoided; but when they have to be faced, they will lead to anxiety and negative self-perceptions. In short, they will lead to the helpless pattern of responding to failure. By contrast, for people who believe that intelligence is changeable, the need for effort leads to the investment of the needed effort in order to demonstrate mastery, and they see difficult tasks as challenges and ways to demonstrate self-esteem. That is, they lead to the mastery-oriented pattern of responding to failure. This complex chain of processes is outlined in Table 6.1.

Intuitive theories, classroom activities and learning

The work described above on cognition and motivation has marked implications for the goals children set for themselves in the classroom. It seems clear, for example, that children will avoid tasks demanding time and effort if they believe that they will fail at the task and if they also believe that achievement is due to some innate ability, or to luck. In other words, belief in an entity theory of intellectual attributes, coupled with low self-esteem, means that neither children nor adults are likely to initiate or persist in effortful learning. Indeed, these maladaptive beliefs may even be fostered by classroom practices. For example, Nicholls (1978, 1984) has observed that most children begin their school careers with an incremental view of intelligence. However, by the late elementary years (that is, by 10 or 11 years old) some children may come to believe that effort and ability are inversely related, and that if success requires a great deal of effort it may mean that the

Table 6.1 Sequence of processes in achievement situations in helpless and mastery-oriented children

	Helpless children	*Mastery-oriented children*
Theory of intelligence	Entity theory: ability is fixed	Incremental theory: intelligence can be improved
Self-concept	The self consists of unchangeable characteristics	The self consists of characteristics that can be improved
Self-esteem	Obtained by demonstrations of high ability	Obtained by demonstrations of mastery and improvement
Goal orientation	Performance goals	Learning goals
Response to the need for effort	Perceptions of low ability	Perceptions of mastery
Response to easy tasks (low effort)	Perceptions of high ability	Irrelevant to mastery
Response to sucess	High self-esteem	Perceptions of progress, high self-esteem
Response to failure	Feelings of failure and low self-esteem, reduction of effort	Persistence and maintained effort

person lacks ability. That is, experience in school leads some children to change their theory of intelligence to an entity one.

Children are likely to gain such a belief if the classroom setting favours performance goals. For example, competition in classrooms seems to support the belief that intelligence is fixed and leads to self-attributions concerning ability (Ames, 1984). It is also possible that the intuitive theories held by teachers influence children's beliefs. Teachers who themselves hold an entity theory of intelligence and who set themselves performance goals may interpret children's performance in similar terms. This may lead teachers to foster the setting of performance goals, which may, in turn, reinforce children's own beliefs in an entity theory. Certainly Ames and Archer (1988) have noted that classrooms display either a predominantly performance or a predominantly learning orientation. In classrooms where the former is the case, students are concerned about being able, about outperforming others, and about achieving success with very little effort. In classrooms where the latter is true, students are concerned about acquiring new skills, about learning and about using effort. Ames and Archer found that capable junior-high and high-school students who rated their classrooms as performance-oriented reported using fewer learning strategies than peers who rated their classrooms as mastery-oriented. Students who reported using learning strategies did so in situations where they thought performance might be enhanced and effort was valued in the classroom. Thus it appears that the overall organization in the classroom can affect the students' goal orientation, and indeed, may even influence their implicit theories of intelligence. Such a view coincides with the arguments made by Schoenfield (1985) concerning the formation of beliefs about mathematics.

It also seems that a concentration on problem solving may encourage the choice of performance goals, particularly when the problems are difficult. Kanfer (1990) has argued that setting specific and difficult goals leads to a performance orientation. She found that such setting during the early stages of learning disrupts performance. However, performance is not disrupted by a non-specific goal where the learners are simply told to do their best (Kanfer and Ackerman, 1989). Kanfer and Ackerman (1989) suggest that these results probably arise because the early stages of learning require extensive use of working memory. However, if the goal is specific and hard to find, then attention is diverted by negative thoughts about performance. These negative thoughts will also occupy working memory, leaving little spare capacity for learning activities. Thus it seems likely that problem solving, which involves the setting of specific goals, contributes to the choice of performance goals, particularly if the task is difficult. In these circumstances, learning will be poor, because negative thoughts about performance may occupy working memory when it is already overloaded.

Overall, therefore, there are a number of ways in which activities in the classroom can affect both the beliefs children hold about intelligence and the goals that they choose for themselves. Competitive classrooms support the belief that intelligence is a fixed entity, and thus encourage the choice of performance goals. It also seems likely that teachers organize their classrooms according to their own intuitive beliefs and goal orientations. Some classrooms appear to be predominantly performance oriented while others appear to be predominantly learning oriented. Finally, a preoccupation with problem solving may also favour performance goals, particularly when the task is difficult. Indeed, children who appear indifferent to learning, and who are labelled as lazy or unmotivated by their teachers, may in fact be protecting themselves against feelings of failure as a result of self-attributions of poor ability (Covington, 1985). As Dweck (1986) has pointed out, even very able students may give up as a result of such ability attributions.

Emotion, motivation and learning

The view that distracting negative thoughts divert attention from the task itself, by occupying working memory, points to a link between emotion and motivation that has been investigated by Eysenck (1979, 1992). Eysenck has distinguished between the emotional component of anxiety and the cognitive one. The *emotional* is responsible for changes in physiological arousal and accompanying states of uneasiness; the *cognitive* is commonly thought of as worry. It involves concern about one's level of performance, negative task expectations, and negative self-evaluations. Eysenck argues that worry is responsible for the observed effects of anxiety on performance. First, he suggests that task-irrelevant worries occupy working memory and so leave less capacity for dealing with the task itself. This has the effect of increasing the effective task difficulty, since both task-relevant and task-irrelevant activities must be dealt with. Second, he suggests that anxious subjects attempt to compensate for this increased difficulty by increased effort. However, as task difficulty increases, increased effort will only partially compensate and so performance will begin to decline. Third, he emphasizes an important modification to the increased effort and motivation of high-anxiety subjects. When the likelihood of success is moderate – greater than 50 per cent – then motivation will increase. However, if the likelihood of success is low – less that 1 per cent – then motivation will decline and helplessness will set in.

This analysis can be likened in some respects to Dweck and Leggett's (1988) account of children with performance goals and low perceived ability. These children respond to failure with an increase in worry and a decrease in performance. They attribute their failure to personal inadequacy regarding their intelligence, their memories and their problem-solving abilities. They also report negative feelings about the task itself, such as aversion, boredom, or anxiety over their performance. Similarly, Kanfer and Ackerman (1989) report the effects of specific and difficult goals on initial learning. They found that the setting of such goals resulted in poorer performance than that obtained with a non-specific goal, such as doing one's best. They also found an increase in self-evaluative thoughts and negative effect, leaving less attention for the task itself. These negative feelings are due to what Eysenck calls worry, the cognitive component of anxiety. These effects of anxiety may go some way to explain one of the most striking puzzles about the helpless children observed by Dweck and Leggett (1988). These were the children who were most concerned with their ability, and yet they behaved in ways that limited their abilities. The solution to the puzzle seems to be that not only do such children have a set of beliefs that effort will not change their ability, they are also vulnerable to the negative cognitive and emotional effects associated with anxiety and helplessness.

Thus, worry may explain why children with performance goals and low perceived ability perform badly following failure. The negative thoughts associated with worry overload working memory and so prevent the children from performing effectively. In effect, the task is made more difficult for them, since the attentional demands are greater, involving as they do both task demands and emotional demands.

The analysis of motivation presented by Dweck and Leggett may also contribute to an understanding of the roots of anxiety and depression. If people believe that their performance is an indicator of some fixed ability, then failure to demonstrate high ability and judgements of low ability are likely to result in negative emotions, such as anxiety. When anxiety sets in, resulting in task-irrelevant worries, then greater effort may initially be expended. If the increased effort is sufficient to counteract the increased task demands, then performance will not deteriorate (Eysenck, 1979). But in the face of consistent failure, motivation will decline and helplessness may set in, together with the depression that may be associated with it (e.g. Peterson and Seligman, 1984). Indeed, many people have argued for a cognitive basis to anxiety and depression. For example, Beck (1976; Beck and Clark, 1988) argues on the basis of therapeutic interviews that anxious patients have a negative self-schema that involves an exaggerated vulnerability to personal threat, while depressed patients have a negative self-schema that involves such themes as personal deficiency, worthlessness and rejection. The work of people such as Dweck and Leggett suggests that the roots of anxiety and of depression associated with helplessness may be deeper than this. They may lie in a set of goals that are determined by implicit theories of intelligence. On the one hand, a person's goals may be designed to promote learning and mastery, in which case negative emotional responses to failure are unlikely. On the other hand, personal goals may be designed to exhibit high ability or hide low ability, in which case negative emotional responses to failure will predominate.

These suggestions have some far-reaching implications. For example, most highly valued, long-term goals, such as those involving work, relationships and moral decisions, pose risks and difficult challenges. People who hold intuitive theories of intelligence in which effort does not improve ability may eventually abandon such goals, or fail to tackle them effectively. What is more, a preoccupation with learning through problem solving may foster and reinforce the belief in an entity theory of intelligence, with all its negative consequences. It is only by making deliberate attempts to understand, to evaluate one's pre-existing beliefs in the light of new learning, that maladaptive beliefs can be modified.

Summary

Preconceived beliefs can hinder learning if they contradict the views expressed in the material to be learned. Intuitive theories of the physical world conflict with a Newtonian mechanical theory and are very resistant to change through explicit tuition. This resistance to change is mainly because problem solving and memorization are encouraged in preference to understanding. In general, the former are deficient, because they simply result in new knowledge being added to memory and consolidated without the pre-existing knowledge being affected in any way. Only through efforts to understand can new material be used to revise and update preconceived beliefs. Problem solving and memorization are also deficient in that they promote and maintain intuitive beliefs about the domain itself, as Schoenfield (1985) has demonstrated in the domain of mathematics.

Implicit learning is ubiquitous and goes on whatever the learning circumstances. Hence people bring a range of such theories and beliefs to each new learning situation. Some of these have far-reaching implications for motivation and emotion. Thus, differing theories of intelligence may underlie the goals that people set themselves and how they interpret their own performance. People who hold an entity theory of intelligence believe that their ability is fixed and cannot be improved no matter how much effort is made. This theory leads people to adopt performance goals designed to prove their ability or to hide their perceived inability. In the face of failure, such people attribute the failure to their own inadequacies, develop increasingly negative views of the task and show impaired performance. People who hold an incremental theory of intelligence believe that their ability is malleable and can be improved through their own efforts. This theory leads people to set themselves learning goals that involve challenge and require effort in attempts to improve that ability. When faced with failure, such people try new strategies to overcome their difficulties and show improved performance.

Activities in the classroom may also affect the learner's beliefs and choice of goals, possibly through the beliefs and goal orientations of the teachers. In addition, a problem-solving approach to learning and instruction may induce performance goals, particularly if the problems are difficult. Intuitive beliefs also affect learning outcomes. People who hold an entity theory of intelligence may perform badly when faced with failure, because negative thoughts and worries about themselves take up much needed space in working memory. Such anxiety leads to task-irrelevant thoughts about poor performance and so increases the overall difficulty of the task by overloading working memory. In the short term, or when self-perceptions of ability are favourable, this may lead to increased effort, and so there may be no performance decrement. However, in the longer term and with difficult tasks, such increases in effort will cease to be effective, and so there will be a decrease in motivation, resulting in helplessness and lowered performance. However, people who hold an incremental theory of intelligence perform well and persist in their efforts, even when faced with difficult tasks. Thus, such people are able to persist in the effort needed to engage in learning through understanding.

Finally, in the light of all the discussion in this and preceding chapters, how might we characterize the really successful learner? It seems that he or she is a person who engages in attempts to understand without neglecting the more mundane tasks of repeated problem solving and memorization. The former activity ensures that new material is used to revise and update pre-existing beliefs. The latter activities ensure that the skills associated with the subject being learned can be practised until they can be executed automatically, and that the new understanding achieved is quickly and easily accessible. In the final two chapters, we turn our attention to classroom activities that are the prerequisites for such successful learning.

CHAPTER 7

The Teacher's Task

Overview

This chapter is focused on three questions which are central to the task of any teacher, namely what the students already know as they come to a learning situation, how the teacher sets about the challenge of finding out this information, and what is then done with this knowledge in order to facilitate further learning. A number of issues are addressed which relate to these questions, notably the skills of assessment and diagnosis of learning, matching, and the design and implementation of an appropriate range of tasks for learners to engage in. A range of strategies is considered, which together could be helpful in promoting conceptual learning.

We conclude with a concise statement of the essential components to be matched in the teacher's task of organizing situations for effective learning, and a summary of independent research findings on what constitutes effective teaching.

Context

Evidence and discussion so far presented in this book suggest that three key questions underpin the complex task faced by any teacher. These are:

1. What do the pupils already know?

2. How does the teacher find out this information?

3. What does she or he then do with this information in order to facilitate further learning?

To an extent, the teacher's task in England and Wales is constrained by the statutory orders of the National Curriculum for Schools. The framework of the National Curriculum provides the context in which classroom tasks may be developed.

A number of significant issues emerge from this framework. These include the need for curriculum coverage; the key question of how time is used in classrooms; the need for adequate planning and programmes of work linked to appropriate observation and assessment procedures; and the need to identify the considerable overlaps which exist in content and skills across the curriculum.

At the outside, it must be stressed that the National Curriculum is a framework for implementation rather than a straitjacket of subject-specific content. Legislation allows for some freedom of interpretation and delivery of material. Fulfilling the precise requirements of the Education Reform Act (1988) in an appropriate manner is a particular goal of education in England and Wales. This may be regarded as an important component of the less specific goal of the present debate, which is how to bring about effective learning in classrooms. It is the route to this wider goal with which we are concerned, a route which incorporates the broader aims and tasks of teaching and learning.

It is our belief that teaching styles and methods are not matters to be imposed upon classrooms. An informed consideration of the educational and psychological issues we raise should lead to individual schools and teachers selecting and implementing that combination of strategies which is appropriate for their needs. Our concern is that judgement and decision making should not be based upon the perceived merits of particular teaching methodologies. The spotlight should instead be on the goals and effectiveness of learning.

We therefore offer no simple prescriptions for successful teaching. We do, however, suggest that a theoretical perspective rmed by cognitive research will equip teachers to deal far more factorily with planning, decision making and action in the ssroom. As suggested by Dewey (1929), teachers who adopt a oretical perspective will be helped to make observations about ners that might otherwise escape their attention, and will be interpret some facts about learning that would otherused.

Prior knowledge

We return to the first basic question to be considered by any teacher, which concerns what the pupil already knows and the significance of this information. Various chapters in this book have drawn upon subject-based research evidence which demonstrates that a great deal of prior knowledge is brought to a learning situation (as well as misconceptions and blurred understanding).

Young children coming in to school make persistent attempts to make sense of their complex world. Desforges (1989) elaborates upon a discussion of research findings which suggest that the majority of young children are very good at learning, even though they may not regularly engage themselves in the process. A considerable literature deriving from research evidence (some already mentioned in previous chapters) provides a commentary on learning before school; that is, that which children 'bring with them' into the classroom. Renewed attention is drawn, for example, to studies of emergent literacy (Hall, 1987). Margaret Clark (1976) demonstrates that some pre-schoolers make remarkable progress in learning to read without support from parents. Parallel studies derive from the subject area of mathematics: Gelman and Gallistel (1978) show how young children can conserve small numbers, Carpenter *et al.* (1982) demonstrate that pre-school children can solve word problems on the addition and subtraction of small numbers, and Hughes (1986) concludes that young children understand small numbers and number operations when presented in the form of games.

These examples are selected from many studies in the areas of numeracy and literacy. Further research highlights early learning in other areas; for example, environmental cognition (Palmer, 1993). All confirm that pre-school children are remarkably efficient learners, and bring a range of skills, concepts and subject knowledge as a background to the teacher's task – even if such knowledge is not entirely accurate or complete. Once in school, learners will inevitably continue to extend their knowledge base from a wide variety of sources (parents, experiences outside school, media, etc.) as well as planned classroom activities. Children's ideas and prior knowledge cannot be ignored, at any age or stage of learning.

Taking account of research evidence concerning students' existing ideas and knowledge should assist teaching and learning in a variety of ways. First, it should inform decision making about which concepts are taught. Research evidence reported by Driver *et al.* (1988) suggests that conventional curriculum planning in science education that starts with a conceptual analysis of the subject matter itself is not the best approach. Such schemes may make assumptions that children have already constructed certain basic ideas, which may not be the case. Thus more effective curriculum planning will take account of the learner's ideas as well as the structure of the subject matter. Second, taking account of prior knowledge should inform the design and implementation of specific learning tasks. More will be said about this later; if pupils' existing concepts and ideas are known, then challenging tasks can be provided that extend them in desired ways.

Success in ascertaining prior knowledge depends upon essential teacher skills. These include assessment and diagnosis, which in turn depend upon observation, testing and interaction.

Assessment and diagnosis

Research evidence suggests that teachers are not good at diagnosing. Before elaborating upon this, we point out that the term 'diagnosis' refers to finding out about existing levels of knowledge and experience, and there is not, by implication, a problem or fault to discover. The process should, however, reveal any learning difficulties experienced by individuals and identify future learning needs.

As a result of their data on matching, Bennett and Desforges (1984) conclude that the teachers' lack of detailed knowledge of the child–task interactions in part explains why ill-matched tasks are assigned to learners. This lack of knowledge results from lack of diagnostic activity. These researchers speculate on reasons for the dearth of diagnosing, and highlight several possible factors: perhaps teachers were unaware of the problems posed by lack of diagnosis; perhaps they were aware but lacked the skills to conduct appropriate observations and interviews; perhaps they were aware and had the necessary skills but for other reasons adopted classroom management strategies that did not allow the time and

opportunity for diagnostic work. Focus was then placed on th
skill aspect of these possibilities. Seventeen teachers were giv
an intensive course in diagnostic interviewing in which vide
tapes of interviews were shown. Interviews were then analy
and discussed, individual training in interviewing was g
to teachers in their own classrooms, and detailed feedba
provided. Despite these efforts, the teachers showed
able problems with diagnostic interviewing. Time was
attempts at diagnosis were conducted in the confusion
ruptions and distractions from other pupils. Commit
another: teachers believed that diagnosis was hardly
because problems underlying children's errors were self
'Our in-service venture failed to produce tangible incren
teachers' skills. It did, however, suggest to us that misma.
was at least as much a problem of classroom management a
teachers' skill and knowledge' (Desforges, 1989).

A fundamental problem seems to be teachers' preference f
immediate instruction rather than for the sustained use of diag
nostic activity. We suggest that the improvement of diagnostic
skills should be the focus of increased attention if the quality of
classroom learning is to be enhanced. We do, however, emphasize
that we refer to the need for ascertaining a general appreciation
of pupils' levels of learning rather than a very precise diagnostic
assessment before every learning task of what each child's prior
knowledge consists of. It is highly likely that a group of pupils will
bring to each lesson a widely differing set of views and beliefs on
the subject matter in hand. The crucial task of the teacher is to
activate this prior knowledge, rather than to spend an inordinate
amount of time in a busy classroom finding out every last detail
of it.

It is difficult, if not impossible, to separate the tasks of assessment and diagnosis in our discussion. Both are intimately connected to each other and to learning. Both require evidence
relating to an individual's capabilities and progress. The accumulation of such evidence depends upon skills of observation, testing
and interaction (conversation, questioning and feedback). In
short, assessment and diagnostic activities are about communication between teacher and learner, communication which helps
the learner appreciate what she or he has learned and the teacher

plan tasks that will promote future learning. Communication, therefore, is an integral part of the learning process, and time must be set aside for this purpose. In school classrooms this will involve time for discussion and questioning individual pupils and groups, as well as for written communication. Assessment procedures may be justified by a number of reasons: perhaps to make predictions of future success in examinations or potential for success on advanced courses; perhaps to measure whether specific learning goals (knowledge, skills, concepts) have been acquired; perhaps to increase the motivation of a learner or to test a learner against others so that comparisons and classifications can be made. It is not a purpose of this book to focus on the various reasons for assessment, but to elaborate on one further justification of the procedure, that of diagnosis of teaching and learning.

Figure 7.1 summarizes various reasons for assessing learners, indicating the central role of assessment for diagnosis and providing guidance and feedback between teacher and learner. Assessment of this kind need not necessarily involve formal tests

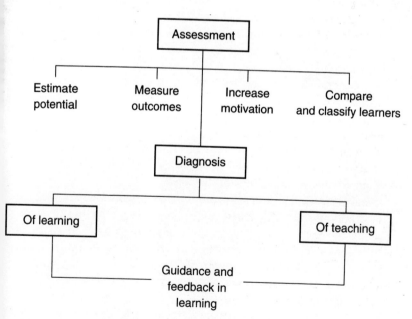

Figure 7.1 Justification for assessment

or measurements, and the term itself may be misleading: we refer to the clarification of learning that has taken place, of learning difficulties being experienced by individuals, and identification of future learning needs and tasks. Such assessments relate to skills and procedures readily accessible to teachers on a day-to-day basis, rather than to formal diagnostic assessment instruments employed by specialists to identify specific learning difficulties. Effective teaching entails constant, conscious and perhaps sub-conscious attempts to assess learning, using in particular the skills of observation and questioning. The major goal of diagnostic assessment is to access information that will help learners to learn, and teachers and learners to communicate feedback that may help overcome learning difficulties. Furthermore, assessment of diagnosis for learning cannot be separated from assessing for diagnosis of teaching or from the crucial skills of self-monitoring which are fundamental to successful teaching.

The implementation of the National Curriculum for Schools has resulted in a great deal more assessment (both formal testing and of an informal nature) than teachers have previously engaged in. In short, it has resulted in an increased trend towards diagnostic activities. If any judgement is to be made about whether a learner has reached a particular level within a Statement of Attainment, then skills of diagnostic assessment need to be employed. We turn our attention to two related skills in this area: observation and testing.

Observation is an essential element of the teaching and learning process, and one which should be approached as a skilled and strategic task. Observations may be either planned or spontaneous in nature. The former will have a clear objective; for example, 'Can Susan organize days of the week in the correct sequence?', 'Does Ted understand why the windmill turns?'. They will be informative and help with future planning, confirming progress made in teaching and learning. In planning observations, it is necessary to decide what exactly will be looked for, ways in which it will be checked, and whether the task will involve interaction with the learner or simply 'seeing' what is going on. Decisions must also be made about whether the interchange will be used to extend the learner's thinking at that time, and how the outcomes of the observations will be recorded. In observation for diagnostic teaching, it is then important to decide whether the learner has achieved the planned outcome of a task, or whether a further period of observation is required. When observations are related to assessment of National Curriculum Statements of Attainment, they will provide not only information about whether an individual has mastered a particular level of learning, but also data relating to learning styles and ability: time spent on task, inter-relationships in group learning situations, and the preferred learning style of individuals. Those who have encouraged independence of learning and the ability of pupils to engage in purposeful time on task activities without constant teacher direction will inevitably find planned observation sessions much easier to slot into a crowded schedule.

Similarly, spontaneous observations are an integral aspect of a classroom in which pupils go about their enquiries in an independent yet purposeful way, knowing what their tasks involve and the availability of the equipment necessary to perform them. Clearly, a teacher cannot possibly record what is happening in the classroom all the time – it is far better to focus on specific features or interactions, and to record significant events in a variety of contexts, than to 'child watch' without a focus. Suitable contexts may include:

- individual tasks, such as constructing a model hut, involving planning, selecting and investigating materials, using appropriate equipment, asking relevant questions, problem solving and communicating the procedure

- group work, such as mapping the playground, involving discussion of ideas, sharing equipment, allocating tasks, sequencing ideas, problem solving, listening to the findings of others and collaborating to produce results.

Spontaneous observations need not occur solely in formal classroom situations. They are important in the playground, at lunch time, in games lessons, in the corridors of secondary schools, and in the domestic role-play corner of infant classrooms. Together with planned observations, they should be recorded carefully to assist the overall assessment procedure and the design of further appropriate learning situations.

The reliability and validity of observations and judgements which arise will of course depend upon the skill of the observer in terms both of what is seen and of how this is interpreted. A recognized disadvantage is that the observer will only see what his or her background, experience and perhaps prefigured focus will allow. An experienced teacher/observer may well detect things that a novice has not previously experienced. Furthermore, anyone can assess only that which is evident. A learner may know and be capable of doing far more than is revealed in any single observation. The observer needs to consider whether an action or behaviour is typical and whether the outcome would be similar on other occasions. In spontaneous observations, for example, it could well be the case that on one day a child gives an answer or action that suggests that he or she has understood a crucial point in learning; on another occasion, she or he may reveal a lack of understanding of the same point. On many occasions, a teacher will face the reality of having overestimated or underestimated the ability of a learner, and repeated observations will be necessary in order to clarify levels of thinking and understanding. For this reason, planned and spontaneous observations may be more reliable than formal tests, which do not allow for the possibility of mistaken judgements that can be checked and followed up.

Observation and *testing* are closely related diagnostic skills. Many forms of test are instruments which systematize or give structure and objectivity to planned observations. Systematic observations may indeed include the use of standardized tests and teacher-devised 'tick' lists. The National Curriculum's Standard Assessment Tasks are intended to complement teacher observations. There may of course be a difference between testing for diagnostic purposes and testing to see whether a particular piece of learning has been mastered. A diagnostic test designed to establish existing understanding, possible problems with learning and ways forward will provide information unique to an individual. Tests of mastery, on the other hand, may provide information that enables learners to be judged relative to their peers, perhaps for the purposes of grouping pupils for learning. While assessing mastery of levels of attainment, the Standard Assessment Tasks combined with teacher assessments and observations serve important diagnostic purposes.

Learning tasks

Progress in teaching beyond the point of ascertaining existing knowledge and ideas depends upon providing appropriate challenges, questioning, and describing, explaining and demonstrating new knowledge, skills or concepts. In other words, it depends upon the design of successful learning activities and situations. Underpinning the success and quality of all classroom learning is the range of tasks which students undertake and the nature of their engagement with these tasks. Such engagement will in turn depend upon successful 'matching' of tasks to their needs.

Before any attempt can be made at matching tasks to the situations of learners, it is necessary to understand what types of task are being considered. In general terms, all tasks should seem purposeful in the eyes of the learner. This book has already drawn attention to the crucial issue of motivation. Learners will be motivated to learn in a non-threatening and supportive classroom environment in which a clear purpose for tasks is communicated by the teacher and appreciated by the learner. Learning will be considerably facilitated if the goals of learning provide meaning to the material in question. All too frequently pupils engage in unchallenging activities, perhaps set in order to occupy their time while their teacher is giving individual attention elsewhere in the classroom. They also spend a considerable amount of time on other non-purposeful, routine activities, waiting for attention and in a range of distractions. As mentioned in Chapter 2, the Alexander study on primary education in Leeds reveals that, on average, children in the classrooms where observation took place spent only 59 per cent of their time working and 41 per cent in routine activities, waiting for attention from a teacher and being distracted from the task which was set (Alexander, 1992).

This reflection of inadequate classroom management may be linked to the fact that the teacher has no adequate depth of understanding of progression of the stages of pupils' learning. It is essential that the task is based on that which the learner is capable of doing, but which, with suitable interventions and interaction, can be extended to bring about further learning. In other words, the teacher needs to make informed judgements about what learning potential is incorporated in a range of tasks and to act on this potential, matching further development of the tasks with the existing experiences and capabilities of the pupils. We illustrate this with examples of 'everyday' practice.

A common activity in primary classrooms is printing autumn leaves to demonstrate their wonderful range of colours. Consider the following methods of going about the task:

- *Classroom X*: the teacher has collected a splendid array of leaves for the children to observe, discuss and use as the basis of their art work. Paints are mixed and beautiful printing results, displayed on the classroom wall.

- *Classroom Y*: the children engage in a series of early autumn visits to the nearby park and comment on the gradual changes in the atmosphere: days get cooler and damper, and the leaves on the trees take on a magnificent display of colours. Each child is encouraged to collect two or three very 'special' leaves – their favourites, chosen for reasons of shape and colour. In school, these are drawn around to reinforce the range of shapes, then the leaves are printed and displayed. Subsequent visits to the park lead to the realization that the colours are short-lived. In reality, leaves fade, wither and die. Creative writing ensues on the 'lost colours of nature' captured in the pictures on display. This work is linked to simple science investigations into chlorophyll loss in leaves and the decomposition of dead leaves. The classroom is in fact the one described as Classroom B in Chapter 3. The art work is a worthwhile task in its own right, set within a more general topic on autumn.

Young learners in both of the classrooms enjoyed their activities. In Classroom X, however, the work had limited purpose. No doubt the children gained satisfaction from the results of their printing, but they had no particular sense of ownership of the leaves used. The final display was an end product, a reminder of the task, adding to the visual attraction of the classroom but perhaps not to the learning experiences of the children. In Classroom Y/B, on the other hand, the printing task was set within a coherent topic. Art was used as a successful bridge between creative and scientific work. The task arose from personal experiences and was seen by the children to have a particular purpose. Indeed, the final display was not only visually enhancing to the room, but was also used as an integral part of further learning – the colours of leaves collected a few weeks later were compared with the colours on display. A sense of chronology and change was thus reinforced, using the children's own experiences, which built upon previous tasks. The teacher in this room consciously engaged in decision making about the learning potential of tasks and attempted to match further activities with existing knowledge. Progress in learning was achieved.

General points thus made are that tasks should be both purposeful in the eyes of the learner and relevant to his or her experiences, and should also have the potential for progression or expansion in order to facilitate further learning in the same or a related curriculum area. The teacher's own task involves making judgements about such relevance and potential, considering whether the pupils are engaged in activities that are purposeful, relevant, rigorous, challenging and sequential.

From general characteristics, planning may take account of more specific analysis of types of task in the context of adequate curriculum coverage. A number of authors in the field of education have described a classification. As discussed in Chapter 2, Bennett *et al.* (1984) identified five types of task, these being incremental, restructuring, enrichment, practice and revision.

Bennett and Desforges (1988) designated four main types of task: incremental, restructuring, enrichment and practice, each with certain 'demand characteristics':

- *incremental*: introduces new ideas, procedures or skills, demands recognition and discrimination

- *restructuring*: demands the invention or discovery of idea, process or pattern

- *enrichment*: demands application of familiar skills on new problems

- *practice*: demands the tuning of new skills on familiar problems.

159

The articulated view of learning from which these classifications derive is that of Norman (1978), who identifies three processes:

1. accretion (the direct acquisition of elements of knowledge or skill to existing knowledge modules)

2. restructuring (using new insights or the reorganization of knowledge already stored)

3. tuning (the process of making intellectual routines automatic, and eliminating unnecessary steps in procedures).

These three processes may occur alongside each other or singly.

> In this view of learning, the acquisition of facts, the growth of understanding, and the deployment of procedural knowledge proceed together. Challenge and practice, rote acquisition and pattern recognition are all significant facets of learning. In these terms, tasks set by teachers might be seen to make different demands on the learner. (Bennett and Desforges, 1988)

We elaborate upon this classification with the addition of discovery tasks and problem-solving tasks and suggest examples of each. This classification model is based on the functions which tasks are intended to achieve.

INCREMENTAL TASKS

These are planned to assist in the progressive acquisition of elements of learning, including knowledge, skills and procedures. In the domestic role-play scene described in Chapter 3 (Classroom A), the teacher's intervention, though far from obvious or intrusive, involved providing an increasing range of materials to be sequenced or selected. A meal of beans on toast followed by jelly requires the selection of more cutlery than a meal of beans on toast only. Gradually these children were introduced to an increasing range of materials and tasks to do, providing opportunities for acquiring skills such as sequencing and selection in a progressive or incremental way. A critical distinction exists between tasks which are truly incremental and those which are practice. Unless close attention is paid to individual children's ability and attainment, many intended incremental tasks could provide practice only. The research findings of Bennett *et al.* (1984) confirm this, reporting, for example, that in the curriculum area of language observed, nearly a quarter of intended incremental tasks were actually practice.

RESTRUCTURING TASKS

Such activities involve the pupils in working with materials that are in the familiar realm in order to discover or invent a new way of looking at or resolving a problem. Intervention by the teacher is likely to involve giving suggestions for proceeding that may not come automatically to mind, or hints which may stimulate original thinking. Mathematics and language work in particular lend themselves to the setting of restructuring tasks. For example, at an appropriate stage, when the basic skills of addition are well mastered, pupils could be asked to add a number repeatedly – 3 add 3, add 3, add 3, etc. – in order to 'discover or invent' the process of multiplication: that is, they are encouraged to use familiar material in a new way. In language work, once pupils are familiar with key words, a variety of word games and puzzles could be provided which aim to provoke the discovery of certain rules of grammar or spelling.

ENRICHMENT TASKS

As with restructuring tasks, these involve the use of familiar knowledge, skills and understandings, but their objective is to use these in unfamiliar contexts in order to expand the learner's ability to apply such skills and concepts. The key to setting enrichment tasks is thus a concern with the application of prior learning rather than with the acquisition of new material. Once again the area of mathematics provides many opportunities for activities in this category. Skills and knowledge of, say, the division process may exist in the pupils' consciousness but they may not understand when to apply division in order to resolve a problem. It may not seem the obvious way, for example, of finding out how long one paving stone is when ten of similar size arranged in a line measure 100 metres.

The leaf-burial activity of Classroom B in Chapter 3 involved tasks of the enrichment kind. When leaves were removed from the

161

soil at the conclusion of the experiment, the area of leaf loss had to be calculated. For many learners it was not obvious that the application of the process of subtraction (of the remaining area from the original area) was the method of finding out what area of leaf had disappeared. Yet all learners were very familiar with basic skills of subtraction. In Classroom C, learners were required to measure the size of holes in various sieves in order to establish conservation of size so that their experiment would be a fair test. Again, this task involved application of a familiar concept (equivalence in size) to a new situation in order that further investigation, and hence learning, could take place.

PRACTICE TASKS

Having added the note of caution under 'Incremental tasks' above, there still exists a key role for those tasks which involve rapid or repeated application of familiar skills, routines or knowledge in order to speed up the process of their application or make it automatic. Mathematics is probably the area of the curriculum where tasks of this kind are most common. A child may be perfectly familiar with the process of addition of numbers between one and ten. It is then a useful and challenging practice to do this task as quickly as possible; for example, seeing how many simple addition sums can be done accurately in five minutes.

In Classroom A in Chapter 3, a great deal of practice activity was taking place. Aside from the planned incremental dimension introduced by the teacher, the young learners were given ample opportunity for 'free play' involving repeated sequencing of, for example, washing and drying routines and ordering and selection of appropriate materials for tasks without any incremental accretion in the acquisition of the skills involved. In Classroom B, the task of drawing round the dead leaves and calculating their area before burial in soil was for some pupils a matter of straightforward routine. It was done speedily and efficiently, a result of regular practice in drawing round shapes and counting the squares they cover. It was an automatic process in the pupils' repertoire of skills, presenting no problem in the sequence of tasks in the experiment as a whole. For others in the group, this aspect of their work was not nearly so automatic. Rather than being a matter

of straightforward practice, the task required interven
teacher and revision.

REVISION TASKS

These involve the use of knowledge and skills previously learnt and
the bringing back of such material into the conscious state. Procedures are not an automatic part of the learner's repertoire. For
some of the learners trying to measure the size of their leaves in
Classroom B, Chapter 3, revision tasks were necessary, while
others clearly did not need to think through the process. The
teacher's intervention was necessary for those requiring revision –
she asked them to think back to the day when they had measured
biscuits to see who had cooked the largest ones. Pupils were
reminded of how counting squares that an object covers helps tell
us about its size, the amount of space it takes up on a piece of
paper: when reminded of the skills involved, and once again
having a conscious understanding of how to go about their task,
meaningful work could proceed. Generally, the children requiring
revision of this nature completed the task far less speedily than
those for whom it was an automatic process. A critical time of
evaluation of their learning was when the leaves were removed
from their bags and had to be measured once again. For the
majority, further revision was no longer necessary, at least in
terms of the method of calculating their area.

DISCOVERY TASKS

These are of an exploratory, open-ended nature, with unpredictable outcomes. They aim to create situations in which the learner
does not know what is likely to happen. Work in drama, music and
other areas of creative expression will involve many tasks of the
exploratory kind. So too will science and a wide range of 'play'
situations in early-years classrooms, when children are exploring
and bringing together the worlds of familiar and unfamiliar materials and situations. Children in Classroom A in Chapter 3 were
undertaking a variety of discovery tasks, such as putting material
into water, and putting wet materials into warm places and airy
places. The burial of dead leaves in soil in Classroom B was a
task of exploratory nature, as was the sowing of seeds in their

containers in Classroom C, and experimentation in Classroom D.

Tasks of this kind may operate in concert with and will lead to a range of more precise tasks of other categories. They are an essential and integral part of the complete act of learning, involving coping with the uncertain, the spontaneous and the unpredictable. Teacher intervention may be minimal in discovery tasks.

PROBLEM-SOLVING TASKS

In some ways related to discovery tasks, these may be open-ended and employ a variety of strategies for solution of the task. The chief difference is that when engaged in problem-solving tasks, the learner will usually have a clear understanding of the end product or what she or he is trying to achieve. The route to that achievement will not be so clear. Teacher intervention in tasks of this nature will encourage the selection or discovery of solution strategies and ensure that the necessary equipment and/or materials are provided. The problem to be solved may be a concrete matter of design or construction (for example, build a bridge, make a model of an Anglo-Saxon village) or it may be of a more abstract, open-ended nature.

The activity as a whole described in Classroom C, Chapter 3, was of a problem-solving type, incorporating specific tasks of other categories. The learners knew what was to be achieved – an investigation into seed sowing and factors affecting the procedure – and their problem was to select an appropriate route to this goal which ensured a fair test of conditions. In Classroom A, the teacher successfully intervened from time to time in order to translate some discovery tasks into ones of a problem-solving variety – instead of a haphazard arrangement for drying clothes, suggestions were made for testing the value of drying them in specific places. In other words, strategies were suggested for investigating outcomes in a more rigorous, scientific manner.

The seven task types exist independently, and each may be identified in specific learning situations. Yet they connect, merge and overlap in the context of the processes of learning, facilitating the acquisition of further knowledge, skills, rules and procedures.

Tasks planned according to this classification should enable pupils to

- consolidate and practise existing skills and knowledge
- build upon such existing understanding
- achieve clearly identified progression within each subject area of the curriculum
- make meaningful intellectual links between subject areas
- engage in imaginative thinking and creative problem solving.

The teacher's task must involve developing insight into the range of activities that pupils engage in, with some vision of how they connect and how they may be extended to bring about learning in its various forms.

An analysis of one straightforward classroom scene demonstrates that this is no easy achievement. In Classroom A in Chapter 3, for example, tasks of incremental, practice, enrichment, discovery and problem-solving natures can all readily be identified. Observation of one child in a classroom throughout a school day will lead to some understanding of the tremendous range and interconnection of learning experiences encountered during this relatively brief period of time. The range and appropriateness of tasks provided seem essential to the quality of learning that will ensue. To provide a diversity of tasks, covering each of the seven categories, is perhaps not a particularly difficult challenge – but to ensure their interconnectedness, appropriateness, balance and quality most certainly is. Research indicates, as discussed in Chapter 2, that teachers do not do this well.

Matching

At a simplistic level, the concept of matching may appear to be straightforward – a question of providing a range of tasks and of matching each task to the individual learner. In the complex world of the classroom, however, a multiplicity of variables to be matched exists alongside other essential elements of planning and organization. Matching cannot exist without assessment and diagnosis, which as we have seen is the ability to find out what the learner already knows about the subject matter in hand so that future decisions can be informed by this. We have identified crucial teacher skills involved in this process, notably observation, communication, formal testing and record keeping.

The key issue is the need to design and match an appropriate range of tasks to the learners' levels of attainment and also to their individual interests, abilities and needs; that is, what they are bringing to the learning situation in terms of prior knowledge and intellectual experiences.

The range of classroom tasks we describe may be interpreted as comprising activities which lie at various stages on a continuum of learning from novice to expert status, and so representing activities which range from rote learning to 'meaningful' learning. In rote learning activities, new knowledge and information are acquired, perhaps by verbatim memorization, and are incorporated into an individual's store of knowledge with no interaction or apparent connection with what is already there. Many practice and revision tasks fall at this end of the continuum. In meaningful classroom learning, on the other hand, the individual is able to relate new knowledge to relevant concepts and mental structures already known and understood. Most restructuring and problem-solving tasks require this level of expertise. Learning has context and is related to experiences with objects and events, thus assisting the incorporation of new knowledge into the individual's cognitive structure. Tasks and learning activities in their various forms can vary from being entirely rote to being contextualized and highly meaningful.

Preceding chapters have demonstrated the theoretical position that it is only by employing a variety of procedures and activities that the three components of learning – acquisition, generalization and consolidation – will be attained. Educational research, as cited above, demonstrates the parallel practical position that in order for meaningful learning to take place, the acquisition of declarative knowledge (facts and concepts) and procedural knowledge (skills) will proceed by the satisfactory completion of an appropriate range of classroom tasks and activities. These need to be carefully selected to match the needs of the learner, and planned so that they are likely to be interpreted by pupils in the way intended.

STRATEGIES FOR EFFECTIVE TEACHING

Integral to the design and implementation of successful learning tasks is the need to take account of strategies related to students' existing ideas that will encourage learning. Driver *et al.* (1988) identify five suggested strategies which together could be helpful in promoting conceptual learning. First, the teacher should provide opportunities for pupils to make their own ideas explicit. Such opportunities could be made available through oral, written or pictorial representation. Second, the teacher should introduce discrepant events. If a student observes something unexpected, then the resulting conceptual conflict will produce thought and perhaps dissatisfaction with misconceptions held. Third, Socratic questioning is valuable, as this may help students to appreciate a lack of consistency in their thinking. Fourth, the generation of a range of conceptual schemes should be encouraged. Students should reflect on their own thinking, and consider and evaluate a range of possible interpretations for events, rather than just seek 'the right answer'. This strategy can be promoted by discussion, brainstorming sessions and the introduction of new ideas by the teacher for the pupils to consider.

Finally, a teacher should encourage practice in using ideas in a range of situations. For example, pupils should be provided with opportunities to apply the results or features of a given scientific experiment in other contexts, leading to the development of skills of generalization and transfer of concepts to alternative areas of learning.

Comments on the engagement of students in successful learning activities and strategies cannot be separated from a reflection on the fact that different teachers will inevitably have different styles of working and approaching the teaching task. Chapter 2 provided details of various ideologies and research studies in the areas of teaching and learning styles and classroom practice. It is evident that because of the complexities of classroom interactions and the multiplicity of variables involved in teaching and learning, no single style or approach to organization can be recommended. Bennett, for example (1976), found that more formal teaching in the basic skills gave better results, but the best results of all in his study were provided by a teacher who worked informally but in a structured way. This suggests that more informal methods can be very successful, provided that sufficient planning and structure are incorporated. Chapter 3 conveyed the key message that in science education, learning will only be accessible and usable if it is well structured, which includes being matched to what the learner already knows. Furthermore, it is not sufficient for the teacher to do the structuring: pupils must have opportunities to sort out and reflect upon their experiences, creating meaning and structures for themselves. How this is achieved in practice in terms of managing pupils as individuals or in groups and product/process orientation is a matter for individual teachers and schools to decide.

We suggest that in reality, few institutions are or will become exclusively 'product' or 'process' dominated. Yet the debate on how to reconcile these two extremes continues in the light of the current trend towards subject specialist teaching.

With this apparent movement towards subject specialism and away from integrated or discovery learning, the pessimistic would argue that perhaps any debate, whether it be on ideological or on epistemological grounds, is becoming increasingly irrelevant. The National Curriculum, non-negotiable in terms of content at least, does little to alleviate such unease and pessimism. Its prescribed subject-based curriculum, incorporating clearly stated aims, content, evaluation and assessment procedures, reinforces a product-oriented view.

The product/process and subject/integration debate is far from irrelevant. It provides the context in which learning may or may not proceed. Decisions must be made on such matters as organization, teaching styles and structure, which take account of ideological, epistemological and practical issues. They must also take account of the processes of learning. There is no reason why consideration of such processes should be lost because there is also a *content*, however organized. It is possible to give both aspects the high profile they warrant in a sensibly planned and implemented curriculum, be it product or process oriented. The organization of classroom work may therefore be examined in terms of content or of different approaches to teaching, *and* as that which cannot be separated from the nature of pupils' learning. Those making decisions on school policies, curriculum development and planning a framework for delivery of the curriculum as a whole need to honour the subject specificity and content of the National Curriculum, while taking account of individual abilities and appropriate tasks. The goal (product) and route to that goal (process) are inextricably linked to each other and to the development of a sound core of subject-specialist knowledge (content).

So far this chapter has identified various components of matching to be incorporated in the design and setting of pupil tasks, in particular the need to match an appropriate range of tasks to the learners' levels of attainment and also to their individual interests, needs and abilities, reflecting their existing knowledge and experiences. This complex task must also be set in the framework of classroom organization; that is, how time and space are used and how subject matter is organized. Linked to this is the need for teachers themselves to have an adequate grasp of the subject matter they aim to teach. Research and publication on the issue of teacher subject knowledge has increased in recent years following the presidential address to the American Educational Research Association in 1985 (Shulman, 1986), when Shulman referred to the lack of attention to subject matter as the 'missing paradigm' in educational research. He set out a research agenda to address how beginning teachers transform their knowledge of subject matter into suitable forms and tasks in the classroom. The case for subject matter knowledge, for readers wishing to pursue this topic, is articulated by Grossman *et al.* (1989) and Ball and McDiarmid (1989). Their arguments include the following:

- if the aim of teaching is to enhance children's understanding then teachers themselves must have a flexible and sophisticated understanding of subject matter knowledge in order to achieve this purpose in the classroom

- at the heart of teaching is the notion of forms of representation, and to a significant degree teaching entails knowing about and understanding ways of representing and formulating subject-matter knowledge so that it can be understood by children. This in turn requires teachers to have a sophisticated understanding of a subject and its interaction with other subjects (McNamara, 1991).

Teacher subject knowledge consists of three interrelated components: content knowledge, which is the actual nature and amount of knowledge the teacher possesses; pedagogic content knowledge, which is knowledge about the subject in forms that are appropriate for teaching it; and curriculum content knowledge, which is knowledge about resources and materials which are the vehicles for teaching the subject (Shulman, 1986).

Figure 7.2 provides a summary of the essential components to be matched in the teacher's task of organizing situations for effective learning. Underpinning this task are the essential skills of teaching, including subject-knowledge application, without which effect learning is unlikely to be promoted.

Independent research findings, introduced in Chapter 2 and summarized in Figure 7.3, confirm this view that effective teaching cannot succeed without certain core skills. These include the ability to provide intellectually challenging activities that are well planned and structured, to match and monitor tasks and pupils' progress, and to motivate pupils to spend time on task.

While classroom organization cannot be neglected, we suggest that perhaps too much emphasis has often been placed by teachers and teacher trainers on this aspect of their work. It is the skills of teaching that are of far greater significance than its organization or delivery styles. Effective teaching is set within a particular mode of classroom organization rather than being determined by it.

Summary

The teacher's task is complex. It is based on an understanding of what individual students are bringing to a learning situation, and involves the related skills of finding this out and building upon it in order to facilitate further learning. We emphasize that teaching styles and methods are not matters to be recommended or imposed upon teachers and classrooms. It is the skills of teaching that are of far greater significance than its organization or delivery styles. Key skills include the ability to make assessments and a diagnosis of individual's learning; also to promote further learning by designing a range of appropriate tasks to be engaged in that are suitably matched to the needs, experiences and prior knowledge of the individual learners. A task classification model is suggested

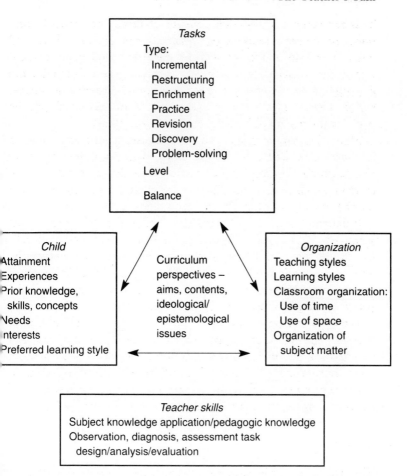

Figure 7.2 Matching teaching for learning: components of the task

which incorporates seven types of task: incremental, restructuring, enrichment, practice, revision, discovery and problem-solving. This classification is based on the functions that tasks are intended to achieve. Tasks planned according to this model should enable pupils to consolidate and practise existing skills and knowledge, achieve clearly identified progression within each subject

171

* Observational Research and Classroom Learning Evaluation Project (Galton *et al.*, 1980)

** Mortimore *et al.* (1988)

Figure 7.3 Effective teaching: summary of independent research findings.

area of the curriculum, make meaningful links between subject areas, and engage in imaginative thinking and creative problem solving. A key role for the teacher is to develop insight into the range of activities that pupils engage in, with some knowledge of how they interrelate and may be extended to bring about learning in its various forms.

Numerous variables comprise the complex process of matching tasks to the individual learners. These components of matching include aspects of the tasks themselves (type, level, balance), curriculum perspectives, details of organization, and teaching and learning styles, as well as the attainment, experiences, prior knowledge, needs and interests of the learner. Underpinning these are the crucial teacher skills we have referred to. We conclude that effective teaching is set within a particular mode of classroom organization rather than being determined by it.

CHAPTER 8

Principles of Learning and Educational Practice

Overview

We began this book by distinguishing between implicit and explicit learning and by describing three different kinds of explicit learning: understanding, problem solving and memorizing. These categories provided the themes that underpinned our discussions of teaching and learning in subsequent chapters. It therefore remains for us to pull these themes together. In doing so we identify two goals of learning and three key learning principles that should underpin practice. The goals of learning are understanding and the consolidation of understood material, while the three learning principles state that successful learning requires the activation of prior knowledge, the right kind of motivation, and good metacognitive skills. We begin with a review of the categories of learning, a review in which we identify our three learning principles. We then discuss these three principles, together with the goals of learning, in relation to classroom practices and we show how an understanding of them can inform good practice.

Categories of learning

IMPLICIT LEARNING, INTUITIVE BELIEFS AND THE IMPORTANCE OF ACTIVATING PRIOR KNOWLEDGE

We saw in Chapter 1 that implicit learning occurs without our conscious awareness and gives rise to implicit knowledge that is also inaccessible to conscious awareness. Sometimes implicit knowledge is conscious in the early stages of learning, but becomes inaccessible through repeated practice. This is the case when newly solved problems are repeatedly practised until the activities that lead to their solution can be executed automatically when needed. The most important thing about implicit knowledge is that it consists of most of our intuitive beliefs about the world.

Intuitive beliefs are reflected in the way a person acts upon the world. That is, they affect what people do rather than what they are able to say. Such beliefs arise out of activities that people constantly engage in during the course of their lives. To take an example from Chapter 6, people's intuitive theories of physical motion affect their ability to anticipate the trajectory of moving objects. As soon as a child starts to walk and to play with moving objects, an intuitive theory of motion begins to develop, which enables the growing child to anticipate what will happen to a moving object and to act accordingly. Intuitive beliefs, therefore, are based on action, and they may be misconceived, as is the case with people's intuitive beliefs about motion. When they are misconceived, they will need to be revised in the light of the new learning gained in school.

All the influences that impinge on a child from birth and that continue into old age affect how a person acts in the world and the intuitive beliefs that underlie his or her acts. Our deep-rooted cultural assumptions are learned in this way, whether they are those of Western technological society, or of a school, or of one's chosen profession. As an example, children form beliefs about the value of literacy well before they learn to read. In a home full of books, newspapers and magazines, where reading is a common activity and is actively encouraged, children will learn intuitive beliefs that reading is worthwhile. By contrast, in a home without books, newspapers or magazines, where reading occurs rarely and is not encouraged, children learn a different set of intuitive beliefs in which reading is not valued and not considered worthwhile. Thus, activities in the home determine intuitive beliefs about the value of reading that children bring with them when learning to read. This is why teaching young children to read is so strongly affected by the home background (Chall, 1979, 1983).

Children's intuitive beliefs and values about literacy will strongly influence their willingness to co-operate in the arduous task of learning to read. If children come from homes where literacy is valued, then they will appreciate the significance of learning to read and will not regard it as a difficult and arbitrary task. But if they come from homes in which literacy is not valued, then learning to read will have no significance for them and will appear to be meaningless and difficult. Such children will have no reason

175

to invest effort in the task and so learning will be further impaired.

Classroom activities also contribute to children's intuitive beliefs. In Chapters 5 and 6, we came across beliefs about the nature of mathematics that arise as a result of classroom practices. Such beliefs are formed when prior knowledge of numbers is not engaged during learning. Without this activation, mathematics is seen as arbitrary and abstract and not related to everyday activities (Brown *et al.*, 1989). This means that it is believed to be very difficult and so only to be learned by a few experts. Students, therefore, confine their learning to problem solving and memorization, since they believe that efforts to understand will not be worthwhile. The emphasis in school on solving mathematical problems quickly and accurately also contributes to the belief that mathematics learning is to do with solving problems. As a result of these beliefs, students frequently give up in the face of failure because they typically assume that the problem is just too difficult for them. Schoenfield (1985) has shown how these beliefs arise and how they can seriously impede learning.

We have encountered discussions of intuitive beliefs and their role in learning on a number of occasions in preceding chapters. It would be surprising if this were not the case, given the important role that prior knowledge plays in successful learning. It is a crucial ingredient in learning through understanding, and without it, new learning will not be fully integrated with prior knowledge, and misconceived beliefs will not be modified and revised in the light of the new material. Thus, prior knowledge was an important issue in the discussion of science (Chapters 3 and 6), reading (Chapter 4), mathematics (Chapters 5 and 6), and motivation (Chapter 6). Chapters 4 and 5 also emphasized the important roles played by reading and writing in clarifying, updating and revising prior knowledge. Prior knowledge, therefore, is the backdrop against which all subsequent learning, including school learning, takes place. Such knowledge usually contains misconceptions about the physical and biological world, hence the importance of using new learning to modify and revise it. Thus, the need to engage the learner's pre-existing knowledge when new learning takes place is of paramount importance.

Overall, then, intuitive beliefs form a major part of the pre-existing knowledge that learners have about a topic, and they are very powerful. If they are engaged when new learning occurs, they will ensure that the new material is understood and that the prior beliefs themselves will be modified and updated in the light of the new information. But if they are not engaged, and hence ignored, when something new is learned about a topic, then the new material will not be properly understood. Instead, the material will seem arbitrary and abstract, since it will appear to have nothing to do with what the learner already knows and with the learner's everyday experience outside the school. In these circumstances, motivation will be poor because the learner will have little reason to invest any effort into learning such arbitrary material. Beliefs about the nature of learning (for example, that it is arbitrary) and about the nature of the subject (for example, that reading is of no value or that mathematics has no practical relevance) frequently lead children to believe that efforts to understand are not worthwhile, and so learning is confined to problem solving and memorization. This influence of prior beliefs on the effort expended on learning points to the importance of motivation, since motivation is responsible for deciding where effort should be invested.

EXPLICIT LEARNING, MOTIVATION AND METACOGNITION

Explicit learning is concerned with two main activities. One is understanding new material, which depends crucially on activating pre-existing implicit knowledge when learning occurs. The second is concerned with consolidating newly understood material so that it can be used automatically and make further explicit learning possible. Consolidation of conceptual knowledge is achieved through memorization: the material is repeatedly revised until it can be retrieved from long-term memory without conscious reflection. Consolidation of procedural knowledge – knowledge of actions and strategies – is achieved through practice of problem-solving skills until they too can be retrieved automatically from long-term memory. Understanding and consolidation need to occur hand in hand, but there is a constant danger that what gets consolidated is material that has not been properly understood. This will happen whenever prior knowledge has not been activated during learning. If understanding is pre-empted by problem solving or memorization in this way, new learning will be considerably

177

impaired, a situation that is likely to get progressively worse as schooling progresses. To avoid such a lamentable state of affairs, it is important to see how learning through understanding makes use of prior knowledge and how understanding is different from problem solving and memorization. Let us, therefore, restate these three basic categories of explicit learning.

1. *Understanding* involves integrating new material with prior knowledge, but it also goes beyond simple integration to a two-way process of evaluation, in which prior knowledge is used to assess how well the new material has been understood, and the new material is used to evaluate and modify pre-existing knowledge. Prior knowledge is thus a key ingredient: first, it is needed to assess the comprehension of new material; second, it is assessed, updated and revised in the light of that material, a process ensuring that misconceived prior beliefs are corrected.

2. *Problem solving* involves discovering, or being told, the solution to a problem and how to arrive at that solution. Once the solution and how to reach it is known, the problem can be repeated many times until it can be retrieved from memory automatically and the individual steps in the problem-solving process become part of implicit knowledge. Without the involvement of prior knowledge to give significance to the task, problem solving becomes an end in itself, as we have seen with respect to mathematics, where what is learned is a set of arbitrary and abstract procedures without any understanding of why or how they work.

3. *Memorization* involves consolidation, through revision of newly understood material until it too can be automatically retrieved from memory without conscious effort. Unfortunately, as was the case with problem solving, memorization too is often seen as a learning goal in itself and material is memorized with few, if any, attempts to understand it. Material learned in this way may be superficially integrated with prior knowledge, but since the two-way process of evaluation is not applied, understanding is also superficial. This use of memorization without full understanding is

implicitly encouraged in schools wherever there is an emphasis on how much has been learned rather than how well it has been understood. Both problem solving and memorization, therefore, need to be seen as ways of consolidating material that has already been understood and making it automatic through practice.

Overall, therefore, understanding through the two-way process of evaluation is the primary purpose of learning. Without it, learning is merely the accumulation of facts and procedures, misconceptions persist, and learning is seen as arbitrary, abstract and needlessly effortful. Unless one constantly keeps in mind the importance of understanding, many classroom activities will be unsatisfactory. For example, a commitment to integrated topic work will not of itself lead to understanding, or even integration. If the learning activities involved in such work are focused on problem solving or memorization alone, then all that will happen is that the learner will accumulate more seemingly arbitrary information that is unconnected to prior knowledge of the individual subjects that were meant to be integrated. This need to foster understanding also requires a sound understanding of the subject matter on the part of the teacher, as well as a knowledge of how to convey that understanding to others. The importance of subject knowledge and pedagogic knowledge has been recognized by Shulman (1986), among others, which may go some way towards encouraging an explicit focus on understanding in the classroom.

In a number of chapters we have emphasized that explicit learning requires considerable effort. This is because it takes up space in working memory and so needs constant attention. The decision to invest this effort depends on motivation, since that determines the goals people set themselves and the amount of effort expended in attaining them. Thus, once again, the importance of motivation is highlighted.

In Chapters 1, 3 and 4 we also said that understanding is more difficult than problem solving or memorization because it requires the involvement of two metacognitive skills. These are:

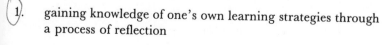

1. gaining knowledge of one's own learning strategies through a process of reflection

2. the ability to use specific strategies in response to changes in comprehension; that is, the ability to monitor and control the use of learning strategies.

Metacognitive skills are not used by everyone, partly because they require considerable effort and hence motivation. However, these skills are crucial for understanding, so it is important that they are learned in school. Thus, as well as addressing the question of motivation, teachers need to encourage the use of metacognition. Furthermore, metacognitive skills enable learners to take control of their own learning. This is because these skills enable people to use learning strategies to their full effect and to control their use of them. Metacognition, therefore, is of paramount importance for enabling children to learn how to learn.

We have now highlighted three crucial principles in learning which need to be borne in mind by the teacher when planning learning activities in the classroom. These principles can be summarized as follows:

1. the activation of prior knowledge is crucial for new learning

2. the learner's motivation determines how much effort the learner chooses to invest

3. learning through understanding depends on metacognitive skills.

In the next section, we turn our attention to classroom practices and examine them in relation to these three principles.

Teaching and learning in the classroom

It is a basic tenet of this book that the best way to decide on suitable classroom activities is by bearing in mind the basic principles of learning. Such an approach requires that the goals of learning be kept in mind, so that learning activities and tasks can be selected as tools that will best achieve them. So what are the goals of learning? They are twofold:

1. understanding new material through the two-way process of evaluation

180

2. consolidation of the understood material through repeated practice at solving problems and repeated revision of understood material.

Without understanding, much learning loses its value, since it will never be applied outside the classroom. Without consolidation, the learned material will not be readily retrieved when needed. Both of these goals need to be borne in mind, therefore, when selecting classroom activities. But understanding is primary, because without that, the material to be consolidated will not make sense to the learner. So the first goal needs to be constantly returned to, lest it be forgotten in the general hurly-burly of classroom life, and in the face of the external pressures on teachers to concentrate on the practice of skills and the learning of facts. The second goal is also important, but it needs to be seen as part of the overall framework of learning through understanding. The simplest way to keep one's sights on the goal of understanding is to keep coming back to the three key principles of learning identified above.

THE ACTIVATION OF PRIOR KNOWLEDGE

Without the activation of prior knowledge, understanding will not be achieved and, despite a teacher's best intentions, rote learning and problem solving will take place instead. The main question to bear in mind is how each child's prior knowledge can be activated, not what that prior knowledge consists of. We saw in Chapter 7 that teachers have difficulty in diagnosing children's current state of knowledge. However, as long as the teacher's goal is to encourage understanding, these difficulties may be resolved. What is needed is for the teacher to select learning activities that engage the learner's prior knowledge, even though the teacher may not know precisely what that prior knowledge consists of. Indeed, it is only through encouraging such activities that the children's prior beliefs can become apparent. But the activities themselves are designed to encourage children to see how the new learning relates to or changes their prior beliefs.

We give an example of how a science lesson could be improved by addressing prior knowledge at the beginning of the lesson. The learning of most subjects could be improved in a similar fashion.

181

The example we take is the secondary science lesson, described in Chapter 3, in which the students constructed a fountain out of a straw by heating the water beneath it. In that class, the activities were exemplary as far as problem solving was concerned. The pupils followed a set of instructions, constructed the fountain, and then wrote up an account of their investigation. Such activities are an important component of science and, repeated again and again, will ensure that problem-solving activities are turned into automatic procedures. But of course there is more to science than this. There is also the need for deep conceptual understanding. The teacher in the excerpt appreciates this need and ensures that the lesson does not stop when the solution (making the fountain) has been reached. Like Schoenfield in his teaching of mathematics, the teacher then encourages the pupils to explain how the fountain works. In these explanations, prior knowledge is used. Thus, a step towards understanding has been taken. But unfortunately, it is not a sufficient step. To see why, we need to consider again the issue of engaging prior knowledge.

Unless prior knowledge is activated during learning, understanding will be poor. More importantly, research has shown that prior knowledge must be activated *before* the new material is presented for successful learning through understanding. If prior knowledge is not activated until after the new material has been presented, then comprehension of the material is poor and learning is impeded (e.g. Bransford and Johnson, 1972). The pupils described in Chapter 3 were not encouraged to relate the new material to prior knowledge until after it had been presented. According to the work of Bransford and Johnson, this means that the prior knowledge would have little effect on what has been learned and that the new material would be seen as arbitrary and difficult. The consequences of this are that the material will be poorly understood because its significance will not be known, and prior misconceptions will not be revised. Both of these consequences have serious repercussions for subsequent learning, since they mean that the prior knowledge that will apply in that learning now contains some poorly understood and poorly integrated new material, and misconceptions that have yet to be revised.

Yet the teacher could have activated prior beliefs by engaging the children's co-operation in the task at the start of the lesson, through encouraging them to contribute their own ideas about fountains and how they might work. That is, the students could have formulated their own hypotheses. Once they had done that, they could then have tested their hypotheses against the evidence derived from following the teacher's instructions. The account of the experiment would then be more than a reporting of what they had done; it would also include their initial hypothesis and end with a discussion of how the results of the activity agreed with or modified it. Not only would such practices encourage learning through understanding, they would also more closely model the practices of expert scientists. Scientists constantly challenge existing beliefs by developing new ideas and testing them in experiments. Experimental procedures and outcomes are thus not an end in themselves. Instead they gain their significance through their contribution to the overall goal of understanding the world we live in.

Prior knowledge, then, needs to be activated before learning begins. Only if that happens will later discussions that address prior knowledge be useful. Furthermore, scientific problem solving needs to be an integral part of the conceptual process of generating, testing and modifying hypotheses, and not presented as a set of arbitrary activities. Notice that there is no need for the teacher to have detailed knowledge of the children's preconceptions when engaging prior knowledge at the start of a lesson. That is, extended diagnosis for its own sake is not needed. What is needed is that the teacher activates that prior knowledge before the activities begin, and then encourages the children to evaluate their preconceptions in the light of the results. Thus, by focusing on learning through understanding, children's prior knowledge will be revealed without the teacher having to engage in difficult and time-consuming diagnosis. In other words, diagnosis need not be seen as an independent activity with its own specific goal. Rather, it can be seen as something that falls out as a consequence of activating prior knowledge.

By bearing in mind the importance of activating prior knowledge, the choice of additional learning tasks and activities will be simplified. The tasks described in Chapter 7, for example, primarily contribute to the goal of consolidation, through either problem solving or memorization and revision. The important point to bear in mind when considering them is that they too only gain their significance by participating in the overall goal of understanding. Thus, when choosing one of those tasks, it always needs to be done in conjunction with a consideration of prior knowledge. That is, teachers need to ask themselves: 'How can I ensure that prior knowledge is activated before this task is carried out?'. As long as that question is successfully answered and put into practice, then they can also ask: 'How can I ensure that the results of the task are referred back to that prior knowledge when the task has been completed?'. The teacher of the science lesson discussed above addressed this second question, but unfortunately failed to address the first, more critical one.

THE LEARNER'S MOTIVATION

Poor learners are those who give up in the face of failure, rather than regarding failure as a stimulus for further learning. They give up because their intuitive beliefs about the nature of intelligence and about their own abilities lead them to believe that they cannot succeed and so there is no reason to expend effort in trying to learn. Such children adopt performance goals rather than learning goals. That is, they aim to display what abilities they have rather than trying to improve them (see Chapter 6). Learning is also poor if the activities lack significance for the learner because prior knowledge has not been activated. Learners will see no reason for expending effort in these circumstances. Learning will be poor, too, if the learner possesses a set of beliefs that devalue the learning goal. Without the relevant set of beliefs, children have no prior reason to invest effort in attaining such goals. Motivation, therefore, has two main aspects:

1. the possession of beliefs that learning is worthwhile and will lead to significant improvements in competence

2. a willingness to invest the effort needed to engage in learning activities.

As far as beliefs are concerned, children come to the classroom with their basic beliefs in themselves and in the nature of learning already formed, so it may seem that the teacher can do little to influence these and the choice of goals that they lead to. But this is not the case. These beliefs may be reinforced or contradicted, depending on the school environment. Indeed, we pointed out in Chapter 6 that many children begin school with learning goals and only come to favour performance goals after several years (Nicholls, 1978, 1984). Recall that intuitive beliefs are the result of habitual actions – of 'doing' rather than 'thinking'. The patterns of activities carried out in schools will therefore contribute to these intuitive beliefs. Schoenfeld has vividly documented how the practice of school mathematics leads to a set of beliefs that mathematics is a discipline that has to be learned without understanding, one that requires rote memorization and problem solving, and one that has no relevance to everyday affairs. As long as classroom practices focus on memorization and problem solving and treat them as goals in themselves, then performance goals will be encouraged in the children. Even within a classroom, the teacher's activities seem to encourage either learning or performance goals (e.g. Ames and Archer, 1988).

So how might a belief in the value of learning be encouraged in the classroom? Basically, by repeatedly showing through one's own actions and one's expectations of the children that understanding is important. A classroom in which the activities are mainly problem solving or memorization will lead children to believe that these are the important learning activities, despite what the teacher might say. Exhortations from the teacher will fall on deaf ears if they are not accompanied by action, since it is through action that intuitive beliefs are formed. Emphasizing, through actions, the importance of understanding will encourage children to form learning goals. To achieve this, the focus on activating prior knowledge at the start of a learning activity is crucial, as we have already indicated above. In addition, understanding will come to be valued by the children if the classroom activities are consistent with that belief. This will be achieved as long as the teacher's main focus is on understanding, so that problem solving and memorization are not treated as ends in themselves but are placed in the context of understanding.

How might the children come to realize that effort expended in learning is worthwhile? Basically, by repeatedly ensuring that they carry out those activities and experience success. Encouraging children to invest the effort needed for learning means that their

attention must constantly be focused on the learning task, so tha
their actions are indeed successful. The maintenance of effor
therefore, and experiences of success are crucial ingredients fc
learning through understanding. Probably the best way for th
teacher to provide these ingredients is through the cultivation c
the children's metacognitive skills.

Before we turn to a discussion of the teaching of metacognitiv
skills, we will pause for a moment to consider another force fc
motivation, which applies when the goals of learning are tran
parent to the learner. Recall from Chapter 5 that what seemed t
mark practical intelligence off from school mathematics was tha
the former is learned in practical domains, such as shopping c
betting, in which the purpose of learning is clear. We will highligl
this observation with another example, that of children learnin
their first language, possibly the most impressive feat of learnin
that any individual ever achieves. Without any formal tuitior
children rapidly acquire one of the most complex human skills. B
the age of 2 years, they are producing two-word utterances t
express their thoughts and feelings, and by the time they go t
school, they are producing a range of complex grammatical cor
structions fluently and without conscious effort. Of course, it
likely that there is a large innate component to language learnin;
children are constrained to notice the universal features of th
language that they hear (see e.g. Stevenson, 1988). Howeve
many aspects of language must be learned: words and their mea
ings, the specific grammar of the language, the use of languag
to communicate thoughts and feelings to others, and so on. Y
children learn to use language without any obvious signs of th
struggle that is evident when learning mathematics in school. S
what makes language easy to learn? The answer probably li
in the fact that its purpose is transparent. Children learn in
context in which language is the primary source of commun
cation. Everything around them reveals its importance, and th
social activities that they engage in require its use. Learnin;
therefore, is not seen as arbitrary and abstract or effortful an
difficult, because its purpose is clear. The learning takes place i
the context of the mature skill so that the goal of the experts – tha
is, communication – is also the goal of the learner. When th

purpose of learning is transparent, therefore, motivation is high and learning is achieved with considerable ease.

METACOGNITION: TEACHING CHILDREN TO USE LEARNING STRATEGIES

Research on the explicit teaching of metacognitive (or learning) strategies is still in its infancy. But it is an exciting development in which practice goes beyond the parochial pendulum swings of policy makers to a view that avoids the extremes of progressivism on the one hand and traditionalism on the other (see Chapter 2). Teaching children to use learning strategies combines the process emphasis of progressivism with the product emphasis of traditionalism, by recognizing the importance of both in the overall learning enterprise. Effective strategies, the *processes* of learning, facilitate understanding and consolidation of the subject matter, and so lead to superior learning outcomes, the *products* of learning. Put another way, the potential in progressivism for aimless activities for their own sake is avoided by focusing on the use of learning strategies that meet the goals of understanding and consolidation. At the same time, the potential in traditionalism for learning facts and procedures for their own sake is avoided by the emphasis on learning through understanding.

Chapter 2 also described Bennett's (1976) research showing that teachers have specific learning styles, ranging from one rooted in progressive attitudes and practices through those combining both progressive and traditional attitudes and practices to one based on traditional attitudes and practices. Further, the mixed styles seemed to predominate. This suggests that teachers themselves naturally adopt a style that avoids the extremes of progressivism or traditionalism, and so they are well placed to develop classroom methods for teaching learning strategies and to take advantage of an approach that does not depend on simple models of progressivism on the one hand or traditionalism on the other.

The work of Brown and her colleagues (e.g. Brown and Day, 1983), described in Chapter 4, has clearly demonstrated what is needed if learning strategies are to be successfully applied. Neither telling children *what* to do, nor telling them *how* to do it, is sufficient to guarantee the successful learning of metacognitiv strategies. Instead, *telling* children what and how needs to b supplemented by *showing* them how to monitor and control th use of strategies. This was evident in Brown and Day's (198? study of summarization skills. Recall that students of all ages fin some summarization rules difficult to apply, particularly that generating a topic statement. Brown and Day found that tellin students to supply a topic statement did not substantially improv performance. Nor did telling them how to supply the topic state ment (by first searching for a topic sentence in the text itself and if there was not one, generating one's own), even with extensiv practice. What did ensure the use of the strategies was showin the students how to check that they had provided a topic sentenc in their summaries, and whether they needed to invent a topi sentence. In other words, the crucial ingredient that needs to b taught is metacognitive: how to assess and monitor performanc and how to regulate the use of strategies by tailoring their use the level of assessed comprehension.

Teachers will be considerably aided in the task of teachin children to be aware of their learning strategies and to use the appropriately if they too reflect on their own learning strategic and assess their success in different situations. Such reflection w increase teachers' metacognitive understanding of their own pra tices, and so enable them to show the children what they are an how to use them. Thus, when we urge that teachers reflect on the own practice, as we did in Chapter 7, this is what we have in min the need constantly to pose and answer questions such as 'How di I do that task?' (for example, getting the children to understan multiplication), 'How successful was I?', 'How else might I hav done it?' and so on. Answers to such questions will help teache to help children do the same kind of thing.

Pressley *et al.* (1987) have reviewed and evaluated the method used to teach strategies. They conclude that two teaching pr grammes are most effective. One, called *direct explanation* (e.? Roehler and Duffy, 1984), is based on Brown and Day's obse vations that strategies are most likely to be used if children a explicitly shown how to use them; that is, how to assess an monitor their performance and select the best strategy in th light of that assessment. The other, called *reciprocal teaching* (e.?

Brown and Palincsar, 1989), is derived from work on practical intelligence (see Chapter 5) and so assumes that the goals of learning must be transparent to the learner and that learning is best achieved by modelling the expert and by being assisted by the expert in tasks that are not yet within the capacity of the learner. The method of direct instruction is more likely to appeal to teachers with a style in which traditional attitudes predominate, while reciprocal teaching is more likely to appeal to teachers with a style in which progressive attitudes predominate. We will conclude this chapter by describing these two teaching programmes. During the course of these descriptions, we will show how they address the key learning principles of activating prior knowledge, of encouraging the formation of intuitive beliefs that lead to good motivation, and of giving the children experience of success after the expenditure of effort.

DIRECT EXPLANATION

This addresses the motivational principles by giving explicit instruction in how to use learning strategies. The programme teaches strategies that can be applied immediately and so give immediate experience of success where failure might normally be expected. Thus, the learners' intuitive beliefs about themselves can be directly modified and they can discover that effort leads to success. The emphasis is on mastery learning, on gaining control over coping with failure by adopting learning strategies that turn failure into success. Thus the helplessness behaviour pattern of the poor learner, observed by Dweck and her colleagues (Dweck and Leggett, 1988), is avoided.

Direct explanation does not directly address the issue of the activation of prior knowledge: the emphasis is on learning the strategies themselves rather than on learning, through understanding, a specific subject. However, there is much emphasis on understanding how and why the strategies work, and so they do make sense to the learners and their significance is grasped. The programme aims to get the children using the strategies quickly so that they can gain mastery over them and begin to use them spontaneously in future learning. Once the strategies are repeatedly used in subject learning, prior knowledge will be activated as a consequence of their use.

Borkowski *et al.* (1990) also show that direct instruction concerning self-attributions can considerably improve the performance of underachievers. This is because, as we have already argued in Chapter 6, underachievement is due not so much to lack of knowledge of learning strategies as to lack of a full understanding that learning strategies in combination with effort result in successful learning and mastery. Thus, Borkowski *et al.* emphasize to the learner the significance of learning strategies and how the effort invested in them is what is needed for success. In their study, Borkowski *et al.* gave direct instruction in the use of comprehension strategies: each step in a strategy was modelled by the teacher and practised and understood by the children before the next was attempted. At each step, the teacher repeatedly emphasized the need for effort in the form of attentiveness to the strategy.

Many teachers already use direct instruction of strategies in their classrooms. Here is a description of one teacher's use of direct instruction:

> Consider a main idea lesson taught by Teacher B. The content of Teacher B's talk patterns reflected an explanation of what one needs to do to find the main idea of a paragraph. Information was initially presented about (1) what the mental process was, (2) how to use salient features of the skill, and (3) why the mental process is useful in connected text. After this direct explanation of what was to be learned, why it was important, and how to do it, Teacher B moved to a turn-taking model where he checked the students' restructuring. Finally, when the students demonstrated that they understood, practice was provided. (Roehler and Duffy, 1984)

Direct explanation, therefore, involves the teacher presenting a lot of specific strategy knowledge: what the strategy is, how to use it, and why it is important. After this, the teacher shows the students how to do it, and checks their understanding by watching them do it and by helping them to get it right, giving additional explanation as required. Then, when the students have demonstrated that they have understood, there is extensive practice.

RECIPROCAL TEACHING

In reciprocal teaching, there is less emphasis on direct instruction and more on learning by doing. The programme specifically addresses the activation of prior knowledge by using learning procedures that enable learners to discover and evaluate their own implicit beliefs. It also addresses the motivational issues by using procedures that foster adaptive beliefs rather than maladaptive ones, and that provide learning experiences that are consistent with adaptive beliefs about learning and about the value of making an effort.

Reciprocal teaching was designed primarily to assist students with learning difficulties. It involves an adult teacher and a group of students who each take it in turns to lead the discussion on the contents of a section of text that they are jointly attempting to understand. In the discussions, four specific strategies are practised routinely. These are *questioning, clarifying, summarizing* and *predicting*. The teacher takes the first turn at leading the discussion, after which each of the group members takes a turn as leader. This is the reciprocal aspect of the procedure. The group leader begins by asking a question about the main content of the text and ends by summarizing the gist. If there is disagreement, the group rereads and discusses potential candidates for questions and summary statements until they reach a consensus. Attempts to clarify any comprehension problems are also an integral part of the discussions. Finally, the leader asks for predictions about future content. Throughout, the adult teacher provides guidance and feedback tailored to the needs of the current discussion leader and his or her respondents. A sample dialogue from an early session with seventh graders is shown in Table 8.1.

The dialogue in Table 8.1 illustrates the use of the questioning strategy. Each of the four strategies facilitates learning rather than problem solving, since each is open-ended rather than specifying specific performance goals, such as answers to questions. For example, if the students cannot summarize a section of text, it is regarded as an important indication that comprehension is not proceeding as it should, not as a failure to perform a particular skill. Similarly, clarifying only occurs if misunderstandings are generated by some unclear aspect of the text or by a student's interpretation of the content. However, the main goal is not refining the strategies but understanding the text, although improvement in the use of such strategies turns out to be a welcome side effect.

Table 8.1 Dialogue from an early session of reciprocal teaching

Text:		Can snakes sting with their tongues?
		No – snakes' tongues are completely harmless. They're used for feeling things and for sharpening the snakes' sense of smell. Although snakes can smell in the usual way, the tongue flickering in the air picks up tiny particles of matter. These particles are deposited in two tiny cavities at the base of the nostrils to increase the snakes' ability to smell.
1.	A:	Do snakes' tongues sting?
2.	K:	Sometimes.
3.	A:	Correct. This paragraph is about do snakes sting with their tongue, and different ways that the tongue is for and the senses of smell.
4.	*T:	Are there any questions?
5.	C:	Snakes' tongues don't sting.
6.	*T:	Beautiful! I thought, boy, I must have been doing some fast reading there because I missed that point. A___, could you ask your question again?
7.	A:	Do snakes' tongues really sting?
8.	*T:	Now, A___, since you asked the question, can you find in that paragraph where the question is answered?
9.	A:	No, snakes' tongues are completely harmless.
10.	*T:	So we'll try it again. Can you generate another question that you think a teacher might ask?
11.	A:	What are the tongues used for?
12.	*T:	Good!
13.	L:	The sense of smell.
14.	*T:	Is that correct? A___, do you disagree? Yes.
15.	A:	That answer was right, but there are other things that the tongue can do.
16.	L:	But she only said tell one, she didn't say tell all of them.
17.	*T:	OK.
18.	B:	It is used to pick up tiny particles.
19.	*T:	OK. I think that this is an important point. You have the basic concept which is correct, OK, but what the question really is saying is, is it used for smell? OK?
20.	B:	They are used for feeling things for sharpening snakes' sense of smell.
21.	*T:	OK. They are used for sharpening the snakes' sense of smell. Are they used for smelling? That's the point we weren't clear on.

Table 8.1 *continued*

22.	L:	In my answer I said it is for the sense of smell.
23.	*T:	This is fine; this is what the technique is all about. What it means is not that you are right or wrong or good or bad. What it says is that we have just read something and have had a disagreement about what it says. We need to work it out.
24.	A:	My prediction is that they will now talk about the different things about snakes. Where they live, and what they eat and stuff like that.
25.	*T:	OK. Good. What do you think they eat?
26.	A:	Animals.
27.	A:	Deserts.
28.	C:	I challenge. Snakes, all of them, don't live in the desert. They live in the woods and in the swamp areas.

Note: *T indicates turns taken by adult teacher; the remaining letters refer to the children.

Source: Brown and Palincsar, 1989

An important aspect of the strategies is that they teach the children what they need to do in order to understand and learn from a text. Summarizing, clarifying, predicting and questioning are all activities that experienced learners engage in while studying independently. The reciprocal teaching procedure renders such internal attempts at understanding *external*. They are modelled by the teacher and observed and practised by the children. In addition, these strategies are readily taught in that the novice can begin participating early. Retelling what one has just read is the first step in more sophisticated attempts to state the gist of a text. Similarly, asking about the meaning of unknown words is a clarification exercise that lays the ground for more subtle comprehension monitoring of unknown or unclear ideas or referents. Easy access to the use of such strategies is important to show that improvement is possible through attempts to understand, and so serves as an example of an incremental view of intelligence.

The role of the teacher is important in a number of respects. First, the teacher provides a model of expert behaviour, and so expertise can be seen as within the grasp of the learner and not as something that only experts can do (Schoenfield, 1985). Second, the teacher has a clear instructional goal of keeping the discussion focused on the content and ensuring that enough discussion takes place to ensure a reasonable level of understanding, but no more. This is in contrast to many forms of co-operative learning where the students are left to construct their own learning goals for themselves. As would be expected from the differing beliefs about learning that children bring with them to such situations, these latter students often construct goals far different from those envisaged by the teacher (e.g. Barnes and Todd, 1977). Third, the teacher provides feedback that is tailored to the students' existing levels, encouraging them to progress gradually towards full competence. However, the responsibility for the comprehension activities is transferred to the students as soon as is possible. The idea is for the teacher to take control only when needed and to hand over responsibility to the students whenever they are ready. The students are therefore guided to perform at an increasingly mature and challenging level without being confronted with dramatic failure. The dialogue in Table 8.2 shows the effects of such guided instruction on the acquisition of question asking by a weak student.

In reciprocal teaching specific goals are not set, as is done in problem solving, and effort is maintained at all phases of learning by the teacher constantly monitoring the changing task demands and presenting new challenges. Such an approach also fosters adaptive beliefs about learning and effort by showing rapid gains in the early stages, thus providing an example of successful learning. The programme also facilitates understanding by modelling learning strategies that lead students to question what they read and to evaluate it with respect to other things that they know about the topic. Thus they learn to evaluate both new information and prior knowledge in attempts to understand what they read. Such activities provide a context in which prior knowledge can be evaluated and revised in the course of learning. This applies not only to prior knowledge about the topic of the text, but also to implicit but maladaptive theories of intelligence that are inconsistent with the activities encouraged in reciprocal teaching.

Table 8.2 Acquisition of question asking by a weak seventh-grade student (approximately 13 years old)

Day 1

Text: The water moccasin, somewhat longer than the copperhead, is found in the southeastern states. It lives in swampy regions. It belongs, as do also the copperhead and the rattlesnakes, to a group of poisonous snakes called pit vipers. They have pits between their eyes and their nostrils which, because they are sensitive to heat, help the snakes tell when they are near a warm-blooded animal. Another name for the water moccasin is 'cottonmouth'. This name comes from the white lining of the snake's mouth.

1.   S: What is found in the southeastern snakes, also the copperhead, rattlesnakes, vipers – they have. I'm not doing this right.

2.   T: All right. Do you want to know about the pit vipers?

3.   S: Yeah.

4.   T: What would be a good question about the pit vipers that starts with the word 'why?'.

5.   S: (No response).

6.   T: How about, 'Why are the snakes called pit vipers?'

7.   S: Why do they want to know that they are called pit vipers?

8.   T: Try it again.

9.   S: Why do they, pit vipers in a pit?

10.   T: How about, 'Why do they call the snakes pit vipers?'

11.   S: Why do they call the snakes pit vipers?

12.   T: There you go! Good for you.

Day 4

Text: Spinner's mate is much smaller than she, and his body is dull brown. He spends most of his time sitting at one side of her web.

13.   S: (No question).

14.   T: What's this paragraph about?

15.   S: Spinner's mate. How do spinner's mate . . .

16.   T: That's good. Keep going.

17.   S: How do spinner's mate is smaller than . . . How am I going to say that?

Table 8.2 *continued*

18.	T:	Take your time with it. You want to ask a question about spinner's mate and what he does, beginning with the word 'how'.
19.	S:	How do they spend most of his time sitting?
20.	T:	You're very close. The question would be, 'How does spinner's mate spend most of his time?'. Now, you ask it.
21.	S:	How does spinner's mate spend most of his time

Day 7
Text:

Perhaps you are wondering where the lava and other volcanic products come from. Deep within our earth there are pockets of molten rock called magma. Forced upward in part by gas pressure, this molten rock continually tries to reach the surface. Eventually – by means of cracks in the crustal rocks or some similar zone of weakness – the magma may break out of the ground. It then flows from the vent as lava, or spews skyward as dense clouds of lava particles.

22.	S:	How does the pressure from below push the mass of hot rock against the opening? Is that it?
23.	T:	Not quite. Start your question with, 'What happens when?'.
24.	S:	What happens when the pressure from below pushes the mass of hot rock against the opening?
25.	T:	Good for you! Good job.

Day 11
Text:

One of the most interesting of the insect-eating plants is the Venus's flytrap. This plant lives in only one small area of the world – the coastal marshes of North and South Carolina. The Venus's flytrap doesn't look unusual. Its habits, however, make it truly a plant wonder.

| 26. | S: | What is the most interesting of the insect-eating plants, and where do the plants live at? |
| 27. | T: | Two excellent questions! They are both clear and important questions. Ask us one at a time now. |

Day 15
Text:

Scientists also come to the South Pole to study the strange lights that glow overhead during the Antarctic night. (It's a cold and lonely world for the few hardy people who

Table 8.2 *continued*

'winter over' the polar night.) These 'southern lights' are caused by the Earth acting like a magnet on electrical particles in the air. They are clues that may help us understand the Earth's core and the upper edges of its blanket of air.

28.	S:	Why do scientists come to the South Pole to study?
29.	T:	Excellent question! That is what this paragraph is all about.

Note: T stands for the adult teacher; S stands for the student.
Source: Brown and Palincsar, 1989

Summary

In this chapter, we have returned to the categories of learning identified in Chapter 1 and discussed their influences on teaching and learning. In so doing, we have shown how principles of learning should inform educational policy and practice. We reviewed intuitive beliefs and explicit learning and identified three key principles of learning: the activation of prior knowledge, motivation and metacognition. We also identified two goals of learning: understanding and consolidation, the latter requiring practice of problem-solving activities and memorization.

Intuitive beliefs are gained through implicit learning and through the repeated practice of familiar problems. They pervade all our daily activities and profoundly influence learning in school. If this prior knowledge is activated at the outset of new learning, then understanding of the new material can begin; but if this prior knowledge is not activated at the outset of learning, the new material will not be understood and will seem arbitrary, abstract and difficult. As long as prior knowledge is activated, difficult diagnostic skills can be side-stepped because the learning activities themselves will reveal the prior knowledge. The skills that teachers need are those that enable them to view classroom activities as stages on the route to an overall goal of understanding. These skills will lead the teacher to make sure that prior knowledge is activated at the start of a task and that the outcomes are referred back to that knowledge. Thus, the activation of prior knowledge is a key learning principle.

This activation leads to understanding if it is followed by the two-way process of evaluation, in which prior knowledge is used to assess one's understanding of the new material, and the new material is used to update and revise one's prior knowledge. This two-way process required for understanding contrasts with problem solving and memorization, each of which can occur – although with great difficulty – in the absence of understanding. Problem solving involves finding the solution to a new problem, followed by repeated practice at reaching it. Memorization involves the accumulation of new information. If prior knowledge is activated, the new information will be linked to it; but if it is not activated, then the new information will be stored in long-term memory as a set of isolated and arbitrary facts. Thus, understanding should guide and govern the use of problem solving and memorization.

Unfortunately, understanding is very difficult. It requires that teachers themselves have a sound understanding of the subject matter, and it requires metacognitive skills that enable people – teachers as well as pupils – to have knowledge of their own learning strategies and to apply those strategies after monitoring their current state of comprehension. Investment in the effort required to use these skills depends on the learner's level of motivation. Thus, a second key principle of learning concerns motivation: whether a person believes such effort is worthwhile. Motivation can be addressed in two main ways: by ensuring that the classroom activities are consistent with the belief that learning requires understanding; and by ensuring that children's efforts lead to success and so are seen as worthwhile. Motivation is also enhanced when the purposes of learning are evident.

The need for metacognitive skills when learning through understanding is our third key principle of learning. These skills can be taught by explicit instruction or by reciprocal teaching. Both teaching programmes address the principles of learning that we have identified here. As its name implies, explicit instruction focuses on the explicit teaching of learning strategies, and the main emphasis is on motivation, through the development of adaptive beliefs about learning and through the immediate experience of success as a result of effort. Reciprocal teaching focuses on learning by doing rather than on explicit instruction. It emphasizes the activation of prior knowledge as well as motivation, and makes the learning strategies an integral part of understanding the subject matter itself. Explicit instruction may appeal to teachers with a predominantly traditional teaching style, while reciprocal teaching may appeal to teachers with a predominantly progressive learning style. In both cases, though, the extremes of traditionalism and progressivism are avoided, and learning is encouraged by structured activities that emphasize both process and product and that are harnessed to the twin goals of understanding and consolidation.

Successful teaching, therefore, requires a wide knowledge of tasks that can be used to foster consolidation. It also requires a clear focus on learning through understanding. The successful marriage of these two requirements means that tasks of consolidation must be embedded in an overall set of activities that encourage understanding. These cannot be pinned down to a set of routine tasks; instead they depend on the teacher's ability to allow children to bring forward their own thoughts and feelings. The successful marriage, then, is between mundane tasks of consolidation and daring flights of imagination that together may lead to understanding. The challenges of such a marriage make up the goals of teaching, the attainment of which can bring untold rewards. Thus, while the skills of teaching lie in implementing routine tasks, and the art of teaching lies in a focus on understanding, a true science of teaching will only be achieved when the skills and the art are successfully co-ordinated.

References

Adams, M. J. (1990) *Beginning to Read: Thinking and Learning About Print*. Cambridge, MA: Bradford Books/MIT Press.

Alexander, R. J. (1991) *Primary Education in Leeds: Twelfth and Final Report from the Primary Needs Independent Evaluation Project*. Leeds: University of Leeds.

Alexander, R. J. (1992) *Policy and Practice in Primary Education*. London and New York: Routledge.

Alexander, R. J., Rose, J. and Woodhead, C. (1992) *Curriculum Organisation and Classroom Practice in Primary Schools – A Discussion Paper*. DES.

Amaiwa, S. (1987) 'Transfer of subtraction procedures from abacus to paper and pencil.' *Japanese Journal of Educational Psychology* 35, 41–8 (in Japanese with English summary).

Ames, C. (1984) 'Achievement attributions and self-instructions under competitive and individualistic goal structures.' *Journal of Educational Psychology* 76, 478–87.

Ames, C. and Archer, J. (1988) 'Achievement goals in the classroom: students' learning strategies and motivation processes.' *Journal of Educational Psychology* 80, 260–7.

Anderson, J. R. (1983) *The Architecture of Cognition*. Cambridge, MA: Harvard University Press.

Anderson, R. C., Hiebert, E. H., Scott, J. A. and Wilkinson, I. A. G. (1985) *Becoming a Nation of Readers: The Report of the Commission on Reading*. Washington, DC: US Department of Education, National Institute of Education.

Baddeley, A. D. (1978) 'The trouble with levels: a re-examination of Craik and Lockhart's framework for memory research.' *Psychological Review* 89, 708–29.

Baddeley, A. D. (1982) 'Domains of recollection.' *Psychological Review* 89, 708–29.

Baddeley, A. D. (1986) *Working Memory*. Oxford: Oxford University Press.

Baddeley, A. D. and Hitch, G. (1974) 'Working memory.' In G. A. Bower (ed.), *Recent Advances in Learning and Motivation. Vol. 8*. New York: Academic Press.

Baker, L. (1985) 'Differences in the standards used by college students to evaluate their comprehension of expository prose.' *Reading Research Quarterly* 20, 297–313.

Baker, L. (1989) 'Metacognition, comprehension monitoring and the adult reader.' *Educational Psychology Review* **1**, 3–38.

Baker, L. and Anderson, R. I. (1982) 'Effects of inconsistent information on text processing: evidence for comprehension monitoring.' *Reading Research Quarterly* **17**, 281–94.

Ball, D. K. and McDiarmid, G. W. (1989) *The Subject Matter Preparation of Teachers*. East Lansing: The National Centre for Research on Teacher Education, Michigan State University.

Bandura, M. and Dweck, C. S. (1985) 'The relationship of conceptions of intelligence and achievement goals to achievement-related cognition, affect and behaviour.' Manuscript submitted for publication. Cited in C. S. Dweck and E. L. Leggett (1988), 'A social-cognitive approach to motivation and personality.' *Psychological Review* **95**, 256–73.

Barnes, D. and Todd, F. (1977) *Communication and Learning in Small Groups*. London: Routledge and Kegan Paul.

Bartlett, E. J. (1982) 'Learning to revise: some component processes.' In M. Nystrand (ed.), *What Writers Know: The Language, Process, and Structure of Written Discourse*. New York: Academic Press.

Beck, A. T. (1976) *Cognitive Theory and the Emotional Disorders*. New York: International Press.

Beck, A. T. and Clark, D. A. (1988) 'Anxiety and depression: an information processing perspective.' *Anxiety Research* **1**, 23–36.

Beck, I. L. and Carpenter, P. A. (1986) 'Cognitive approaches to understanding reading.' *American Psychologist* **41**, 1088–105.

Bekarian, D. A. and Baddeley, A. D. (1980) 'Saturation advertising and the repetition effect.' *Journal of Verbal Learning and Verbal Behaviour* **19**, 17–25.

Bennett, S. N. (1976) *Teaching Styles and Pupil Progress*. London: Open Books.

Bennett, S. N. and Desforges, C. (1988) 'Matching classroom tasks to students' attainment.' *The Elementary School Journal* **88**(3), 221–50.

Bennett, S. N. and Kell, J. (1989) *A Good Start? Four Year Olds in Infant Schools*. Oxford: Basil Blackwell.

Bennett, S. N., Desforges, C., with Cockburn A. and Wilkinson, B. (1984) *The Quality of Pupils' Learning Experiences*. Hove: Lawrence Erlbaum.

Bereiter, C. and Scardamalia, M. (1982) 'From conversation to composition: the role of instruction in a developmental process.' In R. Glaser (ed.), *Advances in Instructional Psychology Vol 2*. Hillsdale, NJ: Lawrence Erlbaum.

Bereiter, C. and Scardamalia, M. (1989) 'Intentional learning as a goal of instruction.' In L. B. Resnick (ed.), *Knowing, Learning and Instruction: Essays in Honour of Robert Glaser*. Hillsdale, NJ: Lawrence Erlbaum.

Bereiter, C., Burtis, P. J. and Scardamalia, M. (1988) 'Cognitive operations in constructing main points in written composition.' *Journal of Memory and Language* **27**, 261–78.

References

Berry, D. C., and Broadbent, D. E. (1984) 'On the relationship between task performance and associated verbalizable knowledge.' *Quarterly Journal of Experimental Psychology* **35A**, 39–49.

Berry, D. C. and Broadbent, D. E. (1988) 'Interactive tasks and the implicit-explicit distinction.' *British Journal of Psychology* **79**, 251–72.

Borkowski, J. G., Carr, M., Rellinger, E. and Pressley, M. (1990) 'Self-regulated cognition: Interdependence of metacognition, attributions and self-esteem.' In B. F. Jones and L. Idol (eds), *Dimensions of Thinking and Cognitive Instruction*. Hillsdale, NJ, Hove and London: LEA.

Bransford, J. D. and Johnson, M. K. (1972) 'Contextual prerequisites for understanding: some investigations of comprehension and recall.' *Journal of Verbal Learning and Verbal Behaviour* **11**, 717–26.

Bransford, J. D., Vye, N. J., Adams, L. T. and Perfetto, G. A. (1989) 'Learning skills and the acquisition of knowledge.' In A. Lesgold and R. Glaser (eds), *Foundations for a Psychology of Education*. Hillsdale, NJ: Lawrence Erlbaum.

Broadbent, D. E., Fitzgerald, P. and Broadbent, M. H. P. (1986) 'Implicit and explicit knowledge in the control of complex systems.' *British Journal of Psychology* **77**, 33–50.

Brown, A. L. (1977) 'Development, schooling and the acquisition of knowledge about knowledge.' In R. C. Anderson, R. J. Spiro and W. E. Montague (eds), *Schooling and the Acquisition of Knowledge*. Hillsdale, NJ: Lawrence Erlbaum.

Brown, A. L. and Day, J. D. (1983) *Macrorules for Summarizing Texts: The Development of Expertise*. Technical Report No. 270. Champaign, IL: Center for the Study of Reading.

Brown, A. L. and Palincsar, A. S. (1989) 'Guided, cooperative learning and individual knowledge acquisition.' In L. B. Resnick (ed.), *Knowing, Learning, and Instruction: Essays in Honour of Robert Glaser*. Hillsdale, NJ: Lawrence Erlbaum.

Brown, A. L., Campione, J. C. and Day, J. D. (1981) 'Learning to learn: on training students to learn from texts.' *Educational Researcher* **10**, 14–21.

Brown J. S., Collins, A. and Duguid, P. (1989) 'Situated cognition and the nature of learning.' *Educational Researcher* **18**, 32–42.

Brunsen, B. and Matthews, K. (1981) 'The type-A coronary prone behaviour pattern and reactions to uncontrollable stress: an analysis of performance strategies, affect and attributions during failure.' *Journal of Personality and Social Psychology* **40**, 906–18.

Carpenter, T. P. and Moser, J. M. (1982) 'The development of addition and subtraction problem-solving skills. In J. P. Carpenter, J. M. Moser and T. Romberg (eds), *Addition and Subtraction: A Cognitive Perspective*. Hilllsdale, NJ: Lawrence Erlbaum.

Carpenter, T. P., Moser, J. M. and Romberg, T. A. (1982) *Addition and Subtraction: A Cognitive Perspective*, Hillsdale, NJ: Lawrence Erlbaum.

Carraher, T. N., Carraher, D. W. and Schliemannn, A. D. (1985) 'Mathematics in the streets and in schools.' *British Journal of Experimental Psychology* **3**, 21–9.

Ceci, S. J. and Liker, J. (1986) 'Academic and nonacademic intelligence: an experimental separation.' In R. J. Sternberg and R. K. Wagner (eds), *Practical Intelligence: Nature and Origins of Competence in the Everyday World.* Cambridge: Cambridge University Press.

Chall, J. S. (1967) *Learning to Read: The Great Debate.* New York: McGraw-Hill.

Chall, J. S. (1969) 'Research in linguistics and reading instruction: implications for further research and practice.' *Proceedings of the Thirteenth Annual Convention, International Reading Association (Pt 1)* **13**, 560–71. Reprinted in R. Karlin (ed.), *Perspectives on Elementary Reading: Principles and Strategies of Teaching.* New York: Harcourt Brace Jovanovich.

Chall, J. S. (1979) 'The great debate: ten years later, with a modest proposal for reading stages.' In L. B. Resnick and P. A. Weaver (eds), *Theory and Practice of Early Reading. Vol. 1.* Hillsdale, NJ: LEA.

Chall, J. S. (1983) *Stages of Reading Development.* New York: McGraw-Hill.

Champagne, A. B., Klopfer, L. E. and Anderson, J. H. (1980) 'Factors influencing the learning of classical mechanics.' *American Journal of Physics* **48**, 1074–9.

Champagne, B. and Hornig, L. (1987) *Practical Applications of Theories About Learning: Students and Science Learning.* Washington, DC: American Association for the Advancement of Science.

Chase, W. G. and Simon, H. A. (1973) 'The mind's eye in chess'. In W. G. Chase (ed.), *Visual Information Processing.* New York: Academic Press.

Chi, M. T. H., Bassok, M., Lewis, M. W., Reimann, P. and, Glaser, R. (1989) 'Self-explanations: how students study and use examples in learning to solve problems.' *Cognitive Science* **13**, 145–82.

Chomsky, C. (1978) 'When you still can't read in 3rd grade: after decoding what?' In S. J. Samuels (ed.), *Research Implications for Teaching Reading.* Newark, DE: International Reading Association.

Clark, M. (1976) *Young Fluent Readers.* London: Heinemann.

Clarke, K. (1991) 'Primary education: a statement by the Secretary of State for Education and Science.' DES 3.12.91.

Clement, J. (1983) 'A conceptual model discussed by Galileo and used intuitively by physics students.' In D. Gentner and A. Stevens (eds), *Mental Models.* Hillsdale, NJ: Lawrence Erlbaum.

Clement, J. (1991) 'Nonformal reasoning in experts and in social science students: the use of analogies, extreme cases, and physical intuition.' In J. M. Voss, D. M. Perkins and J. W. Segal (eds), *Informal Reasoning and Education*. Hillsdale, NJ: Lawrence Erlbaum.

Covington, M. V. (1985) 'Strategic thinking and the fear of failure'. In J. W. Segal, S. F. Chipman and R. Glaser (eds), *Thinking and Learning Skills. Vol. 1*. Hillsdale, NJ: Lawrence Erlbaum.

Craik, F. I. M. and Lockhart, R. S. (1972) 'Levels of processing: a framework for memory research.' *Journal of Verbal Learning and Verbal Behaviour* **11**, 671–84.

Craik, F. I. M. and Tulving, E. (1975) 'Depth of processing and the retention of words in episodic memory.' *Journal of Experimental Psychology: General* **104**, 268–94.

Davis, R. B. and McNight, C. C. (1979) 'Modelling the process of mathematical thinking'. *Journal of Children's Mathematical Behaviour* **2**, 91–113.

DES (1978) *Primary Education in England: A Survey by HM Inspectors of Schools*. London: HMSO.

DES (1985) *Better Schools*. London: HMSO.

DES (1991) *History in the National Curriculum*. London: HMSO.

DES (1992) *Mathematics 5–16*. London: HMSO.

Desforges, C. (1989) 'Understanding learning for teaching.' *Westminster Studies in Education* **12**, 17–20.

Dewey, J. (1929) *The Sources of a Science Education*. Kappa Delta Pi Lecture Series. New York: Liveright Publishing Corporation.

Diener, C. I. and Dweck, C. S. (1978) 'An analysis of learned helplessness: continuous changes in performance, strategy and achievement cognitions following failure.' *Journal of Personality and Social Psychology* **36**, 451–62.

Diener, C. I. and Dweck, C. S. (1980) 'An analysis of learned helplessness: II. The processing of success.' *Journal of Personality and Social Psychology* **39**, 940–52.

diSessa, A. A. (1983) 'Phenomenology and the evolution of intuition.' In D. Gentner and A. Stevens (eds), *Mental Models*. Hillsdale, NJ: Lawrence Erlbaum.

Doctor, E. and Coltheart, M. (1980) 'Phonological recoding in children's reading for meaning.' *Memory and Cognition* **80**, 195–209.

Donaldson, M. (1984) 'Speech and writing and modes of learning.' In H. Goelman, A. Oberg and F. Smith (eds), *Awakening to Literacy*. London: Heinemann.

Driver, R. (1983) *The Pupil as Scientist*. Milton Keynes: Open University Press.

Driver R., Guesne E. and Tiberghien, A. (1988) *Children's Ideas in Science*. Milton Keynes: Open University Press.

Dweck, C. S. (1986) 'Motivational processes affecting learning.' *American Psychologist* **41**, 1040–8.

Dweck, C. S. and Bempechat, J. (1983) 'Children's theories of intelligence.' In S. Paris, G. Olson and H. Stevenson (eds), *Learning and Motivation in the Classroom*. Hillsdale, NJ: Lawrence Erlbaum.

Dweck, C. S. and Leggett, E. L. (1988) 'A social-cognitive approach to motivation and personality.' *Psychological Review* 95, 256–73.

Education Act (1944) London: HMSO.

Education Reform Act (1988) London: HMSO.

Elliott, E. S. and Dweck, C. S. (1988) 'Goals: an approach to motivation and achievement.' *Journal of Personality and Social Psychology* 54, 5–12.

Ellis, A. W. (1984) *Reading, Writing and Dyslexia*. London and Hillsdale, NJ: Lawrence Erlbaum.

Ellis, A. Y. and Young, A. W. (1988) *Human Cognitive Neuropsychology*. Hove, London and Hillsdale, NJ: Lawrence Erlbaum.

Evans, P. (1989) *Motivation and Emotion*. New York: Routledge.

Eyseneck, M. W. (1979) 'Anxiety, learning and memory: a reconceptualization.' *Journal of Research in Personality* 13, 3363–85.

Eysenck, M. W. (1992) *Anxiety: The Cognitive Perspective*. Hove: Lawrence Erlbaum.

Farrell, E. and Dweck, C. S. (1985) 'The role of motivational processes in transfer of learning.' Manuscript submitted for publication. Cited in C. S. Dweck and E. L. Leggett (1988), 'A social-cognitive approach to motivation and personality'. *Psychological Review* 95, 256–73.

Fischer, P. M. and Mandl, H. (1984) 'Learner, text variables, and the control of text comprehension and recall.' In H. Mandl, N. L. Stein and T. Trabasso (eds), *Learning and Comprehension of Text*. Hillsdale, NJ, and London: Lawrence Erlbaum.

Fitzgerald, A., Livingstone, K. and Purdy, D. (1981) *Mathematics in Employment 16–18: Report*. Bath: University of Bath.

Flavell, J. H. (1970) 'Developmental studies of mediated memory.' In H. W. Reese and L. P. Lipsitt (eds), *Advances in Child Development and Behaviour. Vol. 5*. New York: Academic Press.

Flavell, J. H. (1976) 'Metacognitive aspects of problem solving.' In B. C. Resnick (ed.), *The Nature of Intelligence*. Hillsdale, NJ: Lawrence Erlbaum.

Flower, L. S. (1979) 'Writer-based prose: a cognitive basis for problems in writing.' *College English* 41, 19–37.

Forrest-Pressley, D. L. and Waller, T. G. (1984) *Reading, Cognition and Metacognition*. New York: Springer-Verlag.

Funnell, E. (1983) 'Phonological processes in reading: new evidence from acquired dysgraphia.' *British Journal of Psychology* 74, 159–80.

Galton, M., Simon, B. and Croll, P. (1980) *Inside the Primary Classroom*. London: Routledge.

References

Garner, R. (1990) 'When children and adults do not use learning strategies: toward a theory of settings.' *Review of Educational Research* **60**, 517–29.

Gelman, R. and Gallistel, C. R. (1978) *The Child's Understanding of Number*. Cambridge, MA: Harvard University Press.

Gibbs, G. (1990) *Improving Student Learning Project: Briefing Paper for Participants in the Project*. Oxford: The Oxford Centre for Student Learning, Oxford Polytechnic.

Gick, M. L. and Holyoak, K. J. (1980) 'Analogical Problem Solving.' *Cognitive Psychology* **12**, 306–55.

Gough, P. B. (1972) 'One second of reading.' In J. F. Kavanagh and I. G. Mattingley (eds), *Language by Ear and by Eye*. Cambridge, MA: MIT Press.

Graves, D. H. (1979) 'What children show us about revision.' *Language Arts* **56**, 312–19.

Grossman, P. L., Wilson, S. M. and Shulman, L. S. (1989) 'Teachers of substance: subject matter knowledge in teaching.' In M. C. Reynolds (ed.), *Knowledge Base for the Beginning Teacher*. Oxford: Pergamon Press.

Hall, N. (1987) *The Emergence of Literacy*. London: Hodder & Stoughton.

Harris, M. and Coltheart, M. (1986) *Language Processing in Children and Adults: An Introduction*. London: Routledge and Kegan Paul.

Hart, K. M. (1989) Place value: subtraction.' In D. C. Johnson (ed.), *Children's Mathematical Frameworks 8–13: A Study of Classroom Teaching*. Windsor: Nelson.

Hart, K. (ed.) (1981) *Children's Understanding of Mathematics 11–16*. London: John Murray.

Hasselhorn, M. and Korkel, J. (1986) 'Metacognitive versus traditional reading instructions: the mediating role of domain-specific knowledge on children's text processing.' *Human Learning* **5**, 75–90.

Hatano, G. (1988) 'Social and motivational bases for mathematical understanding.' In G. B. Saxe and M. Gearhart (eds), *Children's Mathematics*. San Francisco: Jossey-Bass.

Hidi, S. and Hildyard, A. (1980) 'The comprehension of oral and written productions of two discourse types.' Paper presented at the annual meeting of the American Educational Research Association, Boston. Cited by Scardamalia *et al.* (1982).

Holyoak, K. J. and Spellman, B. A. (1993) 'Thinking.' *Annual Review of Psychology* **44**, 265–315.

Hughes, M. (1986) *Children and Number*. London: Blackwell.

Jones, M. (1990) 'Children's writing.' In R. Grieve and M. Hughes (eds) *Understanding Children*. Oxford: Basil Blackwell.

Kanfer, R. (1990) 'Motivation and individual differences in learning: an integration of developmental, differential and cognitive perspectives.' *Learning and Individual Differences* **2**, 221–39.

Kanfer, R. and Ackerman, P. L. (1989) 'Motivation and cognitive abilities: an integrative/aptitude-treatment interaction approach to skill acquisition.' *Journal of Applied Psychology Monograph* **74**, 657–90.

Keane, M. T. G. (1990) 'Incremental analogizing: theory and model.' In K. J. Gilhooly, M. T. G. Keane, R. H. Logie and G. Erdos (eds), *Lines of Thinking: Reflections on the Psychology of Thought. Vol. 1: Representation, Reasoning, Analogy and Decision Making.* Chichester: Wiley.

Keig, P. (1989) 'About memory facts and concepts.' *Science and Children* **26**(8), 35.

Kletzien, S. B. (1988) 'A comparison of achieving and nonachieving readers' use of comprehension strategies on different reading levels.' Paper presented at the meeting of the American Educational Research Association, New Orleans. Cited in L. Baker (1989), 'Metacognition, comprehension monitoring and the adult reader.' *Educational Psychology Review* **1**, 3–38.

Kolers, P. A. (1966) 'Reading and talking bilingually.' *American Journal of Psychology* **74**, 357–76.

LaBerge, D. and Samuels, S. J. (1974) 'Toward a theory of automatic information processing in reading.' *Cognitive Psychology* **6**, 293–323.

Lave, J., Murtaugh, M. and de la Roche, O. (1984) 'The dialectic of arithmetic in grocery shopping.' In B. Rogoff and J. Lave (eds), *Everyday Cognition: Its Development in Social Context.* Cambridge, MA: Harvard University Press.

Leggett, E. L. and Dweck, C. S. (1986) 'Goals and inference rules: sources of causal judgements.' Manuscript submitted for publication. Cited in C. S. Dweck and E. L. Leggett (1988), 'A social-cognitive approach to motivation and personality.' *Psychological Review* **95**, 256–73.

Lovett, S. B. and Flavell, J. H. (1990) 'Understanding and remembering: children's knowledge about the differential effects of strategy and task variables on comprehension and memorization.' *Child Development* **61**, 1842–58.

McCloskey, M. and Kargon, R. (1988) 'The meaning and use of historical models in the study of intuitive physics.' In S. Strauss (ed.), *Ontogeny, Phylogeny, and Historical Development.* Norwood, NJ: Ablex.

McCloskey, M. (1983) 'Intuitive physics.' *Scientific American* **24**, 122–30.

McCormack, A. J. and Yager, R. E. (1989) 'A new taxonomy of science education.' *The Science Teacher* **56**(2), 47.

McNamara, D. R. (1991) 'Subject knowledge and its application: problems and possibilities for teacher educators.' *Journal of Education for Teaching* **17**(2), 113–28.

Markman, E. M. (1979) 'Realising that you don't understand: elementary school children's awareness of inconsistencies.' *Child Development* **50**, 643–55.

Marsh, G., Friedman, M., Welch, V. and Desberg, P. (1981) 'A cognitive-developmental theory of reading acquisition.' In G. E. MacKinnon and T. G. Waller (eds), *Reading Research: Advances in Theory and Practice*. New York: Academic Press.

Mikulecky, L. and Ehlinger, J. (1985) 'The influence of metacognitive aspects of literacy on job performance of electronics technicians.' *Journal of Reading Behaviour* **18**, 43–62.

Mikulecky, L. and Winchester, D. (1983) 'Job literacy and job performance among nurses at varying performance levels.' *Adult Education Quarterly* **34**, 1–15.

Miller, G. A. (1956) 'The magical number seven, plus or minus two: Some limits on our capacity for processing information.' *Psychological Review* **63**, 81–97.

Mortimore, P., Sammons, P., Stoll, L., Lewis, D. and Ecob, R. (1988) *School Matters: The Junior Years*. London: Open Books.

National Assessment of Educational Progress (1977) *Write/Rewrite: An Assessment of Revision Skills; Selected Results from the Second National Assessment of Writing*. ERIC Document Reproduction Service ED 141 826. Washington, DC: US Government Printing Office.

NCC (1990) *Curriculum Guidance 3: The Whole Curriculum*. York: NCC.

Neisser, U. (1963) 'The multiplicity of thought.' *British Journal of Psychology* **54**, 1–14.

Newell, A. and Simon, H. A. (1972) *Human Problem Solving*. Englewood Cliffs, NJ: Prentice-Hall.

New York State Education Department (1985) *Elementary Science Syllabus*. Albany, NY: Division of Program Development.

Nicholls, J. G. (1978) 'The development of the concepts of effort and ability, perception of academic attainment, and the understanding that difficult tasks require more ability.' *Child Development* **49**, 800–14.

Nicholls, J. G. (1984) 'Achievement motivation: conceptions of ability, subjective experience, task choice, and performance.' *Psychological Review* **91**, 328–645.

Norman, D. A. (1978) 'Notes toward a theory of complex learning.' In A. M. Lesgold, J. W. Pellegrino, S. D. Fokkema and R. Glaser (eds), *Cognitive Psychology and Instruction*. New York and London: Plenum Press.

Oatley, K. G. (1977) 'Inference, navigation and cognitive maps.' In P. N. Johnson-Laird and P. C. Wason, *Thinking: Readings in Cognitive Science*. Cambridge: Cambridge University Press.

Owen, E. and Sweller, J. (1985) 'What do students learn while solving mathematics problems?' *Journal of Educational Psychology* **77**, 272–84.

Palmer J. A. (1993) 'From Santa Claus to sustainability.' *International Journal of Science Education* **15**(5), 487–95.

Paris, P., Lipson, M. Y. and Wixson, K. K. (1983) 'Becoming a strategic reader.' *Contemporary Educational Psychology* **8**, 293–316.

Patterson, K. E. (1982) 'The relation between reading and phonological coding: further neuropsychological observations.' In A. W. Ellis (ed.), *Normality and Pathology in Cognitive Functions*. London: Academic Press.

Paulu, N. and Martin, M. (1991) *Helping Your Child Learn Science*. Washington, DC: Department of Education Research and Improvement.

Perera, K. (1984) *Children's Writing and Reading: Analysing Classroom Language*. Oxford: Basil Blackwell.

Perfetti, C. A. (1985) *Reading Ability*. Oxford: Oxford University Press.

Perfetti, C. A. and Hogoboam, T. (1975) 'The relationship between single word decoding and reading comprehension skill.' *Journal of Educational Psychology* **67**, 461–9.

Perry, W. (1970) *Forms of Intellectual and Ethical Development in the College Years: A Scheme*. New York: Holt Rinehart and Winston.

Peterson, C. and Seligman, M. E. P. (1984) 'Causal explanations as a risk factor for depressions: theory and evidence.' *Psychological Review* **91**, 347–74.

Philips, W. C. (1991) 'Earth science misconceptions.' *The Science Teacher* **58**(2), 21–2.

Plowden, Lady B. H. (1967) *Children and their Primary Schools. Vol. 1*. The Plowden Report. A Report of the Central Advisory Council for Education (England). London: HMSO.

Pressley, M., Snyder, B. L. and Cariglia-Bull, T. (1987) 'How can good strategy use be taught to children? Evaluation of six alternative approaches.' In S. M. Cornier and J. D. Hagman (eds), *Transfer of Learning*. London: Academic Press.

Pressley, M., Goodchild, F., Fleet, J., Zajchowski, R. and Evans, E. D. (1989) 'The challenges of classroom instruction.' *The Elementary School Journal* **89**, 301–42.

Proffitt, D. R., Kaiser, M. K. and Whelan, S. M. (1990) 'Understanding wheel dynamics.' *Cognitive Psychology* **22**, 342–73.

Resnick, L. B. (1981) 'Syntax and semantics in learning to subtract.' In T. Carpenter, T. Moser and G. Romberg (eds), *Addition and Subtraction: Educational Perspectives*. Hillsdale, NJ: Lawrence Erlbaum.

Rigden, J. S. (1983) 'The art of great science.' *Phi Delta Kappan* **64**(9), 613–17.

Roehler, L. R. and Duffy, G. G. (1984) 'Direct explanation of comprehension processess.' In G. G. Duffy, L. R. Roehler and J. Mason (eds), *Comprehension Instruction: Perspectives and Suggestions*. New York: Longmans, Green.

Roth, K. J. (1991) 'Reading science texts for conceptual change.' In C. M.

References

Santa and D. E. Alvermann (eds). *Science Learning: Processes and Applications*. Newark, DE: International Reading Association, pp . 48–63.

Rothkopf, E. Z. (1988) 'Perspectives on study skills training in a realistic instructional economy.' In C. E. Weinstein, E. T. Goetz and P. A. Alexander (eds), *Learning and Study Strategies: Issues in Assessment, Instruction and Evaluation*. San Diego: Academic Press.

Rubenstein, H., Lewis, S. S. and Rubenstein, M. A. (1971) 'Evidence of phonemic recoding in visual word recognition.' *Journal of Verbal Learning and Verbal Behaviour* 10, 645–57.

Säljö, R. (1979) 'Learning about learning.' *Higher Education* 8, 443–51.

Scardamalia, M. and Bereiter, C. (1979) 'The effects of writing rate on children's composition.' Paper presented at the annual meeting of the American Educational Research Association, San Francisco. Cited by Scardamalia *et al.* (1982).

Scardamalia, M. and Bereiter, C. (1984) 'Development of strategies in text processing.' In H. Mandl, N. L. Stein and T. Trabasso (eds), *Learning and Comprehension of Text*. Hillsdale, NJ and London: Lawrence Erlbaum.

Scardamalia, M. and Bereiter, C. (1985) 'Development of dialectical processes in composition.' In D. R. Olson, N. Torrance and A. Hildyard (eds), *Literacy, Language and Learning: The Nature and Consequences of Reading and Writing*. Cambridge: Cambridge University Press.

Scardamalia, M. and Bereiter, C. (1986) 'Writing.' In R. F. Dillon and R. J. Sternberg (eds), *Cognition and Instruction*. Orlando, FL: Academic Press.

Scardamalia, M. and Bereiter, C. (1987) 'Knowledge telling and knowledge transforming in written composition.' In S. Rosenberg (ed.), *Advances in Applied Psycholinguistics. Vol. 2. Reading, Writing and Language Learning*. Cambridge: Cambridge University Press.

Scardamalia, M. and Bereiter, C. (1991) 'Literate expertise'. In K. A. Ericsson and J. Smith (eds), *Toward a General Theory of Expertise: Prospects and Limits*. Cambridge: Cambridge University Press.

Scardamalia, M., Bereiter, C. and Goelman, H. (1982) 'The role of production factors in writing ability.' In M. Nystrand (ed.), *What Writers Know: The Language, Process, and Structure of Written Discourse*. New York: Academic Press.

Scardamalia, M., Bereiter, C. and Steinbach, R. (1984) 'Teachability of reflective processes in written composition.' *Cognitive Science* 8, 173–90.

Schoenfeld, A. H. (1985) *Mathematical Problem Solving*. Orlando, FL: Academic Press.

Schoenfeld, A. H. (1991) 'On mathematics as sense-making: an informal attack on the unfortunate divorce of formal and informal mathematics.' In J. F. Voss, D. N. Perkins and J. W. Segal (eds), *Informal Reasoning and Education*. Hillsdale, NJ: LEA.

Scribner, S. (1988) 'Thinking in action: some characteristics of practical thought.' In R. J. Sternberg and R. K. Wagner (eds), *Practical Intelligence: Nature and Origins of Competence in the Everyday World*. Cambridge, New York and Melbourne: Cambridge University Press.

Sewell, B. (1981) *Use of Mathematics by Adults in Daily Life*. Leicester: Advisory Council for Adult and Continuing Education (ACACE).

Seymour, P. H. K. and Elder, L. (1986) 'Beginning reading without phonology.' *Cognitive Neuropsychology* 3, 1–36.

Shuard, H., Walsh, A., Goodwin, J. and Worcester, V. (1990) *Children, Mathematics and Learning: Primary Initiatives in Mathematics Education*. London: Simon and Schuster.

Shuard, H., Walsh, A., Goodwin, J. and Worcester, V. (1991) *Primary Initiatives in Mathematics: Calculators, Children and Mathematics*. London: Simon and Schuster.

Shulman, L. S. (1986) 'Those who understand: knowledge growth in teaching.' *Educational Researcher* 15(2), 4–14.

Smith, N. V. (ed.) (1982) *Mutual Knowledge*. London: Academic Press.

Spring, C. (1985) 'Comprehension and study strategies reported by university freshmen who are good and poor readers.' *Instructional Science* 14, 157–67.

Stevenson, R. J. (1988) *Models of Language Development*. Milton Keynes: Open University Press.

Sweller, J. (1988) 'Cognitive load during problem solving: effects on learning.' *Cognitive Science* 12, 257–85.

Tulving, E. (1962) 'Subjective organisation in free recall of "unrelated" words' *Psychological Review* 69, 344–54.

Van Rossum, E. J. and Schenk, S. M. (1984) 'The relation between learning conception, study strategy and learning outcome.' *British Journal of Educational Psychology* 54, 73–83.

Vygotsky, L. (1962) *Thought and Language*. Cambridge, MA: MIT Press.

Whitehead, H. I. (1929) *The Aims of Education*. New York: Macmillan.

Name Index

Subject Index

Subject Index

early learning 150, 163, 174
education 4, 12, 27, 81
  changes in 25, 28, 35–37, 46
  formal 99, 129, 186
  goals of 149
  higher 82
  national curriculum and 32–35
  primary 27, 28–31, 36, 37–47, 50–63,
   102, 124, 157
  progressive 29–32, 36, 187
  scientific 48–65
  traditional 36, 37, 38, 40, 187, 189,
   199
elementary schools 140
enrichment tasks 41, 159, 161–62, 165,
  171
enquiry skills 51–52
entity theory 136–37, 138–39, 140,
  141–42, 146
evaluation 11, 19, 25, 163, 179
examinations 5, 100, 124, 153
experiential learning 29–30, 67–68
expertise 10–11, 193
explicit knowledge 3, 88, 129, 179
explicit learning 1, 3–4, 89, 127, 174
  types of 4–25

facts 62, 64, 81, 121
  accumulation of 5, 6, 20, 41, 166, 181
  scientific 50

generalization 16–17, 19, 166
grammar 161, 186
group work 44–45, 47, 155, 191

higher education 82
hypotheses 183

ideas 9, 64, 81, 159, 167
imagination 63, 165, 199
implicit knowledge 3, 6, 24
implicit learning 1–3, 5, 8, 9, 15, 24, 146,
  174, 177
incremental tasks 41, 42, 159, 160–61,
  162, 165, 171
incremental theory 136–37, 139
individual abilities 45, 47, 160
individual tasks 155, 165
inert knowledge 89–90, 95
infant schools 155
information 5, 8, 20–21, 67–68, 85, 88,
  115–17, 154, 166, 194
  inconsistent 92–94, 114, 127
  understanding of 9–10, 23–24, 64,
   83–84, 97
intelligence 127
  intuitive theories of 133–43, 145, 184
  practical 99–100, 186, 189
intuitive theories 127–32, 174–77
  and motivation 132–40, 184–85
IQ 100

knowledge 2, 15, 34, 80, 112, 151
  application of 41, 89–90, 95, 161–63,
   171
  communication of 110, 116–20, 193
  conceptual 11, 17, 19, 105
  consolidation of 197–99
  increase in 4–5, 96, 150

integration of 30, 68, 105, 114–15, 124
mathematical 99–101, 103, 105, 107,
  131
metacognitive 88–90, 95, 130
new 157, 160, 166
and reading 81–87, 97
scientific 48, 49, 64–66, 68
retrieval of 6–7, 15–16, 25, 160
see also prior knowledge

language 161
  development of 79, 80
  learning of 2, 35, 186
  spoken 72, 79, 111–12
  teaching of 40–41, 42, 44, 45
  use of 3, 24, 186
  written 69, 111–12
learning 1–6, 16–17, 25–26, 46, 88, 109,
  119, 157, 159
  arbitrary 100–2, 124, 177
  assessment of 152–56, 170
  child-centred 28, 29–31
  and culture 76–79, 100, 175–76
  early 150, 163, 174
  implicit 1–3, 5, 8, 9, 24, 77–78, 146,
   174
  mathematical 16–19, 45, 98–102,
   107–10, 124
  as memorization 19–24, 38, 146, 147,
   166, 178–79
  and memory 6–7, 9, 12–16, 67–68
  motivation for 95, 120, 133–45, 153,
   157, 170, 177, 180, 184–87, 191, 198
  and prior knowledge 127, 152, 166,
   176–78
  and problem solving 12–16, 24–25, 98,
   105, 147
  purpose of 35–36, 149, 153, 177–79
  of reading 69–75, 77, 80–82, 175–76
  from reading 69, 82–96
  science 48–63, 64–67, 68, 100–2, 127,
   168
  success in 147, 167, 174
  and teaching methods 37–47, 157–58,
   187–97
  and understanding 7–11, 16–19, 23–24,
   83–85, 98, 105–6, 122, 124, 126, 169,
   177–81
  and writing 110, 120–24, 130
learning difficulties 151, 154, 191
learning goals 4, 137–38, 139, 184, 194
learning strategies 187–97
learning tasks 39, 43, 45, 63, 155
  matching 157, 159, 165–66, 169, 170,
   173
  performance of 133–36, 139, 140–47
  types of 41–42, 159–65, 171
linguistic skills 70, 71
literacy 80, 89, 150, 175
  see also scientific literacy
long-term memory 6, 9, 12, 25, 67, 177
look-and-say reading method 75, 76

mathematics 98, 146, 161
  learning of 16–19, 45, 98–102, 107–10,
   127, 176
  practical 99–100
  teaching of 18–19, 98–99, 101–7, 108,
   124–25, 131–32, 185

214

Subject Index

skills 34, 48, 70, 96, 97, 110, 159
  application of 162-63, 165
  acquisition of 5, 6, 15, 17, 25, 31, 41,
    47, 98, 160, 166, 181
  automatic 69, 77, 147, 162
  mathematical 107, 124, 161
  reading 78, 80
  scientific 51-52, 61
  teaching 151, 154, 156, 166, 170, 173,
    197
  writing 117, 122, 125
speech 70, 111-12
specialism 168
spelling 73, 75, 80, 81, 96-97, 113, 114,
  161
spoken language 72, 79, 111-12
subject knowledge 150, 165, 169-70, 179
subject teaching 89, 122, 189
summarization 188, 191
syntax 73

task-centred activity *see* learning tasks
teachers 5, 28
  communication by 151-55, 157, 166,
    187
  intentions of 42
  role of 36, 148
  self-monitoring by 154
  training of 35
teaching methods 28, 35, 37-47, 91-92,
  149, 151
  diagnostic assessment of 151-55
  effective 167-73, 187-99
  of maths 18-19, 98-99, 101-7, 108,
    124-25, 131-32
  and National Curriculum 35-36
  progressive 29-31, 187
  reading 69, 75
  science 48-49, 52-63, 65, 67-68
  task-centred 45, 157-67
  traditional 36, 37, 38, 40, 187
  of writing 121-24
teaching skills 151, 154, 156, 166, 170,
  173, 197, 199
teaching strategies 187-97
technology 100

test scores 76
testing 38, 153, 154, 156, 166
texts 122-23
  information in 85, 88, 116-17
  comprehension of 69-70, 83-87, 91-94,
    97, 193
textual understanding 10-11, 85, 95
thought 3, 167, 199
  conscious 3, 6-7
  original 161
  processes of 7, 67, 68, 87, 88
topics 45, 46, 114-15, 116, 117, 127,
  176-77
traditional education 36, 37, 38, 40, 187,
  189, 199

underachievment 190
undergraduates 11, 19, 85, 94, 109
understanding 34, 133, 197-99
  explicit 8-9
  and learning 4, 5-6, 7-8, 16-19,
    23-24, 83, 100, 103, 105-6, 122, 124,
    126, 174, 177-81
  and memory 20, 84-85
  and problem solving 16, 18, 108-10,
    130
  of science 49
  of texts 10-11, 85-87, 97
university students 5-6, 85
unstructures activities 106

values 34
vocabulary 72, 76, 78-79, 94

Western culture 100
whole-class teaching 46
whole word reading method 75, 77
word recognition 69-75, 77-78, 80, 81
working memory 6-7, 9, 14-15, 18, 25,
  143, 147, 179
writing 45-46, 47, 69, 70, 98
  as communication 110-13, 158
  goals of 113-21, 125-26
  and learning 130-31
  teaching of 121-24